WHAT THEY'RE SAYIN

"STUNNING" SYFY CHANNEL

"Brings to mind VINCENT PRICE and Victorian Era full moons!"
NY TIMES

"It's doubtful any show could capture H.P. Lovecraft's spooky enigmatic quality better than Radiotheatre, which mounts six Lovecraft stories performed by four actors speaking into microphones in solitary spotlights. Creepy music, a few light cues and a burst of smoke are the only design. This chilling production concentrates attention on the voice, the words and, most importantly, the darkness. Like so many Lovecraft tales, this story takes place in blackness." INTELLLIGENT LIFE MAGAZINE, Jason Zinoman, author of "Shock Value"

"Radiotheatre offers HOT AURAL ACTION using all the tricks up writer/director Dan Bianchi's classic radio sleeve!" TIME OUT NY

"Spooky, SHOCKING, Horrific!" POP CULTURE MAGAZINE

"CHILLING and THOUGHT PROVOKING... superbly crafted, fast paced and perfectly scored...Bianchi's sound design conjures up sets and action to rival the most expensive Broadway mega-musical or a blockbuster enhanced with computer-generated imagery. This is a MUST SEE show...or rather a must hear and must imagine for yourself show!" OFFOFFONLINE

"How, precisely, might someone translate Lovecraft's peculiar brand of weird horror to the stage? His nightmarish dreamscapes, his indescribable monsters, and his ever-expanding cast of ancient gods...charming tentacle beasts like Cthulhu, Yig and Nyarlathotep ...invariably lose their power as soon as they are made visual. But, Dan Bianchi has a solution: he lets his audience do the work for him. By dispensing with visuals, Dan Bianchi has found a way to stage ambitious work that is nimble, cheap and popular. In an Off-Off-Broadway scene where most companies are content to produce a show a year, Radiotheatre averages more than six!" NY OBSERVER

"The Radiotheatre actors do an outstanding job...the music and sound effects are terrific! If you are a fan of H.P.Lovecraft or radio dramas, I recommend you attend this festival!" STAGE BUZZ

"A SOUND EXTRAVAGANZA!" VARIETY

"Of all the treasures of New York's contemporary avant-garde scene, it is difficult to find a performance art company as innovative, yet, traditional as Radiotheatre!" TOTAL THEATRE MAGAZINE, London

"Radiotheatre claims that it is not an old time radio show and it is not. But, if you close your eyes and just listen...you may be transported away to another time and place, just the way radio shows used to do for listeners decades ago...Dan Bianchi does a great service to the lost art of radio drama by adapting it to the live stage of today. In that way, he truly creates a new and vibrant theatrical style...BRAVO RADIOTHEATRE!" NORWALK CITIZEN

"Radiotheatre's annual H.P.LOVECRAFT FESTIVAL is a cult hit in the East Village!" NY TIMES

"Amid today's plethora of theatrical bells, whistles and videos, it's reassuring to know that vocal agility and a smart yarn can still conjure up ATTENTION GRABBING theater or, at least, Radiotheatre!" PLATINUM BROADWAY

"RadioTheatre sticks to what makes HORROR really great...the audience's imagination...achieving the best translation of LOVECRAFT to another medium that I've seen!" THEATER IS EASY

"Bianchi does a fine job of spooking up the place! Fans will find much to love in these well-constructed adaptations. For everyone else, if you're not into Lovecraft, then this is a perfect time to remedy that. AN INDIE THEATRE MASTERSTROKE!" NYTHEATRE.COM

"Dan Bianchi has more up his sleeve than just monster stories. There's definitely an allegory regarding modern society at work here and contemporary urban legends is the conduit to a bigger, more monstrous question at hand. THE MOLE PEOPLE is a serious socio-political treatise on terrorism delivered to us encased in a pop culture nod to Tales From The Crypt. That's something we don't often see in modern theatre. It could be the most profound work to date by this prolific performance group." FAIRFIELD NEWS

"INCREDIBLE SCIENCE FICTION! For those of you who love your story telling turned up to 11...this is for you!" AISLE SAY

"The truly amazing discovery is the orchestral score. I'VE NEVER HEARD ANYTHING LIKE IT BEFORE IN LIVE THEATER. This isn't that fake synthesizer sound track stuff. Using advanced software technology, Bianchi has created the kind of carefully composed and edited score one hears only in Hollywood motion pictures. Even though Radiotheatre's simplicity is, in Bianchi's words, 'poor man's theater,' the sumptuous scoring, alone, is far and away a 21st Century technological feat that should not only garner awards, but, open up a whole new field in music composition for the live stage. Is the audience aware of this technological achievement? On the contrary, they're too wrapped up in the excitement of it all! " VARIETY

"GREAT FUN! Crack-brained humor! Unending drive!" NY TIMES

"Radiotheatre has gained something of a reputation for mounting productions of classic horror stories that rely exclusively on sound and voice to get audiences to imagine crazy, gory scenes that can never be realistically staged." CULTURE VULTURE

"Reminds audiences why they were once afraid of the dark. Tremendous performances..." WASHINGTON SQUARE NEWS

"Well conceived and executed, the latest installment of Lovecraft Fest is highly entertaining genre theater that is respectful but not slavish to its source material. RECOMMENDED beyond Lovecraft enthusiasts to general audiences..." J.B.SPINS

"The final key element in this show's success is the evocative musical score. Much more than incidental music it works like a top notch movie score alternately cradling and illuminating the action. IT'S JUST PERFECTt!" STAGE MAGE

"To be frightened by horror is one thing, but, to be moved by it is a much greater thing and that is what this production of The H.P.Lovecraft Festival has accomplished..." THE HAPPIEST MEDIUM

"A TON of FAST PACED FUN! An offbeat treat for those who believe that the best live entertainment is participatory...Bianchi has artfully adapted a cinematic story into an engaging hybrid of live performance and brilliantly crafted soundscapes...They keep you engrossed with a kickass storyline, a lighting crew that specializes in mood control and, of course, a flawless sound effects professionalism that has become their signature statement at all of their shows." VILLAGER

"This seasoned production company has done quality of work consistently enough to be considered one of NYC's best Indie groups!" RETROVISION

"The excellent Radiotheatre has done it again! If you are looking to have a good time, bring your imagination and be prepared for a unique experience! The sound effects are worth the price of admission!" BROADWAY BOX

"Dan Bianchi's sound design, a key component for Radiotheatre, is MARVELOUS!" VILLAGE VOICE

""Ominous, EERIE, Monster Movie Sound FX! A typically spirited offering done with real affection for the source material and completely untainted by camp..." BACKSTAGE

"I have watched his work grow over the years with considerable delight at Bianchi's sensitivity and talent for using the Epic Style of production. His works are ambitious, literate, intelligent and entertaining. Bianchi has joined Beckett at the periphery of existence to contemplate the future of mankind. I am sure that he has the makings of a major artist." HISTORY OF AMERICAN THEATER, Editor, S. Hart, Phd.

"As Renaissance man behind the entire operation, Artistic Director Dan Bianchi is also the Director, Author, Composer and Sound Designer. For his company to have attempted and pulled off a work of this scope, this complexity and length is alone worth commendation ...but, on many levels his work can stand against more commercial and better-funded productions, especially, technically." NY STAGE

"Bianchi's productions are clearly thought out and good natured in their approach, making them both timely and absorbing at a juncture in our history when political trends make it easy to simply fall into apathetic retreat..." THE LONDON TIMES

"A ghastly good time!" NYC TOURISTS GUIDE

"As a horror junkie and a reformed tabletop role-playing gamer, the works of Lovecraft have always been a source of reference for me, although I somehow have never managed to read them directly. In the evocative hands of this company, I'd be happy to listen to the 38 tales that were not performed the night I attended." THEATER IS EASY

"ELEGANT AND VIVID STORYTELLING! Bianchi deserves much credit as adaptor, director, composer and sound designer...the radio play format works extremely well reminding us of the power of a good story and an even stronger imagination ...the great sound design never overwhelms the actors but is a feat for creating the right mood throughout." NYTHEATRE.COM

"RADIOTHEATRE is a VIBRANT force for NYC Stage Shows!" HYREVIEWS

"EERIE! FIENDISH! CREEPY! Dan Bianchi conjures nostalgic campfire ambiance...the right kind of kindling to ignite a HAUNTING night of storytelling...send shivers down your spine and makes hair on the back of your neck stand on end! " AMERICAN THEATRE MAGAZINE

"HORRIFIC! EVOCATIVE! ROUSING! ENGAGING! CHILLING!" OFFOFFONLINE.COM

"I HAD A GREAT TIME! BIANCHI'S adaptation has a brilliant arc that rises to a powerful climax and leaves us with a lot to think about...You feel the audience's energy change as the action rises and falls...One of the most integral aspects of this production is the fantastic and utterly evocative sound design ... Story telling is an art that is slipping away but Bianchi and his company are working hard to keep it alive and thriving. I think he deserves our support!" THEATRE SCENE

"RADIOTHEATRE'S KONG is the only take I've seen on the giant ape that comes close to replicating the magic of the original movie." CBS RADIO MYSTERY THEATRE

"A Sound Spectacular that's totally unique in both its presentation and story...Dan Bianchi delivers a sound track and score that's equivalent to a $30mil movie! A REAL GEM!" NYC TOURIST GUIDE

"Without any more set dressing than a pair of lights and a fog machine, Radiotheatre spins a set of gruesome tales with the help of a sonic collage designed to rake up the hairs on your arm...along with the horror movie frills of music, it pushes viewers to suspend their disbelief long enough to be truly creeped out!" EDGE MAGAZINE

"So how do you get a beast of KONG's proportions to fit inside an intimate theater? You use sound! Music, Noise, screams of terror, tropical bird calls, natives chanting, gorilla calls! That's how

Radiotheatre does it!"   UNITED STAGES

"For writer and director Dan Bianchi, the answer is simple: you use a combination of sound and imagination. The mission of Bianchi's RadioTheatre is to marry the audio drama style of an old-time radio broadcast with the shared intimacy of modern-day experimental theater. He fills the small stage with a sound engineer and six talented actors standing before microphones. It's up to you to fill in the visuals!" DOWNTOWN EXPRESS

"INVOKES ORSON WELLES AND THE MERCURY THEATRE COMPANY in a polished production that takes its pulp roots seriously and proves that Halloween doesn't just happen once a year...using a heavy battery of sound effects and creepy music, it is by turns hokey and unnerving and never less than totally effective...and with such juicy material to play with the entire company sinks their teeth in and presents the spooky tales with relish...as directed by Dan Bianchi those moments carry chilling crediblity... "   NYTHEATRE.com

"If you ever find yourself wondering what a modern WAR OF THE WORLDS would look like without Tom Cruise, then look no further!" WASHINGTON SQUARE NEWS

"Radiotheatre claims that it is not an old time radio show and it is not. But, if you close your eyes and just listen...you may be transported away to another time and place, just the way radio shows used to do for listeners decades ago...Dan Bianchi does a great service to the lost art of radio drama by adapting it to the live stage of today. In that way, he truly creates a new and vibrant theatrical style...BRAVO RADIOTHEATRE!"   NEWSDAY

"FIVE STARS! RADIOTHEATRE DOES IT AGAIN!   Radiotheatre is PERFORMANCE ART AT ITS GREATEST! If you come looking to see a traditional play, stay home. When the lights go down and Dan Bianchi's magnificent score starts playing, you know you're in for something quite different than anything else playing around New York tonight. The multi-talented cast creates a whole world of cinematic action and excitement one doesn't ordinarily find in traditional theater at any level. The hundreds of sound effects are ASTOUNDING!" WORLD THEATRE MAGAZINE

"Dan Bianchi has more up his sleeve than just monster stories. There's definitely an allegory regarding modern society at work here and

contemporary urban legends is the conduit to a bigger, more monstrous question at hand. It's a serious sociopolitical treatise on terrorism delivered to us encased in a pop culture nod to Tales From The Crypt. That's something we don't often see in modern theatre. It could be the most profound work to date by this prolific performance group."
FAIRFIELD NEWS

"ELEGANT AND VIVID STORYTELLING! Bianchi deserves much credit as adaptor, director, composer and sound designer...the radio play format works extremely well reminding us of the power of a good story and an even stronger imagination...the great sound design never overwhelms the actors but is a feat for creating the right mood throughout." NYTHEATRE.COM

"In its minimalist and charmingly retro way, Radiotheatre's KING KONG strikes closer to the heart of the myth than Peter Jackson's overlong, overbaked movie on a budget that wouldn't have covered Jackson's catering bill!" BACKSTAGE

"I've been going to New York's Radiotheatre shows for several years now and love them all. Once again, the Renaissance man behind the live audio project is Dan Bianchi who creates a great sound track and terrifying score, as well as, writing and directing the show, too...Don't miss this one!" THE RECORD (NJ)

"This is the scariest show I have ever seen...All of the actors were great in their roles but the real genius behind the whole production is Dan Bianchi who wrote, directed and also designed the great music and sound effects...I don't know when I had a more enjoyable night in the theater!" WCBS NEWS

"BOY, HAVE WE GOT A RECOMMENDATION FOR YOU! I thought to myself, how the hell are these folks going to pull this off....I actually closed my eyes and let the actors, music and script do all the work ...they did indeed accomplish their goal of giving a new generation an appreciation for entertainment from past eras." RETROVISION

"LIKE ORSON WELLES AND COMPANY, Radiothteatre has polished up an unusual and effective story telling technique...the cast assume all their roles in a spookingly convincing manner...the stories themselves are terrifying and Radiotheatre's technique of providing voices and sound effects forces the audience to recreate the horror's visual aspects as mental theatre...much more horrific than any B Movie moment are true stories Bianchi has unearthed... Bianchi finds New York's haunted most chillingly by the effects of poverty and injustice..."   FEARS MAGAZINE

""AN ENJOYABLE RIDE!...I love Horror, the supernatural, pulp fiction and radio dramas...DAN BIANCHI delivers it all with an exquisite script and, above all, a fabulous score and sound effects design. And yet, it's a simple little show. I was enthralled by the sheer simplicity without all of the visual elements seen in traditional theater....Bianchi produced the first ever live stage production of KING KONG. I don't know if even Disney can pull that off. But, Radiotheatre did. Whether or not you like that kind of fare, Radiotheatre offers shows you won't find anywhere else in NYC. And, judging by audience reception I've seen, they always seem most satisfied when they leave. I know I was!"
SHOW BUSINESS WEEKLY

Edgar Allan Poe
On Stage

26 Stories Adapted For
Stage, Screen, Audio By
Dan Bianchi

HOUSE OF FEAR
NYC NY
2015

For CYNTHIA and ELIZABETH

THE RADIOTHEATRE SERIES

EDGAR ALLAN POE ON STAGE
His Stories Adapted For Stage, Screen, Audio

Copyright © 2015 Dan Bianchi

ISBN-13: 978-1514103425

ISBN-10: 1514103427

BISAC: Drama / Anthologies

CONTENTS

THE RADIOTHEATRE SERIES

RADIOTHEATRE is New York City's critically-acclaimed, award-winning Performance group that creates Audio Theatre live on stage. Though it is inspired by the Golden Age of old time radio dramas...make no mistake, Radiotheatre does NOT seek to re-create quaint, period radio programs, nor does it stage traditional plays.

By combining 21st Century Hollywood sound technology, uniquely written cinematic scripts, casts of storytellers with great voices, original orchestral scores unheard of anywhere on the live stage and a plethora of sound effects, Radiotheatre produces a new hybrid, environmental art form. Its content is also unique in that it draws its inspiration from pulp genres usually ignored by the traditional Theatre world, ie; Adventure, Science Fiction, Horror, and Crime.

Radiotheatre's cinematic scripts and presentational format allow a live acting troupe to deliver nearly anything...from King Kong roaring atop the Empire State Building... to an explosive invasion from outer space ...to the inner voice of a demented mind...all of which you won't experience anywhere else on the live stage.

But, in order to provide a memorable, live theatrical experience, there is one ingredient that is required from the audiences...their *imaginations!* Like the earliest form of Theatre...telling tales around a campfire in the dark...storytelling requires all of a an audience member's attention to be focused upon the Narrator. However primitive that might sound, it's still the most powerful means of intellectual stimulation, wherein, the audience is invited to *participate* by conjuring the visual images in their own minds! That's something they are not required to do very often in today's world of elaborate video games and $200 million movies.

Over the years, many Theatre makers from around the world have inquired if the scripts used by Radiotheatre are available to stage by others or just to read for enjoyment. And, so, The House Of Fear presents The Radiotheatre Series in specially formatted scripts which may also be produced as recorded works, radio broadcasts...or, they may even be used as the basis for film and video projects.

All scripts in the Radiotheatre Series are expertly crafted for simple presentation by Dan Bianchi, Radiotheatre's Artistic Director and founder. . He has worked over 40 years as writer/director in stage and film media, and, to date, he's the most produced, living dramatist in NYC. Founded in 2004, Radiotheatre has presented over 80 stories live on stage including over 20 stories by H.P.Lovecraft and 20 by Edgar Allan Poe. A great many have been recorded, as well, and can be found on their web site.

These tales are short stories, often running from 10-60 minutes in length. Though most of these scripts have been created to blend both intimate story-telling and cinematic styles requiring recorded sound design, music cues and amplified voices ...in which there are no props, no sets, no costumes...some stories may be adapted to fit traditional play format.

These are tales to be told in near darkness. The scripts require not just great actors with exceptional voices, but, great story tellers, or Narrators. Sometimes, it may be left to the director's discretion to cast the Narrator as either male or female. Both Poe and Lovecraft didn't have many females in their tales, but, these new adaptations to script format allow for changes in casting major and minor roles.. The story may also require actors to play multiple characters...or, a director may choose to cast several actors to play these roles.

In most cases, the archaic language in both Poe and Lovecraft has been updated, but, these new adaptations try to retain their original artistic intention and creation. Characters' names, locations and time frames may be changed. Plots may be condensed, endings may be modified, etc. Remember...the original story was intended to be read as literature and *not* intended to be presented in a different medium using 21st century technology. In every case, Radiotheatre's primary goal is to deliver a great story filled with optimal sound design as a most important part of the production.

Sound effects and dramatic music are an integral part of these stories, as necessary as the actors. To allow easier reading, scripts contain some, but, not all, printed sound/music cues. Directors may wish to add or change cues or even provide live music accompaniment. If you do not wish to create your own sound design, but, instead wish to purchase detailed cue scripts and pre-recorded cues/music, please contact: radiotheatrenyc@aol.com. It is recommended that interested parties listen first to samples of Radiotheatre's unique live sound design at: www.radiotheatrenyc.com.

COPYRIGHT AND ROYALTIES

groups with maximum seating capabilities below 300. Special arrangements must be made by professional groups and amateur groups with larger seating capacity. Send licensing inquiries to: houseoffearnyc@aol.com. Please include details about the planned performance (seating capacity, price per ticket, etc.) Production rights for any play listed on our website, because of circumstances beyond our control, may be withdrawn at any time without prior notice.

For broadcast, film and video rights, please contact: radiotheatrenyc@aol.com

AUTHOR'S NOTES
In most of the following stories, a NARRATOR retells a tale, or, he is conversing with his inner voice. When using amplified voices, this is shown by (REVERB) and the following amplified lines are shown within quotation marks. In traditional theater, these lines may be *asides* to the audience. Even Shakespeare used quite a bit of *asides,* or, *soliloquies.* Using modern technology, an actor doesn't need to be chained to a microphone stand in a radio show format. With tiny, hidden, wireless microphones, stage actors, today, can now roam the stage and audience and use different vocal techniques as opposed to traditional vocal projection. For example, an intimate, suspenseful whisper or a muttering under breath can now be equally heard from the first to last rows in an audience.

Within the dialogue, certain words have been *italicized* which need punctuation and aid in the rhythmic flow of speech. Remember, if one is producing an audio work, even live on stage, the audience needs particular words, descriptions, emotional reasons, etc, as tools in order to help them form images in their mind. If they are momentarily distracted because the dialogue or story telling fails them, or for any other reason, they immediately withdraw from participation.

(SOUND) and *MUSIC* cues printed within these scripts are merely suggestions. They do not indicate a cue's length which may be provided in a more detailed cues script. For instance, a *MUSIC* cue may run several pages, or cross fade into a different *MUSIC* cue. *SILENCE* is used as an indicator of dramatic pause, or, a scene change which may also utilize lighting cues which are not provided here.

The production may simply use a black stage with no props and scenery, or, it may utilize a full set with costumes. Staging and casting are left to the discretion of Directors. For example, in COOL AIR, a student NARRATOR tells the tale. The character can either be male or female. He/She may address the audience using (REVERB) and use (NO REVERB) when conversing with other actors within a scene.

Why amplify the works? Some stories may not require amplification, but, the use of originally designed and edited orchestral music and specially crafted sound cues elevates the nature of suspense and terror, of dread and dramatic punctuation naturally found in these tales. With amplification of both voice and music, a careful balance can be attained. Without a balanced amplified voice, amplified music must be lowered in volume and tends to get lost in the background.

These are all aspects we accept quite readily in the format of cinema, but, rarely experience in staged drama...which is one reason why Theatre has generally ignored the genres of Horror, Science Fiction and Adventure. Unless such tales are adapted into musicals and dance or farce, the traditional Theatre world doesn't know how to adapt and succeed with serious, horrific works for the stage, especially if the production tries to emulate expensive motion picture reality. However, the Theatre can create its own worlds of Horror, Science Fiction and Adventure...played straight...and still succeed in delivering what the authors had intended. And, no other media can duplicate a live presentation, particularly when it requires the participation of its audience. Plus...relatively speaking...it doesn't cost much to produce.

Regarding Lovecraft's stories...alright, if you're looking for the great American novelist, he wasn't that. However, if you're looking for someone who died penniless and forgotten in 1937 at age 46, whose terrifying stories have continued to influence writers, filmmakers, artists, composers, comics, magazines and game makers around the world, then, he's your guy. Every year there are scores of new books written about Lovecraft and his works. Yet, he was a writer of short pulp fiction, most of which were published for little or no money in minor publications. His stories aren't known for the depth of a character's personality or their dramatic relationships. But, now recognized as Poe's successor and a master of early 20th Century American Literary Horror, Howard Phillips Lovecraft practically invented the category of Weird Fiction and some of his works revolutionized Science Fiction and Fantastic literature, as well. Unfortunately, the Theatre world has yet to discover these works and, so, it has been Radiotheatre's mission to adapt them for the stage.

Admittedly, at times, his verbose writing style with over the top descriptions is a bit difficult to fathom for modern day readers, but, his visions and ideas came at a time when few were exploring speculative fiction and forbidden subjects in genre writing. Some of those visions have yet to be topped, which is why every generation discovers him as their own and there are legions of Lovecraftians growing more plentiful year after year. Lovecraft Festivals have become annual events across the Americas, Europe, Japan. There are bars named after him in Oregon and NYC. There's even a beer named Lovecraft! And, his hometown of Providence, Rhode Island has become a Mecca for his followers.

I've tried to stay true to his central vision in most stories, but, as with much of pulp fiction, there are repetitive plots, lines, characters, situations throughout the works. That's okay. No one is producing all of these works on the same bill. To allow for further variety, the simplicity of the scripts allows for different presentations. Radiotheatre has even produced the same story in several versions using a solo actor or a multiple cast. But, unlike much of today's plays which require political correctness, or, a need to produce a story with a moral lesson and even a happy ending, you won't find much love for humanity in Lovecraft's works. He aims for something rarely found in Theatre and I recommend that any Director or Adaptor wishing to produce Lovecraft on stage should further examine his great body of stories, his biography and the author's personal commentary on his own work.
Dan Bianchi   NYC   2015

"Now all my tales are based on the fundamental premise that common human laws and interests and emotions have no validity or significance in the vast cosmos-at-large. To me there is nothing but puerility in a tale in which the human form…and the local human passions and conditions and standards…are depicted as native to other worlds or other universes. To achieve the essence of real externality, whether of time or space or dimension, one must forget that such things as organic life, good and evil, love and hate, and all such local attributes of a negligible and temporary race called mankind, have any existence at all. Only the human scenes and characters must have human qualities. These must be handled with unsparing realism, (not catch-penny romanticism) but when we cross the line to the boundless and hideous unknown…the shadow-haunted Outside….we must remember to leave our humanity and terrestrialism at the threshold."
H. P. Lovecraft

MORELLA

By Edgar Allan Poe
Adapted by Dan Bianchi

CAST – 1m/1w
SYNOPSIS - A man is haunted by the spirit of his wicked dead wife.

MUSIC
(THUNDER, RAIN.)

NARRATOR
(REVERB) "How has it come to this? How? Remember! *Remember!* When? Two? *Three* years ago? Try to recall.
19th C. PERIOD DANCE MUSIC
(PARTY SOUNDS)

"Yes, I remember now…I had attended a *social* gathering in town, at the *Radcliff* house. Music, dancing, drinking. I was bored, *lonely,* about to leave, when…I looked up and *there* she was…all dressed in *black,* as if in mourning. Her *eyes….*

EERIE MUSIC

"Those *melancholy* eyes. Staring *deeply* into mine. Strange. There was some…*force*…between us. Yes, a *spiritual* connection. The both of us, we *knew* right away that our *spirits* were to be *bound* together forever. Oh, I don't mean we would become lovers. Although, I must say, *I* was certainly *infatuated* with *her*…she was so *beautiful*…but, for *love* to exist, there *must* be….

SILENCE

"…well, in any case, a month later, we were married. It was all very official. She didn't want a wedding. She had no family to speak of…at least, no one here in America. Quite simply, she *swore* herself to me and from that moment on, she *shunned* the rest of the world. Yes, completely *devoted* herself to me. What could I say? I was a lucky man. Or, so I had thought.

19th C. PIANO MUSIC

"Time passed. I quickly learned that *Morella* was *not* an ordinary woman. Oh, she was talented…she could sit at a piano and play nearly anything. And, she was *very* intelligent. Well versed in world literature, spoke several languages. Even knew her way around science and mathematics. At times, I felt as if *I* was *her* pupil. She could easily have attended Harvard or Yale...*if* women were *allowed* to attend, of course.

EERIE MUSIC

"But, aside from all that...she also spent a great deal of her time studying what is referred to as...the *dark arts*. *Mystical* writings that no *university* would dare teach."

MORELLA
Come, join me. I want you to read this...and this...and this one here.

NARRATOR
(REVERB) "I couldn't resist her. So, I delved into the *horrid* works laid before me. Foreign books with titles I could *barely* pronounce...written by *authors* who were believed to be *wizards* and Satan worshippers. I had *no* idea such things existed...and, certainly, *I* would never have read such *despicable* books if it were *not* for Morella *bidding* me to do so. It was as if I had *no* will of my own. I was *completely* under my wife's guidance. She was mistress of my mind, as well as, my *heart* and soul. *And* body...though it might not have been considered *lovemaking*, yes, we did *revel* in the *pleasures* of the flesh."

SILENCE

MORELLA
Together, we will enter into another world *beyond* our own.

NARRATOR
(REVERB) "I was helpless. I am ashamed to admit that now, but, back then...

EERIE MUSIC

"...well, Morella just had to place her *cold* hand upon my own and *rake* up the ashes of some *dead* philosophy with an *incantation* whose strange meaning *burned* itself upon my memory and...for *hours,* I'd *listen* to her voice *tainted* with terror. At times, it was an *unearthly* sound...a voice, dare I say, almost *inhuman*...and there would fall a *shadow* upon my *soul!* A *shadow*...dark...deep...

SILENCE

"Who *was* this woman? Where had she come from? Whenever I'd inquire, she'd only say had descended from a very *old* family...a *royal* family...whose ancient roots lie in the *gloomy* mountains of *Romania."*

MORELLA
Deep in the forests primeval...where the gray *wolves* rule the night. I *do* miss their songs...what *music* they make...

MUSIC

NARRATOR
(REVERB) "I saw, I *felt* her longing for a *past* life...which only meant that this *marriage* of ours was *unfulfilling* to her. A disappointment...a *mistake! I* was a mistake. She would not say such things, but, I could tell what she was thinking. The way she'd *respond* to me, or, *look* at me with such *disdain* and...

"Each day, I felt a *rift* growing wider between us. I lost my appetite. I grew *pale* and thin. Soon, what *was* joy began to fade into *horror.* The most *beautiful* became the most *hideous.* Meanwhile, Morella talked incessantly, *obsessively*, about her beliefs..."

SILENCE

MORELLA
Our *identity*...perhaps, it is *not* lost at the time of death forever.

MUSIC

NARRATOR
(REVERB) "What had she *meant* by that? Who knew? *My questions* would often go *ignored,* unanswered. As if *she* had known some *monumental* secret far *beyond* my mere, *mortal* comprehension. I would just have to wait and see.

SILENCE

"Well, *that* situation, living like that, it became *unbearable* for me. My wife's manner... it *oppressed* me as if I'd been under a spell. A *curse!* That's it. *That's* how one may describe it. *Cursed!*

MUSIC

"I could no longer *bear* the touch of her *thin* fingers... nor the *low* tone of her voice... nor the *dull* glow of those *melancholy* eyes. Oh, I know, I know. Why hadn't I *said* something to her? *Complained?* Let *her* know how *I* felt about all of it? Well, I *did.* I *did* ask, but, *she* would not discuss it. I suppose she considered me a *weak* man. Sometimes, she'd just shake her head and say..."

SILENCE

MORELLA
It all has to do with *Fate*...

NARRATOR
(REVERB) *"What?* Had some great *unknown* power beyond *ourselves* caused this relationship to *wilt* and fail?

MUSIC

"Anyway, *months* dragged on, And, then, I began to notice the blue veins in her pale forehead becoming prominent...and her cheeks becoming withdrawn and her eyes were glazed..."

SILENCE

MORELLA
I am with child.

MUSIC

NARRATOR
(REVERB) "Yes, *our* child. Despite the beaming *smile* on my own face, there was no joyous response in *her* eyes For her, this news was *not* a gift...it was a *death* sentence. For you see, it was also *apparent* to the both of us that the poor woman had *little* time to live. In an instant, my anger *and* fear melted into pity. How could I had been so damned *afraid* of her? Stupid, silly man. Immediately, I had decided that I must express my abject *apologies*... but, as I turned my gaze to her eyes...I found them *staring* at me...in such a way...it made my *blood* run cold. I can't explain *how* or why, but...

(MORELLA MOANS IN PAIN)

"Shall I say that I *wanted* her dead? *I did.* Not because I was *afraid* of her, but, I did not want her to suffer. She did not *deserve* to die that way. But, she lingered on. Her fragile spirit clung to *life* for days, weeks, even *months*, until my tortured *nerves* controlled my mind, my actions. As time passed, I grew *furious* at Heaven above! I *cursed* the days, the *hours,* which seemed to lengthen and *lengthen* as her gentle life declined...like shadows in the dying of the day.

(MORELLA MOANS)
SILENCE

"But one autumn evening, Morella called me to her bedside."

MORELLA
Come! *Come!*

NARRATOR
"By then, she had ingested *more* than enough *laudanum*. I tried my best to make her *understand* that *whatever* had happened between us...I did *not* want her to *die* like this. By *God!* It was not right."
MUSIC

MORELLA
Listen to me...I see now...there is a *dim* mist over all the *Earth* and a *warm* glow upon the waters, and, amid the rich *October* leaves of the forest...a *rainbow* from the firmament has surely fallen.

NARRATOR
Save your breath, my darling.

MORELLA
It is a day of days, a *day* of *all* days either to live *or* to die. It is a *fair* day for the sons of Earth and life...ah, *more* fair for the *daughters* of Heaven and death!

NARRATOR
(REVERB) "I remember...I kissed her forehead."

MORELLA
I am dying, yet shall *I* live.

NARRATOR
Morella!

MORELLA
The days have *never* loved me. But, her whom in *life* you did *abhor*, in *death* you shall *adore*.

NARRATOR
Don't say that...*Morella!*

MORELLA
This body...dying. Dying. But, *within* me is a *pledge* of that affection which *you* have given me. You dared to *love* me. I know it. I know it. And, so, when *my* spirit departs... shall the *child* live... *your* child and mine, *Morella's* child.

SILENCE

But, I *also* know that you *hate* and fear me...

NARRATOR
Why do you *say* that?

MORELLA
So, *your* days...your days shall be days of *sorrow*...that *sorrow* which is the most *lasting* of impressions...as the *cypress* is the most *enduring* of trees. For the hours of your *own* happiness...are over.

NARRATOR
Morella! Why do you say that? What have *I* done to...?
                    (MORELLA MOANS, SCREAMS)
                                    MUSIC

(REVERB) "Then, the *midwives* entered and carried out their business and soon...
                              (BABY CRIES)

"After a slight tremor, Morella died. As she had *predicted,* in dying *she* had given birth...and our *daughter,* so I was told, did not draw her first *breath* until the *mother* had stopped breathing.
                                    SILENCE

"Years *whirled* by.
                                    MUSIC

"The child grew *strangely* in stature and intellect... and was the *perfect* resemblance of her dead mother. Oh, I *loved* her with a love *more* fervent than I had *ever* believed possible to feel for *any* human being. But, would it *last?* Not likely. You see...*horror* surrounded us. As I have stated, the child grew *strangely* in *stature* and intelligence. Strange, *indeed,* because her *body* size *increased* quite rapidly. And, as for her *intellectual* development...by the age of *ten,* the child had the powers and *faculties* of an *adult* woman. The *words* that came from her mouth...the *wisdom?* From a *child?* It didn't take long for me to *realize* that something *dark* and sinister was at work behind it all. And, *always* my thoughts returned to the *entombed* Morella.
                                    SILENCE

"And, so, that is the way I lived, *terrified*, year after year...*cursed,* day after day, *gazing* upon her holy, and mild, and *eloquen*t face... and *witnessing* her body turn *mature* while discovering *new* features of *resemblance* to her mother.

MUSIC

"They grew more *definite,* more *perplexing,* more *hideously* terrible. Her *smile* was like her mother's.   I could *bear* that.   Her *eyes* were like Morella's.   I could *endure* that.   But, when they stared *down* into the *depths* of my soul with *Morella's* own *intense* and bewildering *meaning...?*

"Then, there was the *contour* of the high forehead, the *ringlets* of the silken hair, the *thin* fingers ...the *deep* sound of her voice and above all, oh, *above* all, when she *spoke* the *same* phrases and *expressions* ...how could she have *known* these words? *Said* in the *same* tone of voice as...well, It *consumed* me with horror.   It was like a worm *squirming* in my brain...*writhing* and *chewing* and *refusing* to *die!*

SILENCE

"In a sense, I had lost *two* loves of my life.   Do you want to know something? I had never even *named* my daughter. I called her simply, *My Child.* Morella's name *died* with *her* at her death. I'd never *spoken* about her to our daughter. I had *forbid* her to *question* me about her mother...the woman, who, with her *dying* breath*,* *cursed* my remaining years with *unhappiness...*

MUSIC

"Well, there came a time when I was determined to *defy* this curse. I was not going to allow my *daughter* to *suffer* from her mother's blasphemy.   It's true, during the brief period of her existence, my daughter, in her *condition,* had seen *little* of the outside world. What could I do to stop that *travesty* from *progressing* further? And, then it came to me!   Perhaps, if she were *baptized,* we may be spared the *terrors* of destiny. *Fate! Ha!* How *dare* Morella *terrorize* me with the *concept* of *helplessness.* *I* would take *Fate* in my own hands now. *I* decided to have my daughter *baptized!* .

SILENCE

"But, I needed a *name* for her. I couldn't think of many, of course. Gentle, good, *happy* names. Then, I made my choice. I would name her after my mother.

EERIE MUSIC

"But, what happened next...was a *desecration*, a *sacrilege...beyond* human experience! For you see, when I *stood* at the *baptismal* font with the *child* next to me...and the *priest* before me, prompting me for a name... I could not *say* the name *I* had chosen. *No!*   There was something *gnawing* at my thoughts. Some *demon* urging me to *breathe* that sound, that *name,* which, in its very *recollection* would make my *blood* run cold! Some *fiend* speaking from the *recesses* of my soul...
SILENCE

"And so, there, standing in the *dim* aisle, in the *silence* of the night...I answered with a *whisper...Morella!*
(WIND, THUNDER, GLASS CRASH, CHILD SCREAMING)
MUSIC BUILDS

"What devil's work was *this!* My child *convulsing*...her skin turning *white!* Her *eyes* to glass...she *fell* back upon the marble floor as I stared on in utter horror...and then, opening her mouth, she responded..."

MORELLA
(ECHO) *"I am here!"*

NARRATOR
(REVERB) "Those few *simple* sounds fell coldly, *distinctly*, within my ear, and like molten *lead*, it hissed *deeply* into my brain. I shall never forget that moment for as long as I live."

MORELLA
(ECHO) *"Morella!"*

NARRATOR
(REVERB) "The *winds* breathed but *one* sound within my ears and the ripples upon the sea murmured *evermore...!"*

MORELLA
(ECHO) *"Morella!"*
SILENCE

NARRATOR
(REVERB) "Today, my child *died* on that *cold* marble floor before the altar of God...a *god* to whom I shall never again pray. With my own hands I *carried* my beloved daughter to our family mausoleum.
(IRON DOOR CREAKS OPEN)
MUSIC

(COFFIN SLAB PUSHED ASIDE)

"And, after I had *opened* the tomb...and, with some effort, *pushed* aside the stone *slab* atop the family coffin where I would lay the child alongside her mother...I...I...couldn't *help* but *laugh!* *Hahahaha!* You *see?* *Hahahaha!* *You see?* The *coffin!* Why, it was *empty!* You see? The *coffin* empty...*all* that time! *It was empty!*"

(WIND)

MORELLA
(ECHO, WHISPERS) "*Morella!*"

END

WILLIAM WILSON

By Edgar Allan Poe
Adapted By Dan Bianchi

CAST - 3m - Wilson/WW; Reverend/Man/Student; Glendinnig
SYNOPSIS - William Wilson is hounded since childhood by, what he believes to be, a doppelganger, another human being who resembles him in almost every way.

WILSON
(REVERB) "My name is William *Wilson*...a name that has brought nothing but *scorn* and detestable *dread,* fear, *infamy*...not *just* to me, but, to my family. Since I can remember, I've been an *outcast.* If only I could *die* with some *sympathy* from my fellow man. If only *someone* might *believe* that I did *not* plan for this to happen. I was a *slave* to circumstances *beyond* my control. I feel as if I've been living in a *dream* and I am *now* dying a *victim* to the *horror* and the mystery born from the *wildest* of all nightmares.

MUSIC

"It all began when I was a boy at school...

(CHURCH BELL TOLLS)

"Ironically, *now,* at this moment, I can recall it with *such* clarity as if it were yesterday. The *school* house with its *gothic* roof...the *grounds* with a high *brick* wall encompassing it. The gate... *riveted* and studded with iron bolts and *jagged* iron spikes. Almost like a prison...only *we* were *allowed* out of it *three* times a week. Every *Saturday* afternoon, we were *permitted* to take walks in the fields.

CHURCH HARMONIUM MUSIC

"*Twice* on Sunday we were *paraded* to church for morning *and* evening services. Conveniently, the *head master* of our school was also *pastor* of the church. *Six* days a week he'd *scold* us and dole out *punishments* and on the *seventh* day, he'd *forgive* us our *transgressions.*

MUSIC

"But, the old school! When I say it was *old,* I *mean* old. There was really *no* end to its rooms and halls and *closets* everywhere. It had *two* stories and you were *never* sure *which* floor you were on at any given time. Steps and *staircases* everywhere.

(STUDENTS IN HALLWAY, CHATTING

IN CLASSROOM, CHAIR SHIFTING)

"I lived there *five* years with *twenty* other students and we were always getting lost. The school room was the *largest* room, very *long* and narrow, with *pointed* Gothic windows and a ceiling of oak. There was a *pulpit* up front for our teacher, the Reverend *Bransby*. There were innumerable benches and desks, *all* antiques from years past, piled with *time* worn books and pamphlets.

REVEREND
Silence!

(STUDENTS COME TO ORDER)
SILENCE
(TICKING)

NARRATOR
(REVERB) "A *great* mantle clock sat on a fireplace at the other end of the room. I can still hear it's *ticking*...

MUSIC

"So, this is where I spent a good portion of my young life. It wasn't *all* boredom. To a child, *excitement* waits around the corner every day. *Life* is what you make of it. *I* didn't *wait* for it to come to me, *I* sought it out. Yes, there *were* tedious drills, the *nightly* summons to bed, the *recitations*...

(BOYS ON PLAYGROUND)

"But, there were *fights* on the playground and *holiday* celebrations, too. And, *because* of my *enthusiasm* for all that, *I* stood out amongst my fellow schoolmates. Everyone looked *up* to me. Everyone *except one*.
SILENCE

"*Oddly* enough, although he was *no* family relation, he had the *same* name as me, first *and* last. *My* name was *not* an odd name, so, I *supposed* it did not seem *too* remarkable to others that *another* boy held *exactly* the same name. *William Wilson*.

MUSIC

"He was *my* age, too...*and* about the same *height* and weight....so, we were given *many* of the *same* assignments. In *sports*, we played together on the *same* team. But, although the *other* teammates followed *my* instruction, *Wilson* made a *point* of going his *own* way. I must admit, I *was* a bit *frightened* of his *air* of superiority. Even his *equality*.

SILENCE

"*But,* no one *else* acknowledged his actions, his *competitiveness,* his *interference* and *resistance* to me…only *I* saw them as a *threat* to *my* dominance in school.

MUSIC

"Yet, he *seemed* to lack that *spirit* or *ambition* to excel. Why did he *have* to *oppose* me or *beat* me in *every* confrontation? For what *purpose,* if he didn't *really* care about moving *up* the social ladder or *impressing* his teacher? Or, even *winning* an award or the *applause* of his fellow mates? I couldn't figure it out.

SILENCE

"Did I say that we had *entered* the school on the *same* day, as well? That, *and* our name *and* similar looks, gave *everyone* the notion that we were *brothers.* In fact, *they* thought we were *so* close in resemblance that we were *twins.* I didn't learn until *later* when I *left* school that Wilson and *I* were *born* on the *same* day, January *19th*…in the *same* year. That's a *remarkable* coincidence, *no?*

MUSIC

"Wilson *dogged* me *throughout* our school years giving me *continual* anxiety by his *rivalry* and contradiction. Yet, for *some* reason, I did not *hate* him *altogether.* I don't know *why.* Even if I *won* a quarrel with him, he *still* made me feel as if *he* had won. We remained on *speaking* terms, but, *I* wouldn't call him a *friend.* Of course, *some* may say that we had a *lot* in common. And *yet,* there was *one* great difference …

SILENCE

"*Wilson* spoke in whispers. That's right, he did not raise his *voice* at any time. Yet, he had a *wide* vocabulary that could *cut* me down in a second. Our *schoolmates* would take *bets* on our arguments and couldn't *wait* for the next. *Some* eluded to the suggestion that *Wilson* and I meant *more* to each other than it had appeared. As if *we* were *masking* our *true* feelings for each other. *That* was a *ridiculous* assumption.

MUSIC

"Sure, his *imitation of* me, at times, would drive me to the *boiling* point. He'd even *dress* like me. But, it seemed, he couldn't *mimic* the *loudness* of my voice. Yet, his *tone* was identical, even if it *was* a whisper. Yes, he even began to *sound* like me. What seemed *strange* to me was that no one *else* seemed to notice it. Only *I* perceived this *constant* intrusion upon my life. What was he *up* to?

SILENCE

"Even worse, I *hated* when he would *patronize* me and allow *me* to win. Almost *winking* to me and others that he *could* have won, *if* he had so *wanted* to win.

MUSIC

"Once, I remember, *I* decided to *turn* the tables… *instead* of opposition to him…I *welcomed* him with open arms. *Ha! That* threw him for a loop. He *avoided* me for some time after that. *That* didn't last long.

(SCHOOLBOYS YELLING AT FIGHT)

"We found ourselves in a *fist* fight a few nights later. I noticed in his style of *battle* that he *reminded* me of *my* childhood… *wild*, confused … *almost* as if I *sympathized* with the fellow. I held back. I felt as if I *knew* his anguish.

SILENCE

"At least, he didn't *sleep* in the same room with me. One night, during my *fifth* year at school, right after the *fist* fight I mentioned…I got out of bed while *everyone* was asleep and *sneaked* toward Wilson's room. I intended to *end* this rivalry, *somehow,* once and for all.

MUSIC

"There I was in his *tiny* room in the dark. I could *hear* his breathing. I covered my lamp and walked *closer* to his bed and *shined* the light onto his face. As I looked…my whole body grew *numb* and icy. I could hardly *breathe.* My *knees* shook and I nearly *dropped* the lamp. Was *this* the face of William *Wilson?* It was, but, it was *not.* What *was* it that *confounded* me? The *same* name as me? The *same* looks? The *same* day of arrival at my school? His *dogged* imitation of *my* walk, *my* voice, *my* habits, *my* manner? Could it be he was a *different* being *before* he had come here… and, now, I stared at someone who had spent *so* long *imitating* me, he had *become* my double?

SILENCE

"I couldn't think. I put out the light and *left* the room. Not only that…I left the *school.* Never to return again.

MUSIC

"Later, as a young adult, I was able to *rationalize* my years of *anxiety* with Wilson…it was just a *passing* experience…my *own* imagination run wild…a mere *bout* of emotional *instability*. Luckily, I was able to *wash* away the past and *delve* into a *new* life at college.

SILENCE

"But, three years *later,* I had not made *much* advance in life and spent *most* of my time *carousing*, drinking and *gambling* until dawn.

MUSIC

"*One* night, while playing poker, I was about to *win* the next hand when…a fellow student tapped me on my shoulder…"

SILENCE

STUDENT
Wilson! Someone wants to meet you out in the hall…

WILSON
What, *now?* Who is it?

STUDENT
Wouldn't say…but, he said it's urgent.

WILSON
Alright…then let's go see who this *urgent* person is…

STUDENT
Watch it now, you're drunk…

WILSON
Me? *Drunk?* Preposterous.

MUSIC

(REVERB) "I staggered out into the hallway where it was rather dark."

(NO REVERB) Who's there? Is anyone there? I *see* you standing there in the shadows. Who *are* you? Do I *know* you?

(REVERB) "Now, at *that* moment, the figure about my *own* height and *dressed* in a white frock coat, the same *exact* coat as *I* was wearing, stepped forth from the shadows, *very* quickly and *seized* me by the arm."

(NO REVERB) Hey there, get your *hands* off me! Just *who* the *Hell* do you think you are?

(REVERB) "And, then, he whispered in my ear…"

SILENCE

WW
(Whisper) William…*Wilson*.

MUSIC

WILSON
(REVERB) "Instantly, I grew sober. Of *course* I did! I was *shocked* out of my senses. In those two *simple* words, *all* the memories came *flowing* back! Before I could even *catch* my breath, he was gone.

SILENCE

"One can't *imagine* what *effect* that had upon my *disordered* imagination over the next few weeks. I *knew* who it was standing there in the darkness. Now, I was *determined* to find him. Did he think he was going to *interfere* with *my* life once again? Who and *what* was this *Wilson?* Where had he *come* from? What did he *want* from me?

MUSIC

"I asked at the *old* school what had *become* of him. I was *told* that he had left *suddenly* due to an *accident* in his family… *exactly* on the day *I* had left. That fact was *too* much to bear. I transferred to *another* college.

SILENCE

"Time passed again while, unfortunately, *I* had *returned* to my vices. Only, at my *new* college, my fellow *collegians* were *much* wealthier than those at the last school.

MUSIC

"So, when I won at cards, I won big time. I became a *full* time gambler and *quite* knowledgeable about *every* trick and method. My name became *known* around the campus. The young men *vied* to play cards at *my* table, so that *they* could tell *their* friends they had *lost* to William Wilson. Eventually, *I* grew richer.

SILENCE

"A few months later, I found an easy mark in a *wealthy* young freshman named *Glendinnig*. He wasn't very smart, an *easy* mark for me. Each time, I'd let him *win* the first *few* hands until he'd bet *bigger* sums and *then* I'd move in for the kill.

MUSIC

"One day, I thought I'd make a *final* killing by inviting *Glendinnig* and

eight others to a game of high-stakes poker. This was to be a *special* occasion, not *just* an ordinary night of card playing.

"By midnight, the others had *long* been *out* of the game. They now stood about *Glendinnig* and me, *watching* the stakes rise *higher* and higher. For the *first* time, my *opponent* seemed to take the game *seriously,* no longer as *mere* entertainment."

GLENDINNIG
I raise you ten…*and* ten *more*…

WILSON
(REVERB) "As planned, in a very *short* period, he owed me a *great* amount. After having downed *another* glass of port wine, he did *precisely* what I had been *coolly* anticipating…"

GLENDINNIG
In fact, *I* propose that we *double* the stakes.

WILSON
Oh, I don't know about that.

GLENDINNIG
What? Are you *scared* to go further, my friend?

WILSON
That's a *lot* of money. I'm sure all of our friends here can *agree?*
(MEN MUMBLE)

GLENDINNIG
What's *money* to *professional* card players such as *ourselves?*

WILSON
Professional? I see. Alright, alright…let's *double* the pot.
(APPLAUSE)

(REVERB) "Less than an *hour* later he had *quadrupled* his *debt* to me. Now, *any* appearance of being *merely* entertained had *completely* left his face. He had grown fearful, *perspiration* pouring down his brow."
SILENCE

GLENDINNIG
Is it *hot* in here? It's *stuffy* in here, very close…

WILSON
Must be the wine.

GLENDINNIG
Yes, this wine…it's getting to me…yes, must be the wine…

MUSIC

WILSON
"Now, Glendinnig was *extremely* wealthy, so, I doubted if his *losses* might subject him to any *grief.* Or, so I had *thought.* But, a nearby fellow informed me that I had just *wiped* out Glendinnig's *entire* annual *allowance.* He was *devastated.* And, *everyone* knew it. What was I to do? My *dupe* was attracting *pity* from everyone. It was *embarrassing.* They *glared* at me, scornful, *reproachful* of my winning.

(WIND, DOORS SLAM OPEN)

"Just then…the doors flew open and, as if by magic, *all* the lamps in the room were *extinguished!* I was able to perceive that a *stranger* had entered the room. A stranger, *my* height, dressed in a cloak. And, all of us, *standing* in darkness, *knew* he was there in our midst."

SILENCE

WW
(Whispers) Gentlemen…I make *no* apology for this behavior because *I* am fulfilling a duty. You are, *beyond* doubt, *uninformed* of the *true* character of the person who has *tonight* won a *large* sum of money from Mr. *Glendinnig.* Therefore, I will *tell* you who he is. Please *examine* the inner linings of the *cuff* of his left sleeve.

WILSON
(REVERB) "It was so still, one could hear a *pin* drop. Then, he departed as *quickly* as he had come. Can I *describe* my sensations? Must I say that I felt, all at once, the *horrors* of the *damned*? Of course, there was no time to *reflect* upon this *phenomenal* intrusion.."

MUSIC

MAN
Look at his cuffs! Someone *turn* on that light! *Search* him!

GLENDINNIG
Look at *that!* Doubles with *bent* corners! He's been *cheating!*

WILSON
(REVERB) "I said nothing. What *could* I have said?"

MAN
Mr. Wilson, *here* is your coat. We've had *enough* of *your* kind of skills. You will see the necessity, I *hope*, of *quitting* this college and of *leaving* this room, immediately. Meanwhile, you will *hand* back to Mr. Glendinnig the money *you* have *robbed* from him!

WILSON
(REVERB) "I was so *humiliated,* shamed, *mortified,* disgraced. When my cloak was *thrown* at me, I realized that it was *no* different than what the *stranger* had worn. And, *this* was a *rare* coat with a *mink* fur collar. In fact, I had it *specially* made. *One* of a kind. It had cost *quite* a bit of money. And, yet…it was *quite* evident, even in the low light, that the *stranger* wore the *same* coat!

SILENCE

"The *next* day I fled in vain. For *years* to come, my evil destiny *pursued* me.

MUSIC

"In *every* city, just as I had settled in, *Wilson* was sure to appear and *ruin* my life. In *Rome,* he *ruined* my job. In *Paris,* he *ruined* my engagement. In *London,* I was nearly *hanged.* Where could I have gone to *escape* from him? Why had he been *doing* this to me? *All* that time? Hadn't he a *life* of his own? Why spend *years* tormenting me?

"I thought it *weird* that, in times past, I had not even *seen* his face when he would suddenly appear. Of course, I *knew* who it was each time. I could *never* forget that *whisper* in his voice. He *dominated* my thoughts. *Always* present in my fears. He made me *weak* and helpless. So *much* so, I found solace *only* in drink. I *tried* to resist, to fight back.

SILENCE

"Eventually, I hit *rock* bottom and I *knew* I had to raise myself *up* and *face* my fears. *Something* in me, my *willpower*, gained *enough* strength to *free* myself from his *hold* over me.

(CARNIVAL SOUNDS, CROWDS)
FESTIVE MUSIC

"So, I traveled here, to *New Orleans*, in time for *Mardi* Gras where I had been *invited* to a *masquerade* ball given by a wealthy land owner. Here is where my *newly* found strength soon disappeared. How could I *resist* the non-stop *gayety?* So, I didn't. I *drank* like a fish. *Always* drunk. The crowds *suffocated* me. I was nearing madness...

"And, yet, *despite* my condition...I had fallen in *love* with the *beautiful* young wife of my host, the land owner. She had *hinted* to me that she would be wearing a *particular* costume in the ballroom and so, having caught a *glimpse* of her across the room, I was soon on my way to *greet* her. But, before I came within *ten* feet of the woman, I felt a *hand* on my shoulder... and that *damned* low *whisper* in my ear..."

WW
(Whispers) *William Wilson...*

TENSE MUSIC

WILSON
(REVERB) *"That's it!* I could take no more. I turned and *seized* him *violently* by the collar. He was dressed *just* as I had expected...*exactly* in the *same* costume as I wore...*and* wearing a *mask* of black silk. Like me, he wore a *dagger* at his side."

(NO REVERB) *Scoundrel! Impostor!* You *damned* villain! I *curse* you! You shall not...you *shall* not *dog* me unto death! Follow me, or I'll *stab* you where you stand!

(REVERB) "And, I *dragged* him *through* the ball room into the hallway outside and closed the door.

(DOOR SLAM)

"I *threw* him aside. He staggered against the wall."

MUSIC BUILDS

(NO REVERB) Draw your *blade!* Go ahead! I *dare* you to draw upon me!

(REVERB) "He said nothing and did *not* resist my vengeance *even* as I kept screaming *insults* at him...my *bravado* growing stronger. Why wouldn't he fight back? I had him at my mercy, his *back* to the wall and, so...so...I *plunged* my blade with *brutal* force *repeatedly* through his chest!

(CROWD MURMURING, BANGING ON DOOR)

"The crowd was anxious to gain entry. But, they had not yet entered the locked room where my *antagonist* lay dying. What *horror possessed* me to *do* what I had done? I looked *down* at the bloody *spectacle* before me.

CHAOTIC MUSIC

"What was going *on?* The hall itself...it was *changing*...it was *all* very confusing... where his bloody body *had* lain, a large *mirror* now stood before me there...I hadn't noticed it before. So, I stepped up to it, *terrified* to look upon my *own* image, all *pale* and *dabbled* in blood.

"But...that wasn't *me* in the mirror...it was my antagonist...*Wilson*, who stood there, dying. *See?* His *cloak* and *mask* lay on the floor. Only now...his clothes were different, his face...it *didn't* resemble me at all. I didn't *understand!* In the mirror...*Wilson*...it *had* to have been...and, yet, he no longer whispered...in fact, his voice...sounded very much...like my own..."

WW
(REVERB) "*You* have conquered, and *I* yield. Yet, from *here* on, *you* are also *dead* ...*dead* to the World, to *Heaven* and to *Hope!* In me, *you* existed...and, in my *death*, as you *see* by this image, which is your own...*you have murdered yourself!*"

END

THE OVAL PORTRAIT
By Edgar Allan Poe
Adapted By Dan Bianchi

CAST - 2m/2w
SYNOPSIS - Carla tells how she and Peter had discovered an old house and a mysterious portrait.

MUSIC
(FOOTSTEPS WALKING THROUGH WOODS)

CARLA
(REVERB) "Several years ago, my friend *Peter* and I had been hiking in the mountains, when…*leave* it to me…I fell, *tumbling* head over heels down a ravine."

(NO REVERB) *Aaaaaahhhh!*

SILENCE

PETER
Carla! Are you *alright?*

CARLA
Nothing broken I think. Feels like I sprained my ankle.

PETER
Hold on…I'll be right there! Can you *walk* on it?

(DISTANT THUNDER)

CARLA
A bit. Not far. Oooh…no…I don't know…

PETER
Well, it's getting dark. Look at those clouds. A *storm* is on the way. We'll need to find some shelter. Maybe that deserted *house* we saw a quarter mile back that way.

CARLA
That's pretty far.

(THUNDER CLAP)

PETER
Well, we can't stay here. Come on, lean on me...

MUSIC
(THUNDER, RAIN)

CARLA
(REVERB) "Well, we made it back to the house and we *forced* our way in."

(DOOR THUMPS, SMASH DOOR)

PETER
Looks like it's only been abandoned for a short while. The rooms are still furnished. Let's look around.

CARLA
(REVERB) "So, we found one of the *smallest* rooms in the East wing to spend the night. Its decorations were rich, yet *tattered* and antique. On the walls hung old musty *paintings* and *moth*-eaten tapestries...lots of *cobwebs* about. But, there was *one* room filled with a great *many* paintings...more *modern* in style."

PETER
I've closed the shutters and lit the candles. Are you in a lot of pain?

CARLA
Yes.

PETER
There's a bed in there... try to make yourself comfortable.

CARLA
These paintings...they're fascinating. I can't take my *eyes* off of them.

PETER
They're everywhere. They're all so similar, they must have been by the same artist. What's that you've found?

CARLA
A book...it was lying *open* here on the side table. Why, it's a book about these paintings, I believe. Interesting...

PETER
Well, I am going to get some shut eye. Try to get to sleep. Let's hope

that storm lets up by morning.

SILENCE
(CLOCK STRIKES)

CARLA
(YAWNS)
(REVERB) "Was it *that* late already? I supposed Peter was fast asleep hours earlier. But, I had found that book so interesting...yet, hard to read by candlelight.

EERIE MUSIC

"The light was so dim, my eyes...hard to focus...but, then, something strange occurred...I thought my *eyes* were playing *tricks* on me...but, the *light* from the candle, it seemed to fall upon *one* painting...there in a frame on the wall. I hadn't *noticed* it before. A *portrait* of a young woman. Mesmerizing.

"Well, I *should* have stopped *right* then and gone to sleep. At least, I could have closed my *eyes* and gave them a rest. But, *no!* I *had* to *see* that face. That *head*, those *shoulders*. The arms, the *bosom*...such expert *skill* the painter must have had...and her hair, how *radiant* it seemed. The way it *melted* into deep shadows. *Odd*, it was the *only* painting there in an *oval* frame. Richly *gilded*, highly detailed. A frame just right for such a *great* painting. I wondered what it was doing there? It should have been in a *museum*, no? The artist, *whomever* he was, had *truly* captured the girl's immortal *beauty* forever on canvas. It was *uncanny* the way she stared *out* at the viewer...*me?* Yes, it was *almost* as if...she were a *living* person, right there, before me. Of course, I *knew* she was not. It was *just* a painting in an oval frame.

"Still...I couldn't keep my eyes *off* of her. She was in my *brain*, now. That *lifelike* expression of hers...I'd *never* forget it. She was *there* in the room with me. *Sharing* it with me. The way the flickering light played off of it...so *alive*...*alive*...this *maiden* of rare beauty...so *full* of happiness...I remember thinking, if *only* she could speak to me...what might she say?"

SILENCE

WOMAN
(REVERB) "Yes, full of happiness. *Once*. But, I *rue* the day, the *hour*, when I saw and fell in *love* and *married* the painter. Oh yes. He was passionate, *studious*, strict...but, he was *already* married...to his *Art*. My *rival*. I began to *hate* it. I *hated* the pallet and brushes, the *easel*

and paints which kept *him* occupied day and night. And, then...he asked to paint *my* portrait. Of course, I *wanted* that. Just think, *posing* for him, I'd *be* with my love for *weeks* to come, no? Little did I know.

MUSIC

"Oh yes, he took such *glory* in that work. From *hour* to hour, *day* to day...so much *passion* from this *wild* and moody man. *Not* for me...but, for his *painting* of me. So *much* so...he *failed* to notice that *I* was *ill...withering* away...yet, *still* obediently *posing* for him. I was a mere *shadow* of myself, *still* smiling, without complaints. *He* was *so* happy, *so* involved in his painting, how could I *ruin* it for him?

"The painting was becoming a *marvelous* work. A *great* work. A *symbol* of his *love* for me. But...then...*nearing* the end, he allowed *no* one to see it. He had become *too* involved, *too* much in *love* with his *own* work. He barely ate, *nor* slept, he did little *else* but paint. He rarely lifted his *eyes* from the canvas to even *look* at me. So *obsessed* was he...he *repainted* the portrait *again* and again...He was no *longer* painting what was *before* him... but, what he had *remembered* me to be when we *first* met. With *rosy* cheeks and *golden* hair and *eyes* that glowed. Meanwhile, my *spirit* within me had been *waning*...my *health* wasting away. It was as if every *stroke* of that brush had *sapped* my life spirit out of me. Still, I *tried* to remain his subject. But, *she*, the girl in the painting, remained his subject. And, when the *last* stroke of his brush had *completed* his great work of Art, the painter, so *enthralled* with himself and his *ability* and his *accomplishment,* cried out with a *loud* voice... "

ARTIST
This is indeed *LIFE* itself!

VOICE
(REVERB) "But, when he turned to me...*finally*...seeking his *beloved*...it was too late, you see. *I* was dead."

SILENCE

CARLA
(REVERB) "Each year since then, Peter and I *return* to that area, *searching* for that house with the oval portrait...but, to this day, we have *never* found it again."

END

THE OBLONG BOX
By Edgar Allan Poe
Adapted By Dan Bianchi

CAST - 2m/1w
SYNOPSIS - A man brings an odd wooden box on board a ship which causes his friend to wonder…what is in that box?

(SHIP HORN, BELL,CROWD, NOISY DOCK)

MRS.CHARLES
Mr. *Carlisle!*

CARLISLE
Yes, Mrs. Charles?

MRS.CHARLES
Are we on time for departure?

CARLISLE
We are being delayed for a *late* passenger. It shouldn't be long.

MRS.CHARLES
I see that Mr. Cornelius *Wyatt* is on the passenger list.

CARLISLE
You know him, Madame?

MRS.CHARLES
My brother and he went to *Harvard* together. He was a good friend, back then. It's been a while since I've seen him last. He's now a famous *artist*, you know…a *rare* genius. I see that he's reserved *three* state rooms?

CARLISLE
Yes Madame. He's traveling with his *wife* and his two sisters.

MRS.CHARLES
Four people in *three* state rooms? Three *big* rooms for four people? Seems like he might do with just *two* rooms. Ah, maybe it's for a *servant?*

CARLISLE
I don't think so. Look here in the log book... there *was* to be a servant, she's *originally* written down, but, crossed out.

MRS.CHARLES
Ah. Well, maybe he's using the *extra* room for baggage.

CARLISLE
Well, then, it must be something *special* since all baggage *that* big goes into the hold.

MRS.CHARLES
You know what? The *extra* room must be for a *valuable* painting he doesn't want out of his sight. Yes, *that* must be it. So, his two *sisters* are with him? I *do* know them very well. Claudia and Francine. Nice girls. However, I've *never* met his wife. The sisters *have* talked about her. They say she's a *beautiful* woman. Very intelligent. Very witty. I can't *wait* to meet her. Are the *Wyatts* on board, yet?

CARLISLE
Well...*they* are the passengers we're waiting for...

MRS.CHARLES
Really?

CARLISLE
They were *due* to come aboard, but, *Mrs.* Wyatt was indisposed and so they've been detained. Ah, *here* they are now...down there, coming up the gangplank.

MRS.CHARLES
I see them. There's Cornelius...and his sisters...*and* his wife. I wonder if he can *hear* me in all this ruckus? *Hello! Cornelius!* Cornelius *Wyatt!*

CARLISLE
He's looking this way, Madame. I think he sees you.

MRS.CHARLES
It's *me! Henrietta Charles!* That's funny...it seems he recognized me ...but, *purposely* looked the other way. Hmm. And, did you see his *wife?* She was wearing a *veil* over her face. And, when she *lifted* it to speak to him...well, I must say...she was *not* the beauty I had expected.

CARLISLE
True, Madame. I guess *beauty* is in the eye of the beholder.

MRS.CHARLES
Very *plain* looking. And, *that's* putting it mildly
.

CARLISLE
She was sure wearing *expensive* clothes.

MRS.CHARLES
I can only suppose she's *captivated* my friend's heart by the more *enduring* graces of the *intellect* and soul. But, that's no cause for *him* to ignore me. Well, Cornelius *was* always a *temperamental* fellow. He's probably in one of those *moods* artists often have. What's that big *box* on the dock there? That big *oblong* pine box? Does that belong to Mr. *Wyatt?*

CARLISLE
I believe so.

MRS.CHARLES
Well, *that's* an odd shape. I doubt if there's a big *painting* in there. Maybe several *smaller* ones. Or...

CARLISLE
Or what, Madame?

MRS.CHARLES
Hmmm. I *heard* that Mr. Wyatt *bargained* for a *copy* of Leonardo's *"Last Supper"* by *Rubini* last Spring in Paris. It was going for an *astronomical* price. I wonder if *he* had purchased it and is *now* bringing it *North* to New York? S*muggling* the picture into the New York *Art* world *right* under my very nose...*I* am an *art* conneiseur, myself...where he could *sell* it for *five* times the purchase price. Hmmm. But, he's never told *me* that he owns it.

CARLISLE
Well...I can *see* from here...there's *writing* on the box...

MRS.CHARLES
What does it say?

CARLISLE
"Ship to: Mrs. Adelaide *Curtis*, Albany, *New York*. Charge of Cornelius *Wyatt,* Esq. This side up. To be handled with care."

MRS.CHARLES
Mrs. Adelaide *Curtis* of *Albany?* Ah, *she* is his mother-in-law.

CARLISLE
See? It's *not* going to New York City.

MRS.CHARLES
Don't believe it for a second. It's a *ruse.* I'll bet that box won't get *any* further than Wyatt's *own* studio on *Chambers* Street in New York City. *Aha!* I now have a *mystery* to solve.

CARLISLE
Well, everything and *everyone* appears to be on board now. We should be getting under way in another few minutes.
                                        MUSIC
                    (SHIP HORN, WAVES, ENGINE)

MRS.CHARLES
Hello, *Carlisle!* Fine weather we've been having.

CARLISLE
Two days out of Kingsport and we've got *good* weather ahead. We'll stop in *Charleston* and be on our way.

MRS.CHARLES
The passengers seem to be in good spirits.

CARLISLE
Indeed, they are.

MRS.CHARLES
But, I *must* say...I haven't seen the *Wyatts.* The two sisters, I've seen *briefly*, but, they don't seem *well* to me. Didn't have much to say.

CARLISLE
Must be the voyage. Not *many* can take the swells. I haven't seen Mr. Wyatt. But, *Mrs.* Wyatt is out and about on deck and seems *very* agreeable.

MRS.CHARLES
Yes, she's a *chatty* one, that one. The *rest* of the ladies seem to like her.

CARLISLE
And, the *men*, too. She had us *all* laughing just a while ago.

MRS.CHARLES
Well, I *heard* she was witty. But, tell the truth, Carlisle...are they laughing *with* her, or *at* her?

CARLISLE
Ah, well...she's *not* the kind of refined lady I *would* have expected *dressed* in all that finery and jewelry.

MRS.CHARLES
I've even overheard *some* ladies say that she's "a *good-hearted* thing, rather *indifferent* looking, *totally* uneducated, and *decidedly* vulgar."
I just can't imagine *why* Wyatt married her. If she *were* wealthy, that *might* be a reason. But, Wyatt said she hadn't a *penny* to her name. I remember his very words...

WYATT
(REVERB) "I married for *love* and for *love* only. My bride is far *more* than worthy of *my* love."

MRS.CHARLES
Yes, it's *puzzling* to me. He's *always* been so refined, so *intellectual,* so fastidious, with so keen an *appreciation* of the beautiful.

CARLISLE
As you say, Madame, artists *are* a funny lot. Maybe, he's taken *leave* of his senses?

MRS.CHARLES
Alright, perhaps, *she* loves *him* beyond reason. She certainly lets everyone *know* that, always referring to *Wyatt* as her *beloved* husband to the extent that she seems *ridiculous*. And, she's *so* loud.

CARLISLE
That she is.

MRS.CHARLES
It is obvious, the *other* ladies *are* laughing at her. I can only *imagine* that, by some *unaccountable* freak of fate, or perhaps, in some *fit* of *enthusiastic* and *fanciful* passion, Wyatt married a person *altogether* beneath him. Immediately *following* that, he must have *realized* what he had done and became *disgusted*. I say that, because, I haven't *yet* seen *Wyatt* with *her* on deck, in the *dining* room, nor on the *dance* floor.

CARLISLE
Mr. Wyatt has shut himself up *alone* in his state-room. No visitors.

MRS.CHARLES
I *know!* I tried to see him.

CARLISLE
Well, Mrs. Charles…I *do* believe that your *wait* is over.

MRS.CHARLES
I beg your pardon?

CARLISLE
There's Mr. Wyatt now…just came up on deck. Now's your chance to talk to him.

MRS.CHARLES
You're *right!* Oh…*Cornelius!* Hello, it's me…Henrietta *Charles!*
(WAVES. ENGINE)
MUSIC

Cornelius! Where have you been? Have you been sick? You *look* ill? Has something happened? It *couldn't* have anything to do with the *contents* of that box you brought aboard now, *could* it? *Aha!* You thought you could fool *me* with that *odd* shaped box? What's wrong, Cornelius? Why are you *staring* at me like that? Stop that. You look like a *mad* man. It was only a joke.

WYATT
Joke? Yes, a *joke!* Hahahahaa…!

MRS.CHARLES
Your eyes look as though they'll *pop* out of your head. Calm down, man, you're going to *burst* a blood vessel. *Cornelius!* Oh dear…*Help!* Help! Help… *someone!* We need help!

MUSIC

CARLISLE
I don't know what you said to him, but, I *advise* that you *avoid* him for the rest of the passage.

MRS.CHARLES
I didn't say much of anything. He just *looked* at me all *wild*-eyed, as if I wasn't even *there* and then…he just *fell* to the deck.

CARLISLE
His mind is…

MRS.CHARLES
Yes, I understand. But…you see…

CARLISLE
What's that, Mrs. Charles?

MRS. CHARLES
Well, last night…*after* the incident…I was feeling *very* nervous, I couldn't sleep. *Especially* after drinking a *strong* cup of green tea. While *walking* the deck, I *clearly* saw *Mrs.* Wyatt, about *eleven* o'clock …*sneaking* from the Wyatt's *state* room into the *extra* room, the *third* room of theirs…where she *remained* until daybreak.

CARLISLE
You *watched* until daybreak?

MRS.CHARLES
Don't be impertinent. Like I said, I couldn't sleep. So, I've *deduced* that they are *probably* separated, most likely *heading* for divorce. You *see?* That's why they've rented the *extra* state room? *She* spends the night in *there.*

CARLISLE
You could be right. Truth of the matter is…(Whispers) My second mate on *night* duty has reported that she's done *just* that every night since we've shipped out.

MRS.CHARLES
Really? Aha! Well, has he heard…*sounds* coming from Cornelius Wyatt's room…the one she *leaves* each night?

CARLISLE
What sort of *sounds?*

MRS.CHARLES
It's not that *I* am a *nosey* person, Carlisle…well, alright, I *admit* that I am… but, *you* too would not have *ignored* them. So, I stood right *outside* his door and listened.

CARLISLE
So, you were standing outside his door. What did you hear?

MRS.CHARLES
What did I *hear?* It sounded as if the artist was *prying* open that *oblong* box using a *chisel* and mallet.
                              (HAMMERING, LID PRIED OPEN, DROPS)

After that, there was a dead stillness…
                                        (DISTANT SOBS)

…until I heard a low *sobbing*, or *murmuring* sound, hardly audible. Had I *imagined* that? Was the man *weeping* over *Rubini's* copy of *The Last Supper?* In my opinion, it's not *that* great to make a grown man weep. Now, if it were the *original* by Leonardo, I could see…

CARLISLE
Maybe, he was weeping because he realized he would *soon* be a millionaire?

MRS.CHARLES
Could be. But, somehow, I don't think *money* would move him to tears.
                                  (DISTANT HAMMERING)

So…when he's through with sobbing, he *returns* the lid to the box and *nails* it shut again. A few minutes pass and *Mrs.* Wyatt returns to the room. And, *you* say, the Second Mate reports *much* the same thing for the past *four* nights? Hmm, odd, *very* odd…
                                          (WAVES, WIND)
                                             MUSIC

CARLISLE
Good day, Mrs. Charles!

MRS.CHARLES
Carlisle! Where are we now?

CARLISLE
We're off Cape Hatteras. Better get below, there's a *tremendously* heavy *gale* wind coming in from the Southwest. The weather's been *threatening* for some time. We've *battened* down everything.

MRS.CHARLES
I've never been *in* a storm at sea before!

CARLISLE
We'll make it through. She's an *excellent* sea boat.
> *MUSIC*
> (LOUD THUNDER, STORM,
> WAVES, SHOUTS, SCREAMS)

MRS.CHARLES
Carlisle! We've been tossed about for *hours!* Are we going to make it?

CARLISLE
It doesn't look good! The *after*-sail is cut to ribbons…we're taking on water! We've lost three men overboard! The storm-stay sail is *barely* holding…

MRS.CHARLES
Good God! We're done for!
> (THUNDER, LOUD WOOD CRACK)

CARLISLE
It's the mizzenmast! Look out!
> (CRASH, SCREAMS)
> *MUSIC*
> (CALM WAVES)

CARLISLE
Well, folks…the *good* news is that the storm's *almost* past. The bad news is we've got *four* feet of water in the hold! The *pumps* are choked and useless!

MRS.CHARLES
Tell us what to do, Carlisle! *You're* the first mate! Where's the Captain?

CARLISLE
He's up top doing his *best* to keep us afloat…but, not for long. We're to throw as *much* as we can overboard. Make the ship as *light* as we can.
(VOICES GRUMBLE)

MRS.CHARLES
Are we going down?

CARLISLE
We've cut away the *two* masts remaining…but, the water's *rising* quickly below. We may *still* have a chance of keeping afloat!
MUSIC
(WAVES)

CARLISLE
There's a full moon. That should light our way.

MRS.CHARLES
We've been drifting for *three* days, Carlisle…where *are* we?

CARLISLE
We're at the *Ocracoke* Inlet. There are *fourteen* of us and *six* left in the crew and the Captain…who was *struck* by the mizzenmast when it came down…he's *still* unconscious. So…*I'm* in charge now. And, *I* say it's time to *lower* the longboat! We can *row* the rest of the way to shore!
(CHEERS, CROWD NOISES)

MRS.CHARLES
God help us!

CARLISLE
That's it, *everybody* stay calm…pitch in…we'll get through this, ladies and gentlemen! Into the *longboat!* One at a time! Be careful it doesn't get *swamped* when it hits the water. That's it, women *and* children first. Watch your step everyone as you climb *down* the rope ladder. There's no room for anything *except* a few necessary instruments, *some* provisions, and the *clothes* upon our backs. We'll need all the men to help with the *rowing!* Ready now…*everyone* sit still…*grab* your *oars* men! Let's row…
(ROWING)

WYATT
Mr. Carlisle!

CARLISLE
Yes, Mr. Wyatt?

WYATT
This *won't* do! We *need* to bring the box I *brought* aboard with us! *Now!*

CARLISLE
Sit *down,* Mr. Wyatt, you will *capsize* us if you do not sit still. The boat is *already* overloaded.

WYATT
The box! The *box,* I say! You cannot, you *will* not *refuse* me! It doesn't weigh much. It weighs *nothing,* a mere nothing. For the *love* of Heaven, I i*mplore* you to turn round for the *box!*

CARLISLE
Mr. Wyatt, *control* yourself. I cannot listen to you. Sit down, I say, or you will *swamp* the boat. *Somebody!* Grab *hold* of him! *Seize* him! He is about to *spring* overboard!

MRS.CHARLES
Cornelius! Come back!

(SPLASH, PEOPLE SCREAM)

Come back! He'll never make it...

CARLISLE
Mr. *Wyatt!*

MRS.CHARLES
Look...he's *back* at the ship...

CARLISLE
He's *climbing* up the rope ladder!

MRS. CHARLES
The man has gone stark raving mad! We have to get him back!

CARLISLE
We can't do that! The current is taking us away...

MRS. CHARLES
What is he doing now? Can you see him, Carlisle?

CARLISLE
He's *up* on board...looks like he's...running around the deck trying to get *down* to the cabin...but, it must be under water by now...

MRS.CHARLES
Cornelius! Oh, the poor man...he must have lost his mind. All *this* to save a *painting?*

CARLISLE
Mr. Wyatt! Can you hear me? Come *back!* If you don't hurry now, we'll be too far away!

MRS.CHARLES
Carlisle! Is there *any* way we can row *back* to the ship? For the sake of his wife and sisters?

CARLISLE
The waves are too strong. We'll be turned over for sure.

MRS.CHARLES
Then, does that mean...?

CARLISLE
I'm afraid so. *Look!* He's back up on deck...

MRS.CHARLES
What's he doing now?

CARLISLE
He's *dragging* the box! Looks like he's tying a *rope* around it....now around himself...he's *tied* himself to the box!

MRS.CHARLES
Oh my lord! He's not going to...

CARLISLE
He's gone overboard!

MRS.CHARLES
Maybe he can *float* on top of the box, no? Where has he gone? I can't see him.

CARLISLE
I'm afraid… he's gone below.

MRS.CHARLES
So quickly? How can that be?

CARLISLE
He'll rise again…with that box. Once the salt melts.

MRS.CHARLES
The *salt?*

CARLISLE
Quiet. I'll talk to you about this at a more *appropriate* time.

MUSIC
(NEW YORK STREET NOISE)

MRS.CHARLES
Carlisle! Is that you? Why, so it is! How are you *doing,* my friend?

CARLISLE
Hello, Mrs. *Charles!*

MRS.CHARLES
Imagine! Meeting you here on *Lower* Broadway. Why, I haven't seen you *since*…well, since our *harrowing* experience at sea. That was a *terrible* time, wasn't it? I *still* have nightmares of it.

CARLISLE
That was a *close* one, alright.

MRS.CHARLES
Losing those *sailors* and Cornelius *Wyatt* like that…and I *hear* the Captain eventually *died* from his wounds…

CARLISLE
Yes.

MRS.CHARLES
Well, what are *you* doing here, all *dressed* up in a suit and tie? Why aren't you *back* out to sea?

CARLISLE
Oh, I've given up the ships. I'm a *stock* broker now.

MRS.CHARLES
Really? Well, I don't *blame* you. *I'll* never sail again. Listen...we never *did* get to talk after the incident...I've always *wondered* what you were going to tell me on board the *rowboat* just *before* we were rescued? You know, about Mr. *Wyatt?*

CARLISLE
Ah! Yes, indeed. Well, I don't suppose it *matters* much now. You see, he had engaged passage for *himself*, wife, *two* sisters... *and* a servant. His wife was, as *you* said he had told you, a most *lovely*, and most *accomplished* woman. But, on the morning of departure... Mrs. Wyatt suddenly *sickened* and died.

MRS.CHARLES
What? She...*died?*

CARLISLE
Understandably, her husband was *frantic* with grief...but, there was a he *could* not cancel his trip to New York.

MRS.CHARLES
Ah, so, he *did* have the *Rubini* copy after all. It's a *valuable* artwork. But, I guess it's *forever* lost now.

CARLISLE
I don't believe *that* was the reason. You see, it was *necessary* to take to her mother the *corpse* of his *adored* wife.

MRS.CHARLES
To *Albany,* New York, of course! But, *why* all the secrecy?

CARLISLE
Can't you *guess?* There's a universal *prejudice* against bringing a *corpse* on board a *passenger* ship. *Bad* luck and all that.

MRS.CHARLES
Well, in *that* respect, seeing that we were *shipwrecked*, I *guess* the old superstition proved correct.

CARLISLE
But, what's worse…for the *company* that is…*nine*-tenths of the passengers *would* have *canceled* the trip *before* we set sail had they *known* they were sailing with a *dead* woman on board.

MRS.CHARLES
I see. And, they would have demanded *full* refunds, too.

CARLISLE
And, the company couldn't let *that* happen…so, the Captain *arranged* that the corpse, being first *partially* embalmed, *and* packed, with a large quantity of *salt…*

MRS.CHARLES
Ah! The *salt!*

CARLISLE
… in a box of *suitable* dimensions, should be *conveyed* on board as merchandise. *Nothing* was to be *said* of the lady's death. But, it became *necessary* that *some* person should *impersonate* her during the voyage.

MRS.CHARLES
The chatty *servant!*

CARLISLE
Exactly. The *extra* state-room was where the *false* wife, slept, of course, every night…while, in the *daytime*, she performed in *public*, to the *best* of her ability, the *role* of Mr. Wyatt's *wife*.

MRS.CHARLES
What a *fool* I'd been! Too *careless* and too *inquisitive* and too *impulsive*. Well, to tell the truth, *I've* paid the price. As it is, I don't sleep too *soundly* at night. Now, I will *forever* see my friend's face, *desperately* tying himself to his *beloved* dead wife in that *oblong* box. And, I can *still* hear that *hysterical* laughter of his when I had inquired about the *contents* of the box. That *hysterical* laugh…which will *forever* ring within my ears.

WYATT'S VOICE
(REVERB) *"Hahahahaha!"*

END

THE TELL TALE HEART

By Edgar Allan Poe
Adapted By Dan Bianchi

CAST - 2m/1w
SYNOPSIS- The nervous Narrator relates his terrible ordeal of murdering his landlady and disposing of the body.

MUSIC
(THUNDERSTORM)

NARRATOR
(REVERB) "It's *true!* I *am* nervous...I've *always* been very, very *dreadfully* nervous. But*, please* do *not* think I am mad. This *disease* of mine, it hasn't *destroyed,* or *dulled* my senses. It's *sharpened* them. My sense of *hearing* is *razor* sharp. I hear *all* things in Heaven *and* Earth, but *especially* in *Hell*. Does that make me *mad?* Listen, just *observe* how calmly *and* effortlessly I tell you my story.

MUSIC

"It is *impossible* to say how I *came* up with the idea. But, *once* conceived, it *haunted* me day and night. There was *no* object I desired. It had *nothing* to do with *revenge*. Hey, I *loved* the old woman. *She* had *never* wronged me *or* insulted me.

SILENCE

"I didn't want her *gold.* No, *not* her gold. Not at all.

EERIE MUSIC

"No, if you *want* to know what was at the *root* of this problem ...the *cause*...what had *really* bothered me...it was her *eye!* Yes, her...*eye.* She had the *eye* of a vulture...a pale *blue* eye, with a *film* over it. Whenever she *stared* at me, my *blood* ran cold.

SILENCE

"Well, I *had* to get rid of that eye. And so, *very* gradually...I made up my mind to *take* the life of the old woman, and *rid* myself of that *eye* forever.

"Now this is the point. *You* probably think I'm mad. But, *madmen* are *idiots. Me?* You should have *seen* me. You should have seen *how* wisely I proceeded ...with *caution* and *precision* and skill.

MUSIC
(CLOCK STRIKES)

"I was *cunning*, never *kinder* to the old woman than during the *whole* week *before* I killed her.

(DOOR CREAKS)

"And, every night, about *midnight*, I turned the *latch* of her door and opened it...*oh* so gently! And then, when I had made an opening *big* enough to put my *head* through, I took my *flashlight*, and held my *hand* over it so that it wasn't *so* bright, and I looked in. Oh, you would have *laughed* to see how *quietly* and slowly I *moved* my head! *And* my flashlight. I moved *it* slowly ...very, *very* slowly. I had to be careful *not* to wake her. It took me a *whole* hour to put my *whole* head within the opening *so* far that I could *see* her as she *lay* upon her bed.

SILENCE

"*Ha!* I ask you, would a *madman* have been *so* wise as that?

MUSIC

"And then, when my head was *well* in the room, I took my *light* and oh, *so* cautiously, I *aimed* a single thin *ray* upon the *vulture* eye.

SILENCE
(THUNDER)

"And this I did for *seven* long nights. *Every* night just at midnight. But, the eye was *always* closed. So it was *impossible* to do the work. I wasn't *angry* at the old woman. It was her *eye*, her *evil* eye that bothered me. And, every morning, at dawn, I'd *march* into her bedroom and *wake* her and *call* her name, asking her how *she* passed the night. She had *no* idea that *I* had watched her for hours. She *suspected* nothing.

(CLOCK STRIKES, THUNDER)
MUSIC

"So, there I was, just *earlier* tonight, this being the *eighth* night and I was moving cautiously... *opening* the door.

(DOOR CREAKS)

"In fact, I was moving my hand *slower* than the *minute* hand on a *watch* moves. Oh, ...I could *feel* the extent of my *own* powers *and* my wisdom. I could scarcely *contain* my feelings of *triumph*. To *think* that *there* I was, *opening* the door, little by little, and *s*he had *no* idea I was there. I have to say, it made me...smile. *And* chuckle. *Ha!*"

WOMAN
Who's there?

SILENCE

NARRATOR
(REVERB) "Now, at *that* point, someone else *may* have retreated...but, *not* me. Her room was *pitch* dark. Even the *shutters* on the windows were closed...for *security* reasons. I knew that she could *not* see the opening of the door...

MUSIC

"So, I kept pushing it on steadily, *steadily*. My head was in now...I was about to shine my light when..."

(FLOORBOARD CREAKS)

WOMAN
Is somebody *there?*

SILENCE

NARRATOR
(REVERB) "Well, now...alright, I stood dead still, my body frozen...I said nothing. For a whole *hour,* I did not move a muscle. In the meantime. I did not *hear* her lie down. I thought, she must *still* be sitting up in the bed, listening...just as *I* had done, night after night, *listening* to the *rodents* in the walls of my room.

(WOMAN GROANS)

"And *then*...oh, that was not *just* a groan. *That* was the groan of *mortal* terror. Not pain, *not* grief, oh no. It was the low *stifled* sound that *arises* from the bottom of the soul when it is *frightened* to death.

MUSIC

"*I* know that sound well. Many a night, *just* at midnight, when *all* the world is asleep, it *overtakes* me. Echoing, dreadfully. *Dark* terrors of the night. So, I *knew* what the old woman was feeling...I *pitied* her. Although, once again, I *couldn't* help from chuckling. You see, she'd been lying *awake* there for an *hour!* Listening. *Straining* to hear. Her *fears* multiplying."

SILENCE

WOMAN
It's nothing but the *wind* in the chimney...or, it's only a *mouse* crossing the floor.

NARRATOR
(REVERB) "A *mouse* crossing the floor? She was trying to *comfort* herself with all the possibilities."

WOMAN
A *cricket* must have gotten in the front door.

NARRATOR
(REVERB) "All in vain. All in vain. Because *Death* was stalking her, casting a *black* shadow over her, *enveloping* the victim."

WOMAN
I know you're there, *whomever* you are.

NARRATOR
(REVERB) "I couldn't *wait* much longer. I'd been *very* patient. I hadn't heard her *lie* down again. So, I just...took my hand from my flashlight ...*careful*...so slowly...*slowly*...so that a single *dim* ray, like the *thread* of a spider, fell *full* upon that *vulture* eye.

MUSIC

"It was open...wide, *wide* open! That made me *angry*, I'll say! I saw it *quite* clearly enough...a dull blue, with a *hideous* veil over it that *chilled* the very *marrow* in my bones. The *nerve* of her! Sitting there *wide* awake *all* that time! I saw nothing *else* of the old woman's face *or* person. You see, as if by *instinct*, I had directed the *light* beam *precisely* upon that *damned* eye!

(HEART BEATING, GROWING STRONGER)

"Now, I've *already* told you...don't *mistake* my over *acuteness* of the senses for *madness*. If *not* for those senses...*wait*! What's that? A dull, *quick* sound...like a *watch* wrapped in cotton. I *know* that sound well. It is the *beating* of a heart...the *old* woman's *heart*! Pounding, *pounding*...getting me *angrier* by the second. It's like the *beating* of a *drum* stimulating the *soldier* into courage. I stand still. I'm *scarcely* breathing. My flashlight ...I'm *trying* to keep it steady, *focused* on that eye. But, that sound...the *beating* of her heart....growing louder, *quicker* and quicker, and *louder* and *louder* every instant. The old woman's *terror* must be *extreme*! I wonder if *she* hears what *I* hear? It's so damned *loud*!

"I told you. I am a *nervous* being. So, you can *imagine*, in the *dead* of night, in the *dreadful* silence of this old house, that *strange* sound *exciting* me to *uncontrollable* terror. Yet, I remain *standing* here, my feet *glued* to the floor. But, the *beating* is *beyond* loudness. How can a *heart* beat so *loudly*…it must be ready to *burst!*

"Now a *new* anxiety *seizes* me. What if…what *if* the sound can be *heard* by a neighbor? *No! No!* I can't *risk* it any longer. *The old woman's hour has come!* I *throw* open the door and *leap* into the room.
            (WOMAN SCREAMS,   CRASH, HEART BEAT SLOWS)

"In an instant… I *drag* her to the floor, and *pull* the heavy *mattress* over her. I smile…I *chuckle. Ha!* The deed is done. But, for many minutes, the heart beats on with a *muffled* sound. *That* doesn't bother me. No one can hear it *through* the wall.
                              (BEATING STOPS)
                                  SILENCE

"Stopped. It's stopped. The old woman is dead. Let me get her up onto the bed. I must *examine* the corpse. Yes, she's stone, *stone* dead alright. *Shush!* Listen to her heart. *Hear* anything? No? No pulse. She's stone dead. That *eye* will trouble *me* no longer.
                                  MUSIC

"If you *still* think I am mad, you'll change your *view* as *I* describe the *wise* precautions I had taken to *conceal* the body. The hours passed by, and I worked quickly, but, in silence.
                              (SAWING)

"First of all, I *dismembered* the corpse. That involved *cutting* off the head *and* the arms *and* the legs.
                              (PRYING BOARDS)

"Next, I took up *three* planks from the *floor* in the parlor. That's where I *deposited* all of the body parts. I replaced the boards *so* cleverly, *so* cunningly, that *no* human eye…not even *hers*…might *detect* anything wrong. There was *nothing* to wash out…no *stain* of any kind…no *blood-*spot whatever. I'd been *too* cautious for that. An old *wash* tub had caught *all* of the drippings. *Hahaha!*
                        (CLOCK STRIKES FOUR)
                                  SILENCE

"Four o'clock and all is well. Still *dark* as midnight. I *love* the quiet of the *early* hours of the morn.
                        (SHARP KNOCKING)

"The door! At *this* hour? Who might be at the *door* at this hour? Well, I *have* to open it. Of course. What have *I* to fear? Nothing."

(DOOR OPENS)

DETECTIVE
Hello, madame, *sorry* to bother you. I'm Detective *Burton*...these two are officers Mullins and Shippee. My badge?

NARRATOR
Yes, I see. How can I help you, Detective?

DETECTIVE
Well, we're here on a *complaint* that a *scream* was heard by two of your neighbors during the night...coming from *this* house. We have to *investigate,* you understand.

NARRATOR
(REVERB) "I smile...for what have *I* to fear?"

(NO REVERB) Do come in, *absolutely,* Detective. But, I'm afraid you've been sent on a *wild* goose chase. You see, that *scream?* That was *me.* I had a *terrible* nightmare. My landlady is *away* and I'm all *alone* here in this old place and...well, you understand?

DETECTIVE
Do you mind if we *inspect* the premises? We *have* to follow procedure.

NARRATOR
Naturally. Please do. Follow me. I'm so ashamed...

(REVERB) "I lead them *all* through the house. Even to the old woman's bedroom. I show them her *treasures,* secure, undisturbed. In fact, I'm feeling *so* confident..."

(NO REVERB) Please, Detective Burton, gentlemen...sit down, *relax* a bit. I'm *sure* you've got a *lot* of serious work ahead of you tonight. Would you men enjoy a glass of *whiskey?*

DETECTIVE
Don't mind if we do!

NARRATOR
(REVERB) "Oh, this is *wonderful!* I feel *so* triumphant...in fact, I feel *so*

secure, I *boldly* place my *own* chair on the very *spot* where the *corpse* is buried beneath the floor. The officers *seem* satisfied. My *nonchalant* manner has convinced them. *I* have *nothing* to worry about."

(NO REVERB) More whiskey?

DETECTIVE
We really shouldn't...but, why *not?*

NARRATOR
Why not?

(REVERB) "We chat on and on about the *weather,* the *neighborhood,* the latest in *sports* and such. After a while, I feel bored. I've had enough. Haven't I *proven* my point? Now, I wish them gone.

MUSIC
(RINGING NOISE GROWS)

"But..."

DETECTIVE
Are you feeling well? You're holding your head...

NARRATOR
It's nothing, just a headache. There's a *ringing* in my ears.

(REVERB) "I should think *that's* a reason for them to leave. But, the whiskey has *done* its work. They continue to *sit* and chat and drink. The *ringing*...it's becoming *more* distinct. I talk more *freely* to get *rid* of the feeling, but it continues until...I discover that the *noise*...it's *not* coming from *inside* my head! *No!*
(DULL HEART BEATING, GROWS LOUDER)

"I feel the *blood* drain from my face. Feeling faint. But, I keep talking, *talking.* Yet, the sound *increases.* What can I do? It's a low, *dull,* quick sound, you know, like a *watch* makes *wrapped* in cotton? Apparently, the *officers* don't hear it."

DETECTIVE
The way he *batted* in the fourteenth inning, you'd think he was playing for his life. Now, you take the centerfielder, O'Malley...
MUSIC BUILDS

NARRATOR

(REVERB) "Why aren't they *leaving?* Why don't they *hear* that noise? Can't they *see* me pacing the floor? Back and forth, back and forth. Don't they *get* my message? Time to *leave,* gentlemen, time to.... *Oh God! What should I do?* I begin to *argue* with them. Foaming, *raving,* swearing. *Anything* to silence that noise. *They* hear it. They *must!* How can they *not* hear it? So, I swing my *chair* and grate it upon the *floor* boards...but, the noise gets even louder...*louder* ...*louder!* And *still* the men chat pleasantly...and smile. God in *Heaven,* how can they be *so* oblivious to it? *No, no! They hear!* They *suspect!* That's it. They *know!* They're here to *trap* me. They are making a *mockery* of my horror! How *dare* they do that! *Anything* is better than that *agony!* Anything is more *tolerable* than that *noise!* Make no mistake...they are *mocking* me! You *hypocrites!* I can bear their *smiles* no longer! I feel that I must *scream* or die! *Louder! Louder! Louder! Louder!"*

SILENCE

(NO REVERB) *Villains!* You're so *desperate* to know, aren't you? Alright, I *admit* the deed! *Tear* up the planks! There, *right there! That's* where it's coming from...that sound...it's the *beating* of her hideous *heart!*

END

#

By Edgar Allan Poe
Adapted By Dan Bianchi

CAST - 2m
SYNOPSIS - A butler must listen to his wealthy employer obsess over his late fiancée's smile.

MUSIC

PURDY
Misery comes in all forms, *hey,* Carter? So, *how* is it that *I* was chosen to be *cursed* with sorrow from something *so* beautiful?

CARTER
Well, you know what they say, sir…Out of joy, *sorrow* is born?

PURDY
My *family,* Carter…they're *all* gone.

CARTER
They *were* an old and honored family, sir.

PURDY
All I've got left is this *gloomy* place….filled with *things,* Carter. *Priceless* things. Italian *frescoes* in the main hall, medieval *tapestries* in the bedrooms…Greek *sculptures* in the garden, massive paintings along the staircase wall. The *library* in here stocked with books from all *over* the world. My mother *died* in this library.

CARTER
Yes, sir…I remember.

PURDY
That was where *and* when I was born…on the night my *mother* died in that room. *I* came into this world *born* into a fairyland, a *palace* of imagination, into the halls of *thought* and learning and *information*. No *wonder* I spent my boyhood *immersed* in books. A *world* of fantasy, *hey*, Carter? What did *I* care about the *outside* world? *My* everyday existence was in the land of *dreams*.

CARTER
You were an *avid* reader as a lad.

PURDY
And, then…my cousin, *Berenice,* came to live with us…and from then on, we *grew* up here, together. The *two* of us *against* the world, Carter.

CARTER
Yes, sir.

PURDY
Me? I was *always* sickly, *gloomy…* like this place. Berenice was *agile,* graceful*, overflowing* with energy. *I* stayed here in my library. *She* roamed the hillsides. *I* meditated daily, *addicted* to my lifestyle, body *and* soul, like a monk. *She* wandered *carelessly* through life. *Berenice!* I can *still* see her now. *Standing* before me. *Filled* with light-heartedness and joy! A *fantastic* beauty! Like a goddess.

CARTER
She was, *indeed,* beautiful.

PURDY
But, then…*aaah! Why* must *my* life be *engulfed* in *mystery* and terror? It was that *father* of *hers! Died* in *madness* contracted from that infernal *disease.* I blame *him…*the *sins* of the father, hey, Carter?

CARTER
Please, sir, you mustn't get yourself worked up…

PURDY
That filthy, sinful *disease…*it *struck* like a *tornado* upon his *own* daughter. It *ate* up her *spirit* affecting her *mind,* her *character,* and, perhaps the most *terrible* change…it *twisted* her *beauty* into…*oh God!* It *stole* her identity. How could it *not* affect her *personality?* The destroyer *came* and went and the victim… where is *she?* She was *no* longer *Berenice!* Do you remember how it *changed* her, Carter? She wasn't the same, was she? *Suffering* like that…?

CARTER
It was not *her* fault.

PURDY
She'd *rock* her body back and forth, back and forth…and then *settle* into

a *trance*...and, then, she'd *arise* as if it had *not* happened and *hobble* off. Meanwhile, my *own* disease began to take over *my* soul. I *buried* myself even *deeper* in my library. Alone. I'd *lose* myself for *days* at a time in here...*staring* at the way the *window* light might hit a *certain* picture...or, *why* a *particular* typography was *used* in a book. Ha! Imagine *that?* Or, I'd just watch the dancing *flame* of a lamp, or the *embers* dying in the fireplace. I'd *dream* away the hours *inhaling* the *perfume* of a flower. Or, I'd repeat *monotonously* the *same* word over and over and over and over... until just the *sound* itself might introduce some *new* image on my mind.

CARTER
We were *all* worried for you, Sir.

PURDY
Yes, I know, you *all* thought I was insane. But, I was *only* trying to keep my mind on *other* things, you see...*anything* to avoid the *reality* of what was *happening* to Berenice. Her condition caused me *great* pain. And, that was when *I* decided to...turn my *anguish* into a more *creative* pursuit. I would *study* Berenice.

CARTER
Study, Sir?

PURDY
Yes. Now, I *didn't* know if I could *help* her...but, I thought I'd *examine* her *change* in personality as an *intellectual* project. In so doing, I had found a *new* obsession. I'd watch *closely* her *descent* into madness and, finally, into death. Does that sound *cold* of me, Carter?

CARTER
Well, Sir, it's not for *me* to say...

PURDY
Yes, yes, I *know* that my aunt had *hoped* for some *romance* between Berenice and I...but, *truth* be told, I had *never* loved her. Not in *that* way. She may have *flitted* about in *diaphanous* gowns on a *beautiful* summer's day, but....she was *not* a *real* creature to me. She was *not* of this *Earth,* you see? On the *other* hand, *she* loved *me.* Oh, that's a fact, Carter. She told me so...and when she *told* me that, I *shuddered* and withdrew, but...I *must* tell you, later on, I felt *bad* about it, so... *one* day, I *did* ask her to *marry* me.

Don't look *shocked,* Carter. It was a *secret* between the two of us. It made *her* happy, at least. There, you *see? I* made *her* happy. I *am* a *nice* fellow, after all. But, *one* day, I was sitting *alone* here in the library...*thinking* of what I had gotten myself into...when, *suddenly,* I looked up and *there* she was...Berenice standing *right* there in the doorway. She was *naked.*

CARTER
Sir...

PURDY
She was *stark* naked. She said nothing. *I* spoke nothing. But, for *some* reason, an icy *chill* ran down my back. It *frightened* me, I tell you. I *sank* back in my chair. A *consuming* curiosity *pervaded* my soul. I remained that way for *some* time, breathless, *motionless,* my eyes *riveted* upon her. Her body...*infected* with disease, it was *terrible* to behold. So, my gaze fell upon her face. She looked *melancholic.* The eyes were lifeless, *dull,* almost without pupils. Such a *glassy* stare. And, those thin and *shrunken* lips. They parted...and she smiled and...there they *were,* Carter!

CARTER
What, Sir?

PURDY
Why, the *teeth!*

CARTER
The *teeth?*

PURDY
Berenice smiled and slowly, her *teeth* came into view. Every day since, I ask God... *Why* did You *allow* that to happen? I *wish* to *death* I had *never* seen them. In an instant, however, she was gone...
                                                            (DOOR CLOSES)

And, all of a sudden...and this was *probably* a product of my *disordered* brain...her *body* may have been gone, yet, that *smile* with its *white* and *ghastly* rows of teeth... had *not* gone. Do you *understand,* Carter? Not a *speck* on their surface, not a *shade* on their enamel, not an *indenture* in their edges...but, that *brief* moment of her smile had *branded* itself upon my memory. I *see* them *now* even *more* clearly than I beheld them then. The *teeth!* The *teeth!* They were *here,* and *there,* and everywhere, *right* before me…long, narrow, and *excessively* white, with the *pale* lips *writhing* about them.

CARTER
I don't understand, Sir…the *teeth?*

PURDY
They were *irresistible.* I struggled in *vain* to *cast* that *image* from my brain, but, to *no* avail. I thought about *nothing* else, but, teeth. *Teeth!* I began to *long* for them, *desire* them. Nothing *else* mattered to me. Now, those teeth enveloped *every* thought, night *and* day, even my dreams. I *saw* them everywhere. I *dwelt* upon their characteristics. I dwelt upon their *peculiarities.* I *pondered* upon their conformation. I *mused* upon their place in nature. I *shuddered* as I *assigned* to them, in imagination, a *sensitive* and *sentient* power… even when *unassisted* by the lips, I could *see* a *moral* expression. I *coveted* them so *madly!* Does that sound *insane,* Carter?

CARTER
Why, I…

PURDY
Maybe. But, I *knew* that if I could only *possess* them…I could return to *reason* and peace of mind.

CARTER
Oh, Sir…I had no idea. I *knew* something was wrong, but…

PURDY
For *days,* I stay *locked* in here, days and nights, trying to direct my *mind,* my *thoughts* to other things. And, *still,* those *teeth* maintained their hold over me. That *hideous* image…it's *so* distinct, it floats about the *shadows* of my room. If I should *doze* off, they *break* into my dreams, *screaming.*

(CLOCK STRIKES)

CARTER
It's very late. You *should* get some rest, Sir. You've had a long day.

PURDY
Berenice's *funeral*…she's buried in her *grave* now… I must continue *on* without her. *Alone* in my library. I don't even *remember* what had happened today. I *do* know it was a day filled with horror.

(THUNDER, WIND)

Unspeakable, *indefinable* horror. I *hear* something...don't you? *There!*
Do you hear that, Carter?

CARTER
What, Sir? What do you hear?

(DISTANT GHOSTLY SCREAM, WIND)

PURDY
Sounds like a departed *spirit*...you don't hear it?

CARTER
No, Sir.

PURDY
It's like the *shrill* and piercing *shriek* of a female voice *ringing* in my ears.
Reminding me that I have *done* some unholy thing.   But, for the *life* of
me, I can't recall. What did I *do?* *What?* Do *you* know, Carter?

CARTER
No...no...

PURDY
It's a mystery to me. I've been wondering...feeling as if all this has
something to do with this little wooden *box*...where did it come from?
It's *odd*. What's it *doing* here on my desk? I *think* I've seen it before...

CARTER
It's been in the family for years. It is a surgeon's *tool* box. It once
belonged to your *Great* Uncle Reginald. He was an Army Surgeon
during the war. You used to *play* with it as a boy...it still holds the
original instruments, I believe.

PURDY
But, how has it come to be *here*, upon my desk? *I* didn't put it here, did
I? Why would *I* do that? Why?

(DISTANT GHOSTLY SCREAM)

There it is *again!* You don't *hear* that, Carter? How can you *not* hear
it? And, what are *you* doing here, hey, Carter? I remember that you
came in here a little while ago to *tell* me something, no doubt...what's
wrong? Why do you *look* like that? What's *worrying* you, man? Out

with it!

CARTER
It's true, Sir…I came to tell you something…important. But, I didn't want to *disturb* you.

PURDY
Don't be ridiculous! Tell me what you *meant* to tell me! I *demand* you tell me!

CARTER
One of the servants, Sir…she discovered that the *grave*…your cousin, *Berenice's* grave…

PURDY
Yes?

CARTER
It has been *violated.*

PURDY
Violated?

CARTER
Oh, Sir…it's too *horrible* to even say it. Someone has…*dug* up her body and…purposely *disfigured* her.

PURDY
What are you saying? You're… *lying!*

CARTER
No! I *saw* it myself, Sir.…there she was, *poor* Berenice, plain as day…

PURDY
What are you *saying*, Carter? Who would *do* such a thing?   Are you *insane?* Don't be ridiculous. For a moment, there, I thought *I* was the one going insane…but*, you, you* take the cake, Carter.

CARTER
It's *true!* Look here…her garments. They're all *muddy* and clotted with blood. *Someone* has done a *terrible* thing to her…her *face.*   Come, Sir, come with me, please. You *must* see. Wait…*what's this?*

PURDY
What?

CARTER
Lying here in the hallway…a *shovel*?

PURDY
What's that you say? What is *that* you've got there? A *shovel?* And, it's covered with mud. It's filthy. Now, what is a *shovel* doing…? *What is…?* What is…?

CARTER
Sir?

PURDY
Oh *no…now* I remember… what I've done… *No! The box! The box!*

CARTER
Sir…allow me to *see* what's in that *box!*

PURDY
Stop, Carter…Get your hands *off of it!* It's *mine!* It's…*Look out!*
(CRASH)

Look what you've done, *you idiot!* Look what you've done….

CARTER
What *are* those things?

PURDY
Surgical instruments!

CARTER
Not those. *Those!* Those little *white* things…*oh, dear Lord!*

PURDY
Look at them, Carter…don't they *gleam* now…sparkling *white?* I've cleaned the blood off of them.   Every one of them…

CARTER
You maniac! It was you! You did that to…! *Aaahhhh!*

PURDY

Come back, *Carter!* Why are you *yelling* like that? There's *nothing* to be alarmed about!   Can't you *see?* I've *cleaned* them. *All* of them. Each and every *one* of them.   *See?* Polished them good. All *thirty* two of them...

END

THE CASE OF M. VALDEMAR
By Edgar Allan Poe
Adapted By Dan Bianchi

CAST – 2m
SYNOPSIS – A hypnotist uses a dying man as a test subject.

NARRATOR
(REVERB) "You've *heard* about the *extraordinary* case of Mr. *Valdemar?* Of course. *Everyone* has heard of it. But, *what* does the public *know* about it? Only what has made its way into the *society* pages. Vicious *gossip* and scandalous, *unfounded* accusations. Misrepresentations and outright *lies*…but, *not* the facts. No, And, all that *blather* has led people to believe that the story is either a *miracle* or a hoax. But, only *I* know the *true* facts and I shall tell you the *real* story.
MUSIC

"For the last *three* years, I've been interested in *Mesmerism*…the art of hypnosis. Nine months ago, it *occurred* to me that *no* person had ever been mesmerized *"in articulo mortis"*…at the *exact* moment of death. Would a patient, at *that* moment, be subject to the *magnetic* influence? If so, would it increase or *decrease* the patient's condition? For how *long* a period could *Death* itself be *arrested* by the process? Just *think* if *any* of these questions could be answered….what might it *mean* to mankind?
SILENCE

"Well, to begin with…I needed a patient. As it turned out, my friend Mr. Ernest *Valdemar,* the *well*-known author who *resided* in Harlem, New York since 1839…*volunteered* to help me with my experiment. He was a *nervous* man, thin and pale with a face *full* of white whiskers, yet his *hair* was still black. People often *mistook* it for a *wig. I* thought he might be a *good* subject for *mesmeric* experimentation. On several occasions, I *had* put him to *sleep* with little difficulty. However, I was *disappointed* to find that his *will* was not *positively* under my control. I blamed *that* on the *condition* of his health. He had been *diagnosed* with *consumption* and he had *very* little time left to live.
MUSIC

"So, you can *see* why, when those *revolutionary* ideas had *first* occurred to me, I had thought of Mr. *Valdemar* as my patient when the *final* moments of life *ebb* from him. I *knew* he had *no* relatives in America who would likely interfere, so, I *spoke* to him *frankly* about the experiment..."

SILENCE

NARRATOR

Wait —

VALDEMAR
I understand *fully!* What an *idea*, my friend. Of *course,* I agree.

NARRATOR
Are you *certain?*

VALDEMAR
I should feel *honored.* Suppose it *should* work? Think what *that* might mean. What *doors* of knowledge might be opened. I know...when my time *nears*...I shall *call* for you about *twenty*-four hours before death knocks...I'll *alert* my physician so that there will be *no* confusion.

MUSIC

NARRATOR
(REVERB) "Seven months ago, I received, from Mr. Valdemar *himself,* this note..."

SILENCE

VALDEMAR
(REVRB) "My dear friend...You may come immediately. My doctor informs me that I may not last *beyond* tomorrow night. I believe him. ...Valdemar."

MUSIC

NARRATOR
(REVERB) "Fifteen minutes later, I was in the dying man's bedroom. I had not seen him for *ten* days, and was *appalled* by the *fearful* change in him. His face was gray, *lead* white. The *gleam* in his eyes was gone. And, he was *emaciated.* His cheekbones nearly *broke* through his skin. He coughed up *blood* constantly and his *pulse* was barely perceptible. Nevertheless, he retained his *mental* power and *some* physical strength. When I entered the room, he was *propped* up in bed, writing *notes* in his journal. His doctor sat in a chair next to him."

SILENCE

VALDEMAR
Come in, my dear friend. This is Dr. Paulsen. He *assures* me that I will be *dead* by tomorrow...I don't mind, I've lived *long* enough in pain.

There is *no* reason to continue. Dr. Paulsen, you might as well leave. There's nothing more you can do.

(DOOR CLOSES)

NARRATOR
(REVERB) "When Dr. Paulsen left, I spoke *freely* with Mr. Valdemar on the subject of his *approaching* death, as well as, about the *proposed* experiment."

VALDEMAR
Didn't I *invite* you to come at the *right* moment just as I had promised? You can have the room next *door* for the night. A *nurse* will stay here by my bedside. I'll instruct her to *fetch* you at the exact moment.

MUSIC

NARRATOR
(REVERB) "That moment came at *approximately* two in the morning. The nurse *urged* me to hurry. There wasn't a *moment* to lose. Mr. Valdemar was sinking fast. When I arrived at his bed, I told the nurse to *stay* as witness to the experiment."

(NO REVERB) Mr. Valdemar, do you wish to be mesmerized?

VALDEMAR
(Coughing, whispering) Yes...I wish....to be mesmerized. Please ...hurry.

NARRATOR
(REVERB) "And so I began the process I had used on him in the past."

(NO REVERB) Look into the *glowing* glass, Mr. Valdemar....that's it...*stare* into its center...it's *beautiful,* isn't it...*drawing* you in...it's making you *sleepy,* tired, isn't it? *Don't* fight it...*accept* it...go to sleep.

(REVERB) "By this time his *pulse* was *imperceptible* and he was *gasping* for breath. This condition carried on for nearly a *quarter* of an hour and then...

(VALDEMAR GASPS DEEPLY
SEVERAL TIMES AND STOPS)
SILENCE

"At five minutes before three, I perceived *unequivocal* signs of the *mesmeric* influence. The glassy *roll* of the eye was changed for that expression of *uneasy* inward examination which is *never* seen except in cases of *sleep*-waking....and which it is *quite* impossible to mistake."

(NO REVERB) Open your eyes, Mr. Valdemar...that's it, you can do it.

(REVERB) "His eyelids *fluttered* at my command. It was *not* enough. Then, I made his *limbs* stiffen. The legs were *stretched* at full length and the arms...the head was *elevated* a bit."

(NO REVERB) That's it...raise your head....now, *lower* it...that's right. Nurse, will you look *closely* and *remember* what you see?   The patient is in a *trance,* no? He is *not* dead...he is in a trance.

(REVERB) "About dawn, I left Mr. Valdemar. I needed to rest.

MUSIC

"I *returned* in the morning and found him in the *same* condition I had left him. His pulse was still imperceptible, *breathing* was gentle, *scarcely* noticeable. I had to put a *mirror* to his lips to test that fact.   His *eyes* were still closed and limbs were *rigid* and cold as marble. *Still,* I wouldn't claim that the man was dead. Not at all."

SILENCE

(NO REVERB) Mr. Valdemar...can you *hear* me? *Nod,* if you can hear me. *Excellent!*   Now, *lift* your right arm...can you *do* that for me? Lift your *right* arm....that's it....higher, *higher*....*excellent!*   Now, *lower* it....very good.   Mr. Valdemar, are you *asleep?* You *must* answer me...are you *asleep?*   I can *see* you want to *tell* me something. Are you asleep?

MUSIC

(REVERB) "At that moment, his whole *frame* shuddered. The eyelids parted...I could *detect* the *whites* in them. His lips moved *sluggishly.* And, in a barely *audible* whisper..."

VALDEMAR
Yes, *asleep* now. Do *not* wake me! *Let me die!*

NARRATOR
Do you *still* feel pain in the *breast,* Mr. Valdemar?

VALDEMAR
No pain...I am dying.

SILENCE

NARRATOR
(REVERB) "The doctor arrived an *hour* later and when *he* examined the patient he was *amazed* to find him *still* alive."

(NO REVERB) Watch this, Doctor. Mr. Valdemar...do you still sleep?

VALDEMAR
Yes...still asleep...*dying.*

NARRATOR
(REVERB) "It was the *doctor's* opinion that Mr. Valdemar should remain *undisturbed* in his condition until *death* supervened...perhaps, a *few* moments from then. I agreed, but, *spoke* to him once more, *repeating* my previous question."

(NO REVERB) Do you still sleep, Mr. Valdemar?

MUSIC

(REVERB) "This time, a *great* change came over the sleeping man. His eyes *rolled* slowly open, the pupils *disappearing* upwardly. His gray skin had turned to *white* parchment.   Any *color* in his cheeks had *disappeared* as quickly as *snuffing* out a candle. His teeth *protruded,* the upper lip withdrew. The *lower* jaw fell open, leaving the *mouth* widely extended, *exposing* his black tongue. It was a *hideous* apparition before me. Even the doctor *and* nurse, who had *probably* been *used* to death, *withdrew* from the bed.

SILENCE

"I now feel that I have reached a point of this *narrative* at which *everyone* will be *startled* into positive *disbelief.* Nevertheless, I shall proceed...

MUSIC

"There was no longer the *faintest* sign of *vitality* in Mr. Valdemar. The doctor *concluded* him to be dead. We *consigned* him to the nurse when suddenly....

(VALDEMAR GAGGING, THEN TRIES TO SPEAK)
SILENCE

(NO REVERB) Mr. Valdemar? Mr. Valdemar...are you sleeping?

VALDEMAR
(REVERB) "Yes…no. I *was* sleeping…and now…now…*I am dead"*
MUSIC

NARRATOR
(REVERB) "I can find *no* words to *fully* describe the unutterable, *shuddering* horror that *filled* my soul at the *sound* of those few words. The nurse fainted. The doctor *immediately* left the room *refusing* to return.
SILENCE

"Once again, I put the mirror to his lips but *this* time…there were *no* signs of respiration. I *tried* to raise his arm or leg or head by instruction …*each* time failed."
SILENCE

(NO REVERB) Mr. Valdemar…do you *hear* me? You *must* follow my direction.

(REVERB) "The only *real* indication of the *mesmeric* influence, was now found in the *vibratory* movement of the tongue.
(VALDEMAR GAGGING)

"Whenever I *addressed* Mr. Valdemar a question, he seemed to be making an *effort* to reply, but, had no longer *sufficient* desire to do so. All *I* knew was…he was *no* longer under my control.
MUSIC

"I stayed *next* to his bedside for hours. His condition *remained* precisely the same. Should I have tried *harder* to awaken him?   What *purpose* would it have served? It was quite *evident* that *death* had been *halted* by the *mesmeric* process. If I had suddenly *awakened* him, he may have *actually* died.
SILENCE

"Well…that was *seven* months ago. I've *continued* to make daily calls at Mr. Valdemar's house, accompanied, *now* and then, by *medical* professionals and other friends. *All* this time the patient has remained *exactly* as I have last described him. He's had *continual* nursing care.
MUSIC

"This morning I *finally* resolved to make the experiment of *awakening,* or *attempting* to awaken him. It is the *unfortunate* result of this *latter* experiment that has caused so much *controversy* and discussion. Nevertheless, I *began* the process of *relieving* Mr. Valdemar from the *mesmeric* trance. For a time, it *was* unsuccessful. At first, the *eyelids* fluttered and the *iris* descended and then...the *pupil*...and then...from *beneath* the lids a *profusion* of yellowish pus *flowed* out with a highly *offensive* odor."

SILENCE

(NO REVERB) Mr. Valdemar, do you *hear* me? *If* you can hear me ...*raise* your arm...raise your arm, Mr. Valdemar.

(REVERB) "But, he did not."

(NO REVERB) Mr. Valdemar, can you *explain* to us *what* are your *feelings* or *wishes* now? Mr. Valdemar...tell us...

NARRATOR

VALDEMAR
(ECHO) "For God's sake! *Quick! Quick!* Put me to *sleep* or, quick! *Waken* me! *Now!* Don't you *see* what you have done? Can't you *see* how I am? *All* this time?"

NARRATOR
What? What Mr. Valdemar? What do you *mean?*

VALDEMAR
(ECHO) "Can't you understand that.... I've been *dead* for so long...*so long*..."

MUSIC

NARRATOR
(REVERB) "I was *thoroughly* unnerved, and, for a moment, *remained* undecided what to do."

(NO REVERB) No...you have been *asleep,* Mr. Valdemar. But now...you *must* awaken. That's right...awaken. See, you're doing *much* better. You must *listen* to me, follow my instructions...you must *awaken,* my friend, from your deep sleep...

(REVERB) "For what *next* occurred, however, it is *quite* impossible that *any* human being could have been prepared. As I rapidly *attempted* to *raise* him through mesmerism..."

VALDEMAR
(ECHO) *"Dead! Dead!"*

MUSIC BUILDS

NARRATOR
(REVERB) "It *burst* forth from the tongue and *not* from the lips of the sufferer and then, his *whole* body at once....within the *space* of a single minute, or even less, *shrunk....crumbled....*absolutely *rotted* away beneath my hands. Upon the bed, before the doctor *and* nurses, there lay the *results* of my experiment...a nearly *liquid* mass of *loathsome* and detestable *putrescence."*

END

MS. FOUND IN A BOTTLE
By Edgar Allan Poe
Adapted By Dan Bianchi

CAST – 2m
SYNOPSIS – A seasoned traveler survives a ship wreck only to find himself aboard a ghost ship.

MUSIC

NARRATOR
(REVERB) "Of my country and of my family I have *little* to say, as I've had *little* use for either one. I *inherited* my wealth…and *that* afforded me a *decent* education. I studied the *German* moralists…*they* gave me great delight…not *just* because *most* of them were *mad*…but, it came rather *easy* to me to *detect* their *false* claims and propositions. As a *genius*, I have *often* been reproached. And, I've been *accused* of *lacking* an imagination, as if *that* is a crime. You *may* be unaware, but, it's no secret that my *opinions* have often made me *notorious* …especially when it comes to *arguments* regarding the *supernatural*. I am…*was*… the *last* person on Earth to *consider* the *supernatural* as a *credible* answer to *any* unanswered problem. I'd *always* used *science* as the answer to *almost* anything. Almost…*anything*.

SILENCE

"I have *admitted* all this because…well, I have an *incredible* tale to tell and I would not want *anyone* to consider it as the creation of a *crude* imagination, nor the *raving* of a lunatic.

(SEA BIRDS, SHIP BELL, WAVES)
MUSIC

"After *many* years spent traveling around the world, I sailed in the year *1855* on a voyage to the Malaysian *archipelago* of the *Sunda* islands. I went as passenger…having *no* other inducement than a kind of *nervous* restlessness, a *need* to explore, I suppose.

"Our *vessel* was a *beautiful* ship freighted with *cotton*-wool and oil, from the *Laccadive* islands. We got under way with a mere *breath* of wind, and for many days *hugged* the Eastern coast of Java. *During* that time, the trip had been *calm* and rather monotonous.

SILENCE
(WAVES)

"One evening, while the *First* Mate and I were on deck…

(NO REVERB) I say, Mr. Hobart…do you see that *cloud* over there to the Northwest? *Remarkable*, isn't it? It's the *first* cloud I've seen since we left harbor. And, its *color*…isn't *that* something?"

HOBART
Does look rather beautiful. The way it spreads out over the sunset.

NARRATOR
Turning into that *wisp* of gray…like a vapor.

HOBART
Moon is out. Looking *red* tonight. The sea seems to be changing…

NARRATOR
I've noticed. Changing rather rapidly. The water seems *more* than usually transparent. I can *distinctly* see the bottom.

HOBART
Fifteen fathoms, I'd say.

NARRATOR
Phew! It's become *intolerably* hot, hasn't it?

HOBART
It's as if every *breath* of wind has died away. I've never *seen* it this calm. Look, there's a *candle* burning on the poop deck…it's not even flickering.

NARRATOR
This doesn't mean we are in any *danger*, does it? You know, the *calm* before a storm?

HOBART
I don't believe so.

MUSIC

NARRATOR
(REVERB) "I went below. I wasn't *entirely* convinced that we were *not* in danger. I've heard of *typhoons* and waterspouts *sneaking* up on ships and islands out here. My uneasiness *prevented* me from sleeping, and

about *midnight* I went upon deck.. As I placed my foot upon the upper step of the *companion*-ladder, I was *startled* by a loud, *rumbling* noise…sounded like a herd of buffalo…
(RUMBLING, GROWING LOUDER)
MUSIC BUILDS

"Before I could *ascertain* its meaning…I found the ship *quivering* and vibrating…
(ROAR, CRASH, WAVES, SCREAMS, WOOD SPLITTING)

"…and *suddenly* a *wall* of foam *hurled* us on our side as a *monstrous* wave *rushed* over us fore *and* aft, *sweeping* the entire *decks* from stem to *stern!* The ship was *blasted* by the extreme *fury* of the *sea!*
(MEN SCREAM, GURGLING WATER, MASTS SPLIT)

"Fortunately, although *completely* water-logged…and having lost her *masts* overboard…she *rose,* after a minute, *staggering* awhile beneath the *immense* pressure of the tempest and *finally* righted itself!
MUSIC
(WAVES CRASHING)

"By what *miracle* I escaped destruction, it is *impossible* to say. *Stunned* by the shock of the water, I found myself, upon recovery*,* *jammed* in between the *stern*-post and rudder. With great difficulty I *gained* my feet, and looked *dizzily* around…only to find the ship surrounded, *engulfed* by a swirling *whirlpool* of mountainous and *foaming* ocean! This, this was *beyond* all imagination!

"I don't *how* long I stood there, *clinging* to a rope…staring *wide* eyed at the situation before me…until I heard a voice…"

HOBART
(DISTANT) *Hello! Over here!*

NARRATOR
(REVERB) "It was *Hobart!*"

(NO REVERB) *Hobart! Hello!*

(REVERB) "A few moments later, he had found his way over to me. After a few words, we soon discovered…that *we* were the *sole* survivors of this *catastrophe!*"

HOBART
All on deck, *all* the others have been swept overboard. The Captain *and* mates must have *perished* as they slept below.

NARRATOR
Oh dear *Lord!* Are you certain?

HOBART
The cabins are under water. The ship is sinking.

NARRATOR
It doesn't look good for *us,* does it?

HOBART
Wave! Hold on!

(WAVE HITS SHIP, CRASH)

NARRATOR
Are you *alright,* Hobart!

HOBART
Let's hope that's the *last* of em! Looks like it's blown over. But, the ship can't take much more...in its condition, another *swell* and we'll be *swamped* for sure.

MUSIC

NARRATOR
(REVERB) "For *five* entire days and nights...we lived off only a small bit of *cane* sugar, the natives called *jadderee* which Hobart procured with *great* difficulty from the forecastle..."

HOBART
The wind is up! The current's moving rather quickly. Taking us down toward Australia, I should think.

SILENCE

NARRATOR
(REVERB) "On the *fifth* day, the cold became extreme. The sun arose with a sickly *yellow* glow to it...rising a very few degrees above the horizon.

(WIND)

"There were no clouds apparent, yet the *wind* was upon the increase.

About noon..."

HOBART
Look at *that* sun. It's barely giving out any *light* at midday. Never seen *that* before. *Weird,* ain't it?

MUSIC
(THUNDER, RAIN ON WATER)

NARRATOR
(REVERB) "We waited in *vain* for the arrival of the *sixth* day... you see, we were *enshrouded* in patchy *darkness*, so that we could not have seen an object at *twenty* paces from the ship. Eternal *night* continued to envelop us. *More* rain and wind. *Thunder* and lightning. All around us was *horror*, and *thick* gloom, and a *black* sea. Superstitious *terror* crept by *degrees* into the spirit of Mr. Hobart. My *own* soul was *wrapped* up in *silent* wonder. We neglected *all* care of the ship, for It was *useless* to try to save it. We *secured* ourselves, as well as possible, to the *stump* of the mizenmast... and looked out *bitterly* into the world of ocean."

SILENCE
(WIND, WAVES)

HOBART
Any idea what time it is?

NARRATOR
Around midnight, I should think.   Any idea where we are?

HOBART
If I were to guess, I'd say farther to the South than any *previous* navigators. I *suppose* we'll be seeing *icebergs* soon enough.

NARRATOR
(REVERB) "In the meantime every *moment* threatened to be our last ...every mountainous *billow* hurried to *overwhelm* us. The swell surpassed *anything* I had imagined possible. How we were not *instantly* buried is a miracle. Yes, I *know* that miracles are *supernatural* phenomena."

HOBART
This ship has been *well* built to keep us afloat this long, but, not for much longer. Luckily, we've got a light cargo. Every little bit helps.

MUSIC

NARRATOR
(REVERB) "But, I could not help *feeling* the *utter* hopelessness of *hope* itself, and prepared myself for the *end* within the hour. The swelling of the black *stupendous* seas became more *dismally* appalling. At times, we were lifted *up* toward the sky…and tossed *down* with such velocity toward some *watery* hell…we'd grow dizzy, *nearly* fainting…ready to be *swallowed* up by some *sea* monster. But, just as we were *swirling* at the *bottom* of one of these abysses…"

HOBART
See! See! Almighty *God!* See there! *There!* It's a light, a dull red light, but, it's a *light!*

                                MUSIC BUILDS

NARRATOR
(REVERB) "Casting my eyes upwards, I beheld a *spectacle* which *froze* the blood in my veins! At a terrific height *directly* above us, and upon the very *verge* of the *precipitous* descent… hovered a *gigantic* ship of, perhaps, *four* thousand tons! I'd never *seen* a ship her size! Her *huge* hull was of a deep dingy black…I could just see a single *protruding* row of brass cannon. She was at *full* sail but there she *was* just *hanging* there above us, *high* up for a moment of *intense* terror as she *paused* upon the *giddy* pinnacle, as if in *contemplation* of her own *magnificence*… then *trembled* and tottered, and…*down she came!*"

HOBART
This is it, man! It's the end for sure!

NARRATOR
(REVERB) "Staggering as far *aft* as I could, I awaited *fearlessly* our *destruction!*

                               (CRASH, WAVES, SPLASH)

HOBART
Aaaaahhhhh!

                            (WOOD SPLINTERING, CRUNCHING)

NARRATOR
Hobart!

(REVERB) "The *shock* of the descending mass *struck* our ship in that portion of her frame which was *already* under water…and *I* was *hurled* like a *catapult* straight *up* and *into* the *rigging* of the *other* ship!

SILENCE

"But…as *unbelievable* as it sounds…since it was night…*I* was not seen by their crew and I was *able* to make my way *unperceived* down the rigging, *across* the deck and *into* the main hatchway, which was partially open, where I soon found an opportunity to *hide* myself in the hold. I don't know *why* I did that. But, I did not *know* the navigators of this ship…I *might* have been considered an *enemy*. A trespasser. A *spy!*
(WOOD CREAKING, HEAVY FOOTSTEPS APPROACH)

"I had scarcely *moved* some crates below in order to *hide* behind them, when…I heard someone approach…I peeked *out* from the darkness and could see…an *ancient* man…

(MAN MUTTERING)

"Yes, old and *decrepit* tottering on *bent* legs as if carrying a *heavy* burden. He was *muttering* to himself…I couldn't *understand* the language. He was surveying a *pile* of decayed *navigation* charts.
(FOOTSTEPS ASCEND STAIRS)

"Then, he went upside and I saw him no more.
MUSIC

"A feeling then took *possession* of my soul…yes, my *soul*…a *sensation* for which *I* admit, I have *no* scientific explanation…certainly, I have no *prior* experience to rely upon. To a mind like my own, this *feeling*…well, it *is* an evil. I shall never…I *know* that I shall *never*…be *satisfied* with regard to the *nature* of this feeling, but…

SILENCE

"Well, I could not *deny* that this new found sense…it was an *uplifting* entity *added* to my soul. And, what followed could *only* be defined as… something *beyond* a *scientific* description in *favor* of the dramatic.
MUSIC

"You see…as I grew *braver*, I began to *show* myself on deck…and I *found* that the *men* of that ship…they would *pass* by me…and *never* take *notice* of my existence. Yes, as if *I* did not exist…to them, I *wasn't* there! At first, I found that *incomprehensible*, no? They *all* seemed wrapped up in *meditations* of a kind which *I* could not divine. From then on, there was *no* reason for me to *conceal* myself. Why *hide*, if they could not *see* me? The *first* mate looked me *straight* in the eye and did *not* respond to my questions. The *Captain*…well, I went into *his* cabin and took for myself some *writing* materials right before him…and he *never* noticed me, never said a word.

SILENCE

"I have since taken to *writing* my own journal. It is *true* that I may not find an opportunity of *transmitting* it to the world, but, I will *try*, nonetheless. At the last moment I will *enclose* the manuscript in a bottle, and cast it into the sea.

(SEA BIRDS, WAVES)
MUSIC

"I have made *many* observations lately upon the *structure* of the vessel. Although well-armed, she is *not* a ship of war. Her rigging, *build,* and general equipment…I can't *guess* what she might be. I am not familiar with the *wood*…it is *worm*-eaten, of course, even *rotten* in places…which means the ship is *very* old. Might be Spanish oak. Her sheer *size*…her *strange* design, her *oversized* sails and antiquated stern…reminds me of *foreign* tales from long ago. *One* tale told of a sea where a ship might *grow* in bulk like the living body of a seaman.

SILENCE

"About an hour ago, I was *bold* enough to join a group of sailors. They paid *no* attention to me although I *stood* in the midst of them. *All* seemed to be old, *very* old men, *trembling* with infirmities, shriveled skins, *eyes* glazed over, unkempt, *long* gray hair. Around them, on *every* part of the deck, lay scattered, *old* and obsolete *mathematical* instruments.

(ROUGH WAVES, WIND)
MUSIC

"In the *meantime,* the ship sailed *onward* due South…right into the most *appalling* hell of water which a man can imagine. I could no longer stay on deck and *maintain* a footing. Of course, the crew weren't even *inconvenienced.* Though the waves that broke my *former* ship were *unbelievable* in size…these *dwarfed* those, some were *three* times the size of this *tremendous* ship! Continually *thrown* from side to side down in the hold…it's a *wonder* I was not *knocked* unconscious. Surely, we were *doomed* to hover upon the *brink* of Eternity…without taking a final *plunge* into the abyss!

"But, then…from billows a *thousand* times more *stupendous* than any *I* had ever seen…from the *colossal* waters that *reared* their heads above us like *demons* of the deep….we *glided* away from them *seemingly* with ease. *Why? How?*

SILENCE

"*Logically*, I must *account* for such effect using *scientific* deduction …I…I must *suppose* the ship was within the *influence* of some strong current, or impetuous under-tow. Yes, that must be it.

MUSIC
(HEAVY FOOTSTEPS APPROACH)

"The *Captain* entered his cabin again while I *sat* at his desk. Face to face, I *stared* at him. As expected, he did *not* see me. I must say, the *look* on his face…so *intense* and wonderful, the *thrilling* evidence of old age, so *extreme*…*all* of which *excited* within my spirit a sense…an *overwhelming* sentiment. Yes, I know…*me? Sentimental?* His wrinkled forehead seemed to bear upon it the stamp of *countless* years…his gray hairs were *records* of the past… and his grayer *eyes* were tellers of the future.

"The cabin floor was thickly *strewn* with strange, *iron*-clasped folios, and *moldy* instruments of science…and obsolete *long*-forgotten charts. His head was *bowed* down upon his hands, as he *pored* over a paper which *I* took to be a commission…

(MAN MUTTERING)

"…which I *believed* to be signed by some monarch. He was *muttering* to himself, yet, *I* could hear him clearly…as if he spoke into my ear.

EERIE MUSIC

"I suppose I must *accept* the fact that I am aboard a ship like *no* other…one that is *imbued* with spirits, *ghosts* of buried centuries…their *eyes* filled with an eager and *uneasy* meaning…and when they *walked* within my path in the *wild* glare of the lanterns at night…I *feel* as I have *never* felt before…until my very *soul* has become one with them.

"When I look around me I feel *ashamed* of my former apprehensions. The *typhoon* that smashed my ship, the *loss* of all on board, the *loss* of Mr. Hobart…the *storms* that threaten this one…*all* are trivial, even *meaningless* here…

MUSIC
(COLD WIND HOWLS)

"…where *now* the ship has sailed into the *blackness* of eternal night…*surrounded* on either side by *stupendous* ramparts of ice, *towering* away into the desolate sky, and looking like the walls of the universe.

"As the ship *dashes* on…it is utterly *impossible* for me to conceive the *horror* of my new sensations…yet, a *curiosity* to penetrate the *mysteries* of these awful regions…now *predominates* even over my despair…and will *reconcile* me to the most *hideous* aspect of death.

MUSIC BUILDS

"Are we hurrying *onwards* to some exciting knowledge…some *never*-to-be-told secret… whose *attainment* is destruction? Perhaps this current leads us to the Southern *pole* itself. *Why not?* That is not a *wild* assumption…it has *every* probability in its favor.

(MUTTERING, FOOTSTEPS)

"The crew pace the deck with *unquiet* and tremulous step… but there is upon their faces an expression *more* of the eagerness of *hope* than of the *apathy* of despair.

(STORMY WINDS, SAILS WHIPPING, WAVES THRASHING)

"In the meantime the wind is *still* at our backs… and, as we carry a *crowd* of canvas…the ship is at times lifted *bodily* from out of the sea! Oh, horror upon *horror!* The ice opens *suddenly* to the right, and to the left, and we are *whirling* dizzily… in immense *concentric* circles, round and round the *borders* of a gigantic amphitheatre…

(LOUD THUNDEROUS ROARING OF WHIRLPOOL)

"…the summit of whose walls is *lost* in the darkness and the distance. But, *little* time will be left me to *ponder* upon my destiny…the circles *rapidly* grow small…we are plunging *madly* within the *grasp* of the whirlpool…and amid a *roaring*, and *bellowing,* and *thundering* of ocean and of tempest…the ship is quivering… *oh God! And… going down!"*

END

THE BLACK CAT

By Edgar Allan Poe
Adapted By Dan Bianchi

CAST- 2m/1w
SYNOPSIS – A cat drives a demented man to commit murder.

MUSIC

NARRATOR
(REVERB) "I've *always* been considered a *quiet* human being. Gentle, even. Since childhood, *others* have joked that I am *too* kind hearted. *Especially*, to animals. I've had a *lot* of pets. They give me a *great* deal of joy and comfort. If *you're* a pet lover, you *know* what I am talking about. There is something in the *unselfish* and self-*sacrificing* love between a man and a dog, it's *hard* to describe. It often goes *beyond* any trust or friendship *humans* are capable of giving.

"Well...you can *imagine* how happy I was to find a *wife* whose disposition was *much* like my own. She *knew* I loved pets, so, she didn't *mind* my menagerie. We had birds, goldfish, a *fine* dog, *rabbits,* a small *monkey*, and...a *cat*. The *cat*...we named him *Pluto*... was a remarkably *large* and beautiful animal, *entirely* black, and *clever* to an *astonishing* degree."

SILENCE

WIFE
You *know* what they say about *big* black cats? I'm not being *superstitious*, although, perhaps, we shouldn't *ignore* what's been said about them, altogether. They're *witches,* you know? Witches in *disguise*.

NARRATOR
You *can't* be serious?

WIFE
I'm just saying...that's all. *You* treat Pluto as your *favorite* of all your pets. *You* feed him. He follows *you* wherever you go...even *out* into the streets, *if* you let him.

NARRATOR
You're not *jealous*, are you?

WIFE
I'm just saying. For *years,* he's been by your side. Did you ever think, *why?* No, and *why?* Because you're always *inebriated.*

NARRATOR
Are you *implying...?*

WIFE
I'm just saying...you'd better *cut* out your drinking. You're growing *moodier* every day. Irritable. You care *only* about yourself, *not* about others. And, I don't like that *language* you've been using lately. And, if you *ever...ever...*raise your *hand* to me again...*or,* to your pets? That *cat...*it gets everything. The *rest* of the animals...you've neglected. You *kicked* the dog yesterday.

NARRATOR
I didn't mean to...

WIFE
I'm just saying...the rabbits, the *monkey.* You get a few *drinks* in you and you're *mean* to all of them. Except that *damned* cat. I'm warning you, you'd better put a *stop* to all this.
                                             MUSIC

NARRATOR
(REVERB) "Eventually, the demon *alcohol* grew *worse* upon my temper. Poor *Pluto* even began to experience its effects. One night, returning home, *intoxicated,* from the local tavern..."
                                          SILENCE
                                       (CAT HOWL)

(NO REVERB) *What?* Well, then, you shouldn't be *walking* under my feet. What are *you* looking at? Come *here* you...*you....!* OW! You *bit* me! You actually *bit* me! *That's* what you think of me? Why, I'll...*come here!* Come here, you little *bastard! I'll show you!*
                                    (CAT HOWLING)
                                             MUSIC

(REVERB) "I'm thoroughly *disgusted* and *embarrassed* to tell you this, but, I must. I then took from my pocket a *pen-knife,* opened it, *grasped* the poor beast by the throat, and *deliberately* cut out *one* of its *eyes* from its socket!"
                                 (CAT SCREECHING)

SILENCE

"I know, I know…I should be *hanged* for *that* alone.

MUSIC

"The next morning, after I *slept* off my drunkenness…I *realized*…I *saw*…what I had done. I felt…well, how can I *describe* such a *lowly* feeling? I was feeble, *guilty*, remorseful…I don't know. But, then, as the *craving* came upon me *once* again…my *soul* became *hardened* to what I had done. I just wanted to *drink*. I found a bottle of *wine* in the closet and soon *drowned* all memory of my deed.

SILENCE

"In the meantime, the *cat* slowly recovered. The *socket* of the lost eye presented, it *is* true, a *frightful* appearance, but he no longer *appeared* to *suffer* any pain. He went about the house as usual… but, as might be expected, fled in extreme terror at my approach.

(CAT HOWLS)
MUSIC

"At first, I *still* had a *bit* of my old feelings left…it *hurt* me to see him run away whenever I *entered* a room. Eventually*,* *that* feeling grew into irritation. And *then,* it turned to *anxiety*. *That's* what *liquor* will do to you. *And yet,* I continued to drink. I *know* I shouldn't have, but, I did. The more my *wife* told me *not* to, the *more* I had to. In fact, I began to regard *drinking* as an act of *rebellion* by a *free* spirit. *I* could do what *I* want. *You* can't tell *me* to stop doing it!

SILENCE

"*One* morning…."

(CAT MEWLS)

(NO REVERB) *Pluto!* I *see* you there…*staring* at me with that *one* eye of yours. *Accusing* me, aren't you? *Always* accusing me. Well, *you* are not *my* judge.

(CAT HOWLS)

Come here, *you devil!* I'll put an *end* to all this right *now!*

MUSIC
(CAT SCREAMS)

(REVERB) "So, I slipped a *noose* about its neck and *tied* it to the limb of *a tree*. Yes, I *hanged* the damned cat! *Why?* Because I *knew* that it had *loved* me, and because *I* felt it had given me *no* reason to harm it. I *hanged* it because I *knew* that in *so* doing I was committing a *sin*. A *heinous* sin that would *so* jeopardize my *immortal* soul as to place it even *beyond* the reach of the *infinite* mercy of the *Most* Merciful and *Most* Terrible God. Like Lucifer himself... *I* had *rebelled* against *God!*"

SILENCE

"That night...as I lay in my bed sleeping..."

(FIRE CRACKLING)

WIFE
Fire! Fire!

MUSIC

NARRATOR
(REVERB) "The *curtains* around my bed were in *flames!* The whole *house* was blazing! My wife and I had *barely* made our *escape* from the conflagration. The *destruction* was complete. Our entire *worldly* wealth was swallowed up."

SILENCE

WIFE
What are we to do now? We've got nothing left...nothing...

MUSIC

NARRATOR
(REVERB) "I didn't want to *think* that what *I* had done to *Pluto* might have *caused* this disaster. That couldn't be. Impossible. *How* could it be? Well...the next day, we *visited* the ruins. The walls had fallen in. Except for *one* wall which stood about the *middle* of the house. *That's* where the head of my *bed* had been. The *plastering* there was thick. *That's* what probably had saved it. But, now...there was my *wife* examining that wall, *pointing* to it..."

SILENCE

WIFE
Look at that. *That's* very strange...isn't it?

NARRATOR
What is that?

WIFE
Why...it looks as if someone *carved* this dark *patch* into the plaster...

NARRATOR
It looks like...

WIFE
I'd say it looks like a...*cat.*

NARRATOR
A *cat?* What's *that* thing there?

WIFE
It looks like...a *rope.* A *rope* about the animal's neck.

NARRATOR
A...*rope,* you say?

MUSIC

(REVERB) "At *first,* I was trembling. But, *then* I thought, the cat had been *hanged* in the garden, *not* the bedroom. Sure, what had *this* to do with *that?"*

SILENCE

WIFE
Hmmm...How did it get *there* on the wall?

NARRATOR
Yes, I wonder? How *did* it get there?

MUSIC

(REVERB) "Well, *using* the best of logic, I *somehow* concocted a scenario that included the *heat* of fire, the *ashes* of burnt wood, a *beam* falling against the wall, leaving a *blackened* scar, an *imprint, stained* from water thrown on the fire...that, *together* with our imaginations, *resembled* a hanged *cat."*

SILENCE

(NO REVERB) Yes, it's just an *optical* trick that *occurred* from a *combination* of coincidences. You know, the way people are always *seeing* religious figures in a *tree* trunk, or on *wet* pavement?

MUSIC

(REVERB) *"That* might have solved the mystery for the moment, *but,* it did not *altogether* satisfy *me.* For *months* I could not *rid* myself of that *image* of the cat. I began to *miss* my old friend. Every time I went down

to the tavern, I looked about me, *down* the street, *around* the corner, for Pluto. I'd even looked for *another* cat to *replace* him.
(CROWDED TAVERN SOUNDS)
TAVERN ACCORDIAN MUSIC

"*One* night as I sat, *half*-stupefied, in the tavern...I found myself *staring* off into the shadows, into the *far* corner where the barrels were stored ...and *there,* sitting on *top* of a stack of kegs...I saw something *black* ...*a black cat!* As *big* as old *Pluto!* I *approached* it. It surely *did* look like him...*except* that Pluto was *pure* black. *This* cat had a large *splotch* of white on his breast."
(CAT PURRS)

(NO REVERB) Well now...who are *you* then? Do you have an *owner?* If not, would you like to come home with *me? Landlord?* Is this *your* cat?

LANDLORD
No. *I've* never seen it before.

NARRATOR
Aha...alright, my *new* found friend. Do you want to come with *me?*
MUSIC

(REVERB) "I didn't even *have* to pick it up. The cat *followed* me home. And, he made himself *right* at home.
(CAT PURRING)

"My wife took to him immediately. But*, wouldn't* you know?   A *week* passes and I no *longer* have that *good* feeling for it. I begin to *dislike* it, actually. I don't *know* why. *It* loves *me.* But, I begin to become *disgusted* and *annoyed* with it. Sure, I even *hate* it. I *avoid* the creature. Of course, it *reminds* me of my *guilt* and shame, my former *cruelty* to Pluto. But, *now*...I can't *bear* to be in the same *room* with it! *Why?* I hadn't noticed while I was *drunk* in the tavern and *brought* the *beast* home...but, when my *mind* was a bit clearer, I could see...like Pluto*, this* cat has only *one* eye. My wife, having *never* known the *true* facts about what had *happened* to Pluto, *loves* this *poor* thing even *more* so.
(CAT MEWLS)

"I *wish* I could be my *old* self. Maybe, I might feel the *same* sympathy for it. But, I *don't.* The *more* I try to *avoid* the cat, the *more* it clings to my heels, *following* me everywhere. If *I* sit, it's under my chair. Or *leaping* up on my lap, *caressing* me.

(CAT PURRS)

"If *I* walk, *it* gets between my feet, nearly *tripping* me. Sometimes, it *claws* its way *up* my pants leg to my shirt *just* to sit on my chest. I want to *knock* it down with my fist. But, I don't...I *remember* what I had *done* to Pluto. Alright, I *admit*...I am *deadly* afraid of this creature. I'm *scared* that it will do some *harm* to me. I can't *explain* the fear."

SILENCE

WIFE
Have you seen, taken a *good* look, at the *white* spot on this cat? On its chest?

NARRATOR
Why? What about it?

WIFE
Well, when you brought it home...it was just a big *white* shape.

NARRATOR
Yeah...and?

WIFE
Well, if you look at it now...it looks *definitely* like something...

NARRATOR
Like...*what?*

WIFE
Well...what are those things on which they *hang* people? The *gallows!*

NARRATOR
Are you *kidding* me?

WIFE
No! Look at it. *That's* what it looks like...a *gallows.*

NARRATOR
You're *crazy.* It *doesn't* look like a gallows.

MUSIC

(REVERB) "But, it *did.* It did look like a gallows. I could see it *plain* as day. Now, I am frightened even *more,* right? Well, what does it mean? Can it be some sort of *message* from beyond? But, Pluto was just a *cat,* a dumb *beast.* He didn't have a *soul.* He wasn't created in *God's* image like we humans. Now, I'm a *nervous* wreck, right? I barely sleep. My *dreams* became nightmares. I wake up screaming...*aaahhh!*

(CAT GROWLS)

"Only to find the *hot* breath of that *thing* upon my face, sitting on my chest, right over my beating *heart* and I am *powerless* to shake it off. It's *tormenting* me so much...the last bit of *good* that is within me disappears, giving way to the *darkest* and most *evil* of thoughts. I now *hate* all things, *all* mankind. Even my wife. Since the fire, we've been living in a *cellar* in an old building. *Poor* as beggars. And, don't think she doesn't *remind* me of *that* every day.

(CAT MEWLS, FOOTSTEPS DESCEND STAIRS)

"So, a few hours ago...the cat, he was following me down the steep stairs...*causing* me to *trip* and nearly *break* my *neck!"*

(CAT HOWLS, MAN STUMBLING, CRASH)
SILENCE

(NO REVERB) You're trying to *kill* me, *aren't you?* Where is that *axe?* *There it is!* I'll *fix* you, you no good, *rotten...*

WIFE
Just *what* do you think you're going to do with *that?*

NARRATOR
Leave go of my wrist! Who are *you* to interfere?

WIFE
Put it down! You're drunk!

NARRATOR
Leave me alone or I'll....!

(THUD)

WIFE
Stop! Murder! Aaahhhhhh!

(WHACK, WHACK, WHACK!)
MUSIC

NARRATOR
(REVERB) (Whispers) "Well, *now* you've done it. You *killed* her. You *killed* your wife. You buried the *axe* in her head and now her *brains* are all *over* the cellar floor."

(NO REVERB) I didn't *mean* to...she got in the way.

(REVERB) "She *saw* that you were angry. She *saw* you with the axe."

(NO REVERB) That's right! She shouldn't have gotten in the way.

(REVERB) "Well, what are you going to do now? *Confess?*

(NO REVERB) Go to the *police?*

(REVERB) "Don't be ridiculous. *They'll* never believe *you* that it was an *accident.* You have to *hide* her, of course. You have to...

(NO REVERB) Think! *Think!*

(REVERB) "You *can't* remove it from the house without the risk of being *observed* by the neighbors."

(NO REVERB) There *must* be some *other* way.

(REVERB) "Maybe, maybe...you can *cut* the corpse up into tiny *fragments* and throw them into the fire? Or...or...you can dig a *grave* for her in the *floor* of the cellar. Or, throw *bits* of her *down* the well in the yard. No...what if you *packed* her in a box and made it to *look* like a regular *shipping* parcel and you can order a *porter* to pick it up and...Ah, *I* know....what if you did what those *monks* had done to their *victims* back in the Middle ages? Why not *wall* her up in the cellar? *That* can be easily done. The walls are *loosely* constructed. It's been *recently* plastered. The *dampness* has *prevented* it from hardening. You can simply *remove* the bricks, *insert* the corpse, *plaster* it all up again and *no* one would be any wiser."

(NO REVERB) Where's that hammer? I'll start dislodging the bricks...that's it...

(HAMMERING, LAYING BRICKS)

Next...I'll *deposit* the body against the *inner* wall. Like so.

(REVERB) "That's it... prop it up nicely. She'll have to stand. No room to lie down. Now, just start *relaying* the bricks as they were... and some *new* plaster should do the job."

SILENCE

(NO REVERB) Good as new! A work of art. All cleaned up. Can't tell it's been disturbed in the slightest. But, there's *still* one thing on my mind.

(REVERB) "The *cat!* Yes, where is that *damned* beast? The *cause* of all your misfortune! It *escaped* when the wife interfered. Well, just wait, you'll do to that *cat* what you did to *her!* It might have taken *off* for good. Just as well. You can finally have a good night's *sleep* for yourself.

MUSIC

"Well, it's been what? Two days, *three* days? And *still* my *tormentor* hasn't shown itself. Looks like I'm a *free* man. Let's hope it's *gone* forever. For the *first* time in a long time, *I* am a *happy* man. I'm not even feeling *guilty* over what I've done. To cover my tracks, I've even *notified* the police that my *wife* is missing... perhaps, she's taken *off* with a *lover?* But, they're coming *now* to inspect the premises. Of course, they'll find nothing.

SILENCE
(KNOCK)

"There they are now."

(DOOR OPEN)

DETECTIVE
Good day. I am Detective Burton. Here are my credentials. These are my officers Mullins and Shippee.

NARRATOR
How do you do?

DETECTIVE
I understand that you have reported that your *wife* is missing? Do you mind if we come in and have a *look* around? Purely, to complete our *records* and then we'll be out of your way.

NARRATOR
Certainly.

DETECTIVE
The *bureaucracy*, you understand? I must *apologize,* but, if you *allow* us in, we'll make it quick.

NARRATOR
Of course, come right in.

(DOOR CLOSES)
MUSIC

"They are inspecting every *nook* and cranny.   Why, you can even accompany them.   No corner unexplored.   When they enter the *cellar*...well, look, you're not even *quivering* a muscle. Your heart is beating as *calmly* as an innocent man. Go on...let them walk and look wherever they desire."

SILENCE

DETECTIVE
Well, everything looks *fine* to me.

NARRATOR
Sorry to have wasted your time. You must have *far* more *important* work to do tracking down criminals.

DETECTIVE
Oh yes...why just the other night, we had a *helluva* time with a real *looney* he was, *hey* boys? He was *screaming* to high Heaven...

NARRATOR
What did he do?

DETECTIVE
Murdered an old woman and *cut* her up and *buried* her under the *floorboards!* Can you *imagine?*

NARRATOR
Is that so?

DETECTIVE
Would you believe it? Said he heard her heart still beating. We get all kinds, we do. Well, we'll be on our way. Sorry to have bothered you.

NARRATOR
Any time, Detective. I only hope you will be able to find my wife.

DETECTIVE
By the way, looking at this house...this is a well-constructed house. Reminds me when *my* family lived in a house like this. They don't make em like this anymore.

NARRATOR
Uhm, yes, that's true...actually, these *walls* can withstand the *test* of time. *Solid* as a rock.
MUSIC
(TAPS WALL WITH CANE)

(REVERB) "Now why did you just do that? That was the most *unintelligent* thing you have ever done in your miserable life! *You idiot!* Picking up your cane and *rapping* it on *that* wall, that *very* portion of brickwork *behind* which stands the *corpse* of your *wife!*

DETECTIVE
Hmmm...that doesn't sound very solid at all. Rather hollow...

NARRATOR
(REVERB) "But, it's *not* the sound of a hollow *wall* which draws his attention..."
(MUFFLED CAT HOWL)

DETECTIVE
Good Lord, what's *that?*

NARRATOR
What? I...don't hear anything.

DETECTIVE
Why that sounds like...it's...a...*cat*...inside that *wall!*
(CAT SCREAMING GROWS LOUDER)
MUSIC BUILDS

NARRATOR
(REVERB) "At first, it's muffled and broken, like the *sobbing* of a child, but, now, it's *quickly* swelling into one long, *loud,* and *continuous* scream, *half* of horror and *half* of triumph, like something out of *Hell*...the sound of the damned in their *agony* and of the *demons* that *exult* in their *damnation!* I feel like I'm going to *faint.* I *stagger* to the opposite wall. Look at them, the Detective and his police...standing there... motionless, *terrified*, awestruck. What are they going to do?"

DETECTIVE
Men! Tear down that wall!

(HAMMERING, CRASH)

NARRATOR
(REVERB) "Within minutes, the wall falls. The corpse, *already* greatly decayed and *clotted* with gore, stands *erect* before our eyes.

(CAT HOWLING ECHOES)

"Upon its *head,* with red *extended* mouth and that solitary *eye* of fire, sits the *hideous* beast whose *craft* had *seduced* me into murder, and whose *terrible* voice now *consigns* me to the hangman's noose upon the gallows. *You stupid fool!* You *stupid, stupid* fool! You *walled* the *monster up within the tomb!"*

END

HOP FROG

By Edgar Allan Poe
Adapted By Dan Bianchi

CAST – 2m/1w
SYNOPSIS – In this dark, but, comic fairy tale, the King is cruel to his
Fool, but, in the end, the Fool is no Fool.

LIVELY MUSIC

NARRATOR
I never knew *anyone* who liked a *good* joke as much as the King.

KING
Me? Ha! We live *only* for joking. We *love* funny stories. If you can tell
one well enough, we'll make *you* one of our ministers. We've got *seven*
ministers. *All* accomplished jokers. They're all *big* and round as we are.
(MEN LAUGH)

We don't know if being *fat* makes one *funny* to begin with, but, a *skinny*
joker is rare, indeed. Yes, indeed, we don't *like* skinny jokers.

NARRATOR
The King had a *few* rules for the jokers telling jokes...

KING
We *do* like when they keep their stories *short.* If you go on *too* long with
a tale, you will *lose* our interest. Actually, now that we *think* about it...we
prefer *practical* jokes over the verbal ones. Yes, a good *practical* joke!
(MEN LAUGH)

NARRATOR
By that time, court *jesters* were out of fashion in most of Europe. A few
kings *still* retained their fools who still wore *motley* with caps and *bells*
and who were expected to be ready *always* with *sharp* witticisms at a
moment's notice...in consideration of the *crumbs* which fell from the
royal table.

KING
We've *always* retained a fool. We'll *never* give up that little *luxury* of life
just because some *idiots* in another country have deemed it to be

unfashionable. They'd rather *hire* a *professional* jester. Imagine *that?*
(MEN BOO!)

Ha! Foolery that's what we need. It helps to *counterbalance* the heavy *wisdom* it takes to rule this country. *Our* fool is like no other fool. Ha! *He's* special.

NARRATOR
You see, the King *especially* got a *kick* out of *his* fool because *his* fool was *also* a dwarf *and* a cripple.

KING
Ha! Two for one!
(MEN LAUGH)

NARRATOR
Dwarves were as common at court, in *those* days, as fools. But, as I have *already* observed, in *ninety*-nine cases out of a *hundred*, fools are *fat*, round *and* unwieldy. So the King considered himself *extremely* lucky that *his* fool was *also* a crippled *dwarf* and his name was...
(GONG)

KING
Hop Frog!

NARRATOR
I believe the name *"Hop Frog"* was *not* his baptized name.
SILENCE

Since he could *only* get about by *hopping,* leaping, *wriggling,* the ministers *adopted* the name *Hop Frog* for him. Everyone, *including* the King, was *much* amused.
(MEN LAUGH)

KING
Ha!

MUSIC

NARRATOR
Poor Hop Frog. He could move *only* with great *pain* and difficulty along a path, or *road* or floor. His legs were *bent* out of shape, *heavy,* twisted. Because of that, his *arms* had turned into *powerful* limbs. They enabled him to *perform* many feats of *wonderful* dexterity, climbing trees or

ropes. Sometimes, he resembled *more* of a *squirrel,* or a small *monkey,* than a frog.

Now, I don't know from what *country* Hop Frog originally came. I believe it was from *far* away, a *barbarous* region *no* one had ever heard of. Hop Frog, *and* a young girl, another *dwarf* but of *exquisite* proportions and a *marvelous* dancer, were *forcibly* carried off from their homes and *sent* to our King as *gifts* from one of his generals.

Under *these* circumstances, a close *intimacy* arose between the two little captives, Hop Frog *and* Trippetta. Indeed, they soon became *sworn* friends. Hop Frog, *although* he was a *great* jester, was by *no* means popular. But *she,* on account of her *grace* and exquisite *beauty*... *although* a dwarf...was *universally* admired and petted. So she possessed *much* influence and *never* failed to use it, whenever she could, for the *benefit* of Hop Frog.

SILENCE

On some *grand* occasion...I forgot which...the *King* determined to have a *masquerade*...

(GONG)

KING
We want to have a *masquerade!* A grand ball. Invite *everyone* we know to court. Starring Hop Frog *and* Trippetta!

MUSIC

NARRATOR
Now, Hop Frog was *especially* inventive in producing *pageants* and masked balls. He created *novel* characters, and *designed* costumes and *painted* sets and *built* props and special effects...he did it *all.*

(CROWD SOUNDS)

The night of the ball had arrived. The *main* hall had been *gloriously* decorated under *Trippetta's* direction. The whole *court* was in a *fever* of expectation. As for costumes and characters, *various* court members were assigned *beautiful* and *strange* hats and *colorful* capes and *fashionable* clothing. *Some* even designed their *own* original costumes. *Everyone* knew *what* they were wearing to the ball even *weeks* before.

Except for the King and his *seven* ministers. I don't know *why* they hadn't decided on *what* to wear...unless they were *cooking* up a new joke. Or, *perhaps,* it was because they were so *fat,* they couldn't *find* anything to fit them.

SILENCE

KING
We don't know *what* to wear. Send for *Hop Frog* and Trippetta!

(GONG)

NARRATOR
When the two little friends *obeyed* the *summons* of the King, they found him *sitting* at his table drinking *wine* with the *seven* members of his cabinet council.

MUSIC

But, the monarch *appeared* to be in a *bad* mood. He *knew* that Hop Frog was *not* fond of wine...for it *excited* the poor cripple almost to madness... and *madness* is no *comfortable* feeling. But, the *King* loved his *practical* jokes, and took *pleasure* in *forcing* Hop Frog to drink.

KING
We *order* you to drink, Hop Frog...*little* Hop Frog. Come on now, be merry. If you had *any* family, we'd tell you to *drink* to *their* good fortune...but, since you *don't* have any family, you'll drink to *our* good fortune, *no?*

(MEN LAUGH)

You don't want to *anger* us, now, do you? That's it, *swallow* it down...and then, let's *hear* what *ideas* you have for our costumes. We want *characters*...something absolutely *out* of this world, weird, *inconceivable,* strange, *bizarre,* outlandish *and* unbelievable. Are we *forgetting* anything? Come, *drink,* be merry. The *wine* will brighten your wits!

NARRATOR
Hop Frog *tried* his best to *entertain* the King and his ministers. But, it was *too* much because...

SILENCE

...it *happened* to be the poor dwarf's *birthday,* and when he was *reminded* that he had been *stolen* from his family...*that* forced the *tears* to his eyes. Many large, *bitter* drops *fell* into the goblet as he took it, *humbly,* from the *hand* of the tyrant.

KING
Ah! Hahaha! See what a *glass* of good wine can do! Why, your *eyes* are shining already!

(MEN LAUGH)
MUSIC

NARRATOR
Poor fellow! His large eyes now *gleamed* rather than shone…the wine was *taking* its effect. He placed the goblet *nervously* on the table, and looked round upon the company with a *half*-insane stare. *He* was the King's *joke.*

SILENCE

KING
And, *now* to business. Come, Hop Frog, lend us your *assistance.* *Characters,* my fine fellow. We stand in *need* of characters, not just *we,* meaning *me,* but, *all* of us, meaning *them*…ha! ha! ha! Come, come, have you *nothing* to suggest?

HOP FROG
I am *trying* to think of something that is *completely* new, never been seen before.

KING
Trying? What do you mean by that? Ah, we understand. You are *sulky,* and want *more* wine. Here, drink *this!*

NARRATOR
And he *poured* out *another* goblet full and offered it to the *crippled* fool, who merely *gazed* at it, *gasping* for breath.

KING
Drink, I say! Or by the *fiends…*

(MEN LAUGH)

NARRATOR
The dwarf hesitated. The King grew *purple* with rage. The courtiers *smirked.* Trippetta, *pale as* a corpse, *advanced* to the monarch's seat, and, *falling* on her knees before him…

TRIPPETTA
Please, your Majesty…please *spare* poor Hop Frog.

KING
What? What's *that* you say? *Spare* him? As if, *as if*....Oh...well
...then...*get out* of here you *freak! Both* of you! *Freaks!*
                                                                    MUSIC

NARRATOR
The King *pushed* Trippetta to the floor and *threw* the contents of the
goblet in her face. The poor girl got *up* as best she could, and, not
daring even to sigh, *resumed* her position at the *foot* of the table.
                                                                   SILENCE

There was a *dead* silence for about half a minute, *during* which the
falling of a *leaf,* or of a *feather*, might have been heard.

HOP FROG
Grrrrrrrrrrrrrrrr....

NARRATOR
It was interrupted by a *low,* but *harsh* and protracted *growl* which
seemed to come at *once* from every corner of the room.

KING
Hop Frog! Why are you making that noise?

HOP FROG
I...I? How could it have been *me?*

KING
You dare to....? Wait...where *is* it coming from? Oh look...it's our
favorite *hound* chewing on a bone. If I hadn't *seen* it with my own eyes,
I'd *swear* it was the sound of *this* vagabond growling. *HA!*
                                                          (MEN LAUGH)
                                                               MUSIC

HOP FROG
Oh, your Majesty, you are *so* funny! Look at your *Hop Frog* drinking
away...all *night* long if need be!

KING
Good old Hop Frog!

HOP FROG
Your *Majesty!* I have *just* the idea. It *just* came to me when you had

struck down the girl and threw *wine* in her face…just *then,* and when the *dog* was making that *terrible* noise…there *popped* into my mind a *great* idea. I've *done* it before at our *country* frolics…but, *here,* oh, your Majesty, *here* it will be *altogether* new. *But…*

                                                                    SILENCE

KING
But, *what?*

HOP FROG
Unfortunately, however, *this* diversion requires a company of *eight* persons, and…

KING
Here we *are!* There are *eight* of us…including our *seven* ministers.

HOP FROG
Then, it *is* possible after all. I call this diversion…the *Eight Chained Orangutans!* It really is *excellent* sport if well enacted.

KING
Have *no* fear, we will *enac*t it!

HOP FROG
The *beauty* of the game lies in *frightening* the women.

KING
We love it! We love it!

HOP FROG
I will equip the *eight* of you as *orangutans…* leave *all* that to me. The *resemblance* shall be *so* striking, that the company of *masqueraders* will take you for *real* beasts…and of course, they will be as *much* terrified as *astonished.*

KING
Oh, this is *exquisite!* Hop Frog! I will make a *man* of you, yet.

HOP FROG
We need *chains.* They increase the *confusion* by their jangling. You are *supposed* to have *escaped,* all together, from your keepers. Your Majesty, imagine the *effect* produced, at a masquerade, by *eight chained* orangutans believed to be *real* ones by most of the audience…

and *rushing* in with *savage* cries, among the crowd of *delicately* and *gorgeously* dressed men and women. Can you *imagine?*

KING
We love it! It sounds...*exquisite.* We *must* do it! Hop Frog, *hop* to it!
(GONG)
MUSIC

NARRATOR
Now, not many people at *that* time had actually *seen* orangutans. Most had never *heard* of them. So, *who* knew if the *hideous* beast costumes looked *truthful* to the actual creatures?

The King and his ministers were *first* encased in *tight*-fitting stocking shirts *and* underwear. They were then *saturated* with tar. Hop Frog didn't have *hair* to cover their bodies, so, he substituted *sheep* wool *coated* in tar. Indeed, they *looked* like *strange* wild beasts from the jungle...even if they *didn't* really look like *orangutans.* Then, a long *chain* was *tied* around the *King's* waist, and then *tied* to another *and* another, *successively,* in the *same* manner until they were *all* attached together. When finished, they *stood* in a circle and Hop Frog *drew* the chain *crosswise* once, and then again, *and* again.
SILENCE

The main hall, where the *masquerade* was to take place, was a *circular* room and *very* lofty and a big *chandelier* hung by a *chain* down from the ceiling. It could be *elevated,* or lowered, through a *skylight* in the roof.

HOP FROG
Trippetta, dear...*I* think we shall *remove* the chandelier.

TRIPPETTA
Are you *sure?*

HOP FROG
Yes, I have something *special* in mind. Besides, the candle wax drippings will *ruin* some of the costumes beneath it. We can't have that. We'll just have *additional* candles and torches to light the room in *out* of the way places. And, I'd like to have some *incense* burning to *fragrant* the room.
(PARTY SOUNDS)
PERIOD BALL MUSIC

NARRATOR
The eight *orangutans*, taking Hop Frog's advice, waited *patiently* until *midnight* before making their appearance. *Meanwhile,* the great ball room was *thoroughly* filled with *masqueraders* having a grand time of it all…

(GONG)

No sooner had the *gong* been struck…and the beasts *rushed* in, all at once. But, having been *tied* together by the chain, they *tripped* and *stumbled* and fell as they entered.

(SCREAMS)

Many of the women *fainted* with fright. Some of the *men* even fainted. Had the King *not* taken the precaution to *exclude* all weapons from the room, his party might *soon* have ended in bloodshed. One of his generals *rushed* for the doors, but the King had *ordered* them to be locked *immediately* upon his entrance. Hop Frog had *persuaded* the King to leave the *keys* with him.

(FURNITURE CRASH, SCREAMING, YELLING)

Chaos reigned. The excited crowd *pushed* this way and that until it became dangerous.

(CRANKING CHAINS)

Meanwhile, the *chain* that had once held the *chandelier* was being *lowered* from the ceiling. There was a *hook* at the end of it. The King and his fellow *orangutans* wheeled about the room like *crazed* apes *reaching* out for victims until they found themselves moving *toward* the center of the hall. When Hop Frog *saw* this, he *leaped* down from a hidden area and *ran* to the center.

KING
How are we *doing* Hop Frog?

HOP FROG
We are doing *just* marvelous, your Majesty. *Keep it up!*

NARRATOR
That's when Hop Frog took *hold* of the *hook* at the end of the hanging chain and *attached* it to the cross chains in the center.

KING
What are you *doing* now?

HOP FROG
Now...*for the finale!*

(CRANKING CHAINS)

NARRATOR
As the hook was *raised* on its chain....the circle of *chained* orangutans
were *drawn* closer, *closer,* until they were *face* to face.

(CROWD APPLAUSE)

The masqueraders, by *this* time, had recovered, in *some* measure, from
their alarm. At last, they *recognized* that the *whole* thing had been an
elaborate *joke* on them.

(CROWD LAUGHTER)

HOP FROG
Ladies and gentlemen! Don't be alarmed! Leave *everything* to me! I
know these creatures *posing* as creatures. If I can *only* get a good look
at them, I can tell you *who* they are. I need a *torch* to see.

MUSIC

NARRATOR
Scrambling over the heads of the crowd, he managed to *grab* a torch
from the wall, and *returned* to the center of the room, *leaping* like a
monkey upon the *King's* head. He climbed *up* the chain and held the
burning torch *inches* from the ministers' faces.

HOP FROG
I shall *soon* find out who they are!

(CROWD LAUGHTER LOUDER)

NARRATOR
And now, while the whole assembly, the *apes* included, were *convulsed*
with laughter, the crippled joker suddenly *uttered* a shrill order...

HOP FROG
Now!

TENSE MUSIC

NARRATOR
The chain flew *violently* up for about *thirty* feet...

(CRANKING CHAINS)

dragging with it the *dismayed* and *struggling* orangutans, and leaving them *suspended* in *mid-air* between the sky-light *and* the floor.   Hop-Frog, *clinging* to the chain, *rose* up with them. He *pushed* the flickering torch *down* into their faces as if trying to *discover* each of their identities for the crowd below.

HOP FROG
I think I *know* who *you* are....but *who* is this one here?
SILENCE

NARRATOR
Now, the crowd below *hushed*. All were *astonished* at the sight before them.

HOP FROG
You see, your *Majesty*...they are *shocked*.   They've *never* seen anything like *this* before.

KING
Yes, yes, but, these *chains* are tight...can't breathe.   It's time to *end* the joke, Hop Frog. Let us down, you *idiot*.

HOP FROG
(Growls) *Grrrrrrrrrrrr!*

KING
What's that *sound?*

NARRATOR
This time...there was *no* mistaking that growling...it was *not* a dog eating a bone. It came from the *fang-like* teeth of the dwarf, who *ground* them and *gnashed* them as he *foamed* at the mouth, and *glared,* like a *maniac,* into the *upturned* faces of the *King* and his *seven* companions.

HOP FROG
Ah, ha! I begin to *see* who these people are, *now!* Let me look even closer...*closer...*

NARRATOR
And then...as he held the torch *next* to the King's *tarred* woolen coat, the outfit *suddenly* caught *fire* and instantly the King *burst* into flames!
(FIRE CRACKLING, KING AND APE MEN
SCREAM, CROWD SCREAMS)
MUSIC BUILDS

In less than *half* a minute all *eight* orangutans were blazing *fiercely,* amid the *shrieks* of the multitude who *gazed* at them from below, *horror-stricken*, and without the power to *render* them the slightest assistance. As the flames rose *higher* and higher....the crippled *fool* climbed *higher* up the chain, *out* of reach...

HOP FROG
I now see *distinctly* what manner of *people* these maskers are. They are a great *King* and his *seven* privy-councilors...a King without *scruples* who would *strike* a *defenseless* girl, and his seven *councilors* who *assist* him in the outrage. As for myself, *I* am simply *Hop Frog,* the joker...and *this* is my last *joke!*

NARRATOR
The tar and wool *exploded* into *higher* flames and the little joker had scarcely *finished* his speech when the work of his *vengeance* was complete. The eight *corpses* swung in their chains, a fetid, *blackened,* hideous, and *indistinguishable* mass. The cripple *hurled* his torch at them, clambered *leisurely* to the ceiling, and *disappeared* through the sky-light.

LIVELY MUSIC

It is *supposed* that Trippetta, *stationed* on the roof, had been the *accomplice* of her friend in his *fiery* revenge, and that, *together,* they escaped *back* to their own country for *neither* was seen *ever* again.

END

THE FALL OF THE HOUSE OF USHER

By Edgar Allan Poe
Adapted By Dan Bianchi

CAST - 2m
SYNOPSIS - Victor visits his old friend Roderick who is haunted by his soon to be dead sister.

MUSIC
(HORSES, COACH RIDES)

VICTOR
(REVERB) "It's a dark, dull, *soundless* day…the autumn clouds hang oppressively *low* in the sky. Such a *dreary* part of the country. But, I promised Roderick I'd come. Come to that *melancholy* House Of *Usher*. Like a gloomy *castle* in some old *gothic* novel. Hard to believe *anyone* still lives there.   A three-storied *mansion* with windows that *appear* to be staring like vacant *eyes* set into the *blank* walls. *Surrounded* by brown *dead* hedges and *white* trunks of decayed trees.
(COACH STOPS)

"Look at it. It's as if the whole *place* is *dying* from some *sickness* of the spirit.   Cold *and* dreary.   Perhaps, if the *trees* were healthy, if the windows were *lit* and inviting, I *might* have a completely *different* feeling about the place.   As it is, even the *coach* driver can't wait to drive off.
(COACH RIDES OFF)
SILENCE

"It was only a week ago, Roderick Usher had sent a *letter* to me, written in a nervous hand…"

RODERICK
(REVERB) "Victor…I know this will *shock* you but, I am suffering…an acute *bodily* illness, as well as, a *mental* disorder. I need to see you right away. *You* are my only *personal* friend."

VICTOR
(REVERB) "I found that *odd*…his only *personal* friend? I haven't *seen* Roderick since childhood. We were *never* close. *He* came from an old and *revered* family, so, he held himself *above* the rest of us at school, reserved *and* aloof. In fact, both his family *and* their house had been

referred to as *The House of Usher.*

MUSIC

"A building that, from the start, *reeked* of mystery and ancient *horrors* set in an atmosphere of *psychological* depression. But, perhaps, that's a great *exaggeration* on my part. I have to shake myself *free* from that perception. It's *only* a building, after all. True, it's *covered* in vines and *fungi* spread like a tangled *web* over all four sides. It is, beyond a *doubt,* dilapidated, but, I see *no* fallen masonry. Yet, *some* walls *appear* to be crumbling. The *woodwork* must be rotten. *If* the decay is widespread, the building may *even* be unstable. Look, there ...*extending* from the roof in front *down* the wall in a *zigzag* fashion to the high weeds, runs a large *crack.*"

SILENCE

RODERICK
(REVERB) "I *know* a visit from *you* will cheer me up, immensely."

VICTOR
(REVERB) "Well, how could I deny him?

(KNOCK, DOOR CREAKS OPEN)
MUSIC

"Waiting at the front door is a servant who takes me through a Gothic *archway* into the hall...through many dark and intricate passages, past the *carvings* on the ceiling, past the somber *tapestries* on the walls, and the *armor* and trophies. At a staircase, the family *physician* stands waiting. He doesn't have *much* to say, so, I *continue* on to meet the master.

(KNOCKS)

"This room is *large* and lofty. Windows long and narrow and the *black* oak floor must have *once* gleamed like a mirror. A reddish light *pours* in through the *stained* glass window at the *farthest* end of the room. Dark draperies *hang* upon the walls. The furniture is *antique* and tattered. There are many books and *musical* instruments lying about but *they* don't make the room come alive. No, I sense an atmosphere of *sorrow* here. *More* gloom *hanging* over and *pervading* the *House of Usher.*"

SILENCE

RODERICK
Victor! How are you, my *friend!*

VICTOR
Roderick! Glad to see you!

RODERICK
You're looking well. How was your trip?

VICTOR
Fine, fine.

RODERICK
Come in, sit down. We have *so* much to talk about.

MUSIC

VICTOR
(REVERB) "Actually, I am *appalled* to see the man. This *pitiful* looking creature is *Roderick Usher?* It *can't* be, surely. It's hard to *believe* that this pale, *thin* character before me is my *boyhood* friend. His hair is white. He *looks* like a cadaver. He appears to be a *nervous* wreck of a fellow. Sometimes sullen, *sometimes* vivacious. He speaks *oddly*…in an *abrupt* manner. Perfectly *modulated* enunciation…one might think he's a *drunkard* or an *addict* trying to *hide* his addiction."

SILENCE

RODERICK
I suppose you are wondering *why* I asked you here after *so* long a time? Victor, I've *really* needed to see you. I know that *you* might be able to help me. The problem may *mystify* you at first. It has to do with my family. An *evil* in my family. I need to find a *remedy* for it. I have inherited a morbid *acuteness* of the senses. For instance, I can only eat *bland* food. Or, wear *garments* of a certain texture. I can't *bear* the odor of flowers. And, the faintest *light* hurts my eyes. As for music…I can't endure *anything* but the sound of *stringed* instruments. Anything else inspires *horror* in me.

I know I'll *die* from this affliction. I don't *fear* dying. I do *dread* the events leading *up* to dying. And…what's *worse*, I fear this *house* to which I am chained. Yet, for *two* decades, I've *not* left it. It *owns* me. It *possesses* my body and soul. But, *that's* not the *only* reason for my sickness. You see, I *did* have a *companion* all these years…my beloved *sister,* Madeline. I called her *Lady* Madeline. But, after a *severe* illness, my last and *only* relative on this Earth is gone. *I* am now the *last* of the Ushers.

MUSIC

VICTOR
(REVERB) "Now, *just* as he is telling me this...my *eye* strays to a *movement* at the *far* end of the room...and a *woman*...I *take* to be the *Lady* Madeline passes *slowly* by in the hall...having never *noticed* me and then disappears into the shadows."

(NO REVERB) Roderick...who was *that* just now?

RODERICK
No! Did *you* ...*see* her?

VICTOR
I saw a *woman* just now.

(RODERICK SHRIEKS)

(REVERB) "Either my friend is *hopelessly* insane...or *I've* just seen a ghost. I *run* to the hallway and look *straight* down and *there* she is...entering *another* door and closing it behind her."

RODERICK
It's her! Madeline...

VICTOR
(REVERB) "He's got his *head* buried into his *emaciated* fingers, *sobbing* like a child."

(NO REVERB) But, *you* said...she was *dead*.

RODERICK
She might as *well* be. The doctors agree it's some sort of *catalepsy*. It developed a *year* ago. She had been doing well, *battling* it. Then, it began to *eat* away at her. At her body *and* soul...her *brain* and her heart. *Killing* her spirit. She's in *another* world now. *Dead,* yes...the *walking* dead. I never *know* when it will *finally* happen. Perhaps, *that* was the *last* we'll ever see of her.

MUSIC

VICTOR
(REVERB) "For the past *two* days, Usher has not mentioned her name. Meanwhile, I've been *trying* to raise his spirit. We *paint* and *read* together. He plays *guitar,* we sing. But, that *oppressive* gloom *never* raises itself from his soul. My attempt has been a *futile* effort. Life is *light* and *he* lives in darkness.

(CLOCK STRIKES)

"I don't know *how* many hours I've spent with him, the *last* master of the *House* of Usher. I'm beginning to think that *many* of his illnesses are the products of a *hypochondriac*. Whenever he *complains* about them, *I* change the subject."

CLASSICAL GUITAR MUSIC

(NO REVERB) Roderick, what is *this* picture here? This small painting...looks like a white, *rectangular* vault...smooth white walls, low ceiling...no windows or torches, yet, it *appears* to be bathed in light. Did *you* paint this?

(REVERB) "Roderick doesn't answer. Instead, he plays his *guitar* while *I* read one of his *poems* to myself...a *dreary* ode to his *haunted* homestead. But, at the *end* of it, he explains..."

SILENCE

RODERICK
The *house*, Victor, the house *itself* lives...*it* has a life... and *I* belong to it. *I* am a *prime* component. Like an *organ* in our body. It's as if, well...if *I* were taken away, *out* of the body...the house would *cease* to exist. And, there are *parts* of this house...rooms, that *vault* in the cellar, and so forth...the very *heart* of this place. The *soul.*

MUSIC

VICTOR
(REVERB) "Well, since my *morbid* friend *is* a hypochondriac and *claims* to own a *thousand* illnesses and *deformities* and the doctor prescribes all *kinds* of medication... so, *much* of what Roderick says can be taken with a *grain* of salt."

(NO REVERB) I think I'll go to bed now, Roderick. Good night.

RODERICK
Good night, Victor.

SILENCE

VICTOR
(REVERB) "But, just as I slip into bed, do I get even a *moment's* rest?"

(QUICK KNOCKS, DOOR OPENS)

RODERICK
Victor!

VICTOR
What is it?

RODERICK
The *time* has come. Lady *Madeline*…is *no* more.

VICTOR
What? Roderick, are you *sure?*

RODERICK
Yes, of course. Don't you think I *know* death when it presents itself?
Well, I've been *waiting* for this moment. *Come,* you *must* help me. We
will take her body *down* to the family vault.

VICTOR
Can't the *servants*…?

RODERICK
No! We must do it.

VICTOR
But, the *doctor*…

RODERICK
The doctor has been sent away.   It is up to *us* now. *We* will put her
body in a coffin and *carry* it to the tomb. It's *all* prepared. It has been
waiting for her.
                                                              MUSIC
                        (IRON GATE CREAKS OPEN. DRIPPING VAULT)

VICTOR
(REVERB)   "And, so, carrying her body, *down* we go to the *vault*
below…where we *place* her into her *coffin* upon a marble pedestal in
the *center* of the room. I look *down* upon her face. I had not *known* her
in life, but, I am *astonished* at her *striking* resemblance to Roderick."

RODERICK
Look at her, Victor. My *twin* sister.

VICTOR
What? I never knew *you* had a twin sister.

RODERICK
She inherited *all* the beauty from our *awful* family. Look at the *rose* in her cheeks. Her *smile.* You might not *think* she was dead. Let us leave her now and *retire* for the night. Help me with the lid. We'll have to nail it down tight.

VICTOR
Isn't there an *undertaker* in the nearby village?

RODERICK
There *is* no nearby village. *We* must do it ourselves. Come, before I fall *prey* to my *emotions* and the *damp* air down here.

(HAMMERING)

VICTOR
(REVERB) "I do not *approve* of his method, but, I say *nothing* and assist him in his duty.

MUSIC

"Bitter grief follows for the next week. Is Roderick's behavior *changing?* He's not taking care of himself as before...his *hair* is uncombed, his *body* unwashed. He *forgets* or neglects to do many *ordinary* things. He *roams* from room to room, even *hurrying* at times. He seems to be *looking* for something. His *skin* has turned even *paler* than before, almost *ghastly.* And, the *light* in his eyes is now *gone* altogether. His voice *trembles,* as if in *extreme* terror, so he *hardly* speaks. Sometimes, he *wants* to speak to me...but, *something* is holding him back...as if he's *hiding* some great secret. Now, he's sitting there...*staring* for hours ...listening. I think if I stay here *much* longer, *I,* too, will *join* him in his madness. In fact...it's *already* beginning...I'm beginning to *hear* things..."

SILENCE
(DISTANT SCRATCHING)

(NO REVERB) Roderick...are there *rats* in the walls?

RODERICK
What? No...no rats.

VICTOR
(REVERB) "Now, my *own* imagination is taking over. My *nerves* are getting the *best* of me. I'm trying to *ignore* the *oppressive* atmosphere in this place. So quiet I can hear my *heart* beating. Like it's ready to

burst. I'm being *ridiculous,* of course.

(FLOORBOARDS CREAKING)

"Now, I've *never* been a nervous person. I always... *Listen...* what's that? That's *not* my heart beating. But, it is definitely *something* else. Coming from upstairs! Well, I think I'll go and find out right now what's going on!"

(RUNNING FOOTSTEPS ASCEND STAIRS)

(NO REVERB) *Aahhh! Roderick!* What are *you* doing up at this time of night? I thought you had gone to bed.

(THUNDER, WIND HOWLS OUTSIDE)

RODERICK
(Whispers) Have you seen it?

VICTOR
Seen it? What are you talking about?

RODERICK
You *haven't?* Ah. Well then, *stay* where you are. *You'll* see it.

(THUNDER CLAP)

Quite a *storm* out there tonight.

VICTOR
(REVERB) "And, suddenly....

(WINDOW OPENS, WIND, THUNDER)
MUSIC BUILDS

"Roderick Usher *throws* open the window and a *gust* of wind nearly *lifts* us from our feet. The night is *wild* with terror. The *lightning* is blinding. The *look* on Usher's face is frightening."

(NO REVERB) *Roderick! Stop this at once!* You must *not* allow the weather to *affect* you like this. It's only *fog* and lightning... and *wind.* Common, *normal* elements. Close the window. Go ahead. That's it.

(WINDOW CLOSED)
SILENCE

Now, try to calm down. I know... I'll *read* us a book, something *frivolous,* a romance. Let's do that, shall we?

(REVERB) "So, I reach for some antique book on his shelf called *"The Mad Tryst"* and attempt to find him *relief* in its pages. Luckily, though the book is just *terrible*, it *does* lift his spirits somewhat. When I am *twenty*-two pages into the *sordid* adventure, I suddenly stop.
(GHOSTLY SOUND ECHOES)

"Have my *ears* deceived me or was *that* a strange sound *emanating* from *somewhere* in the house? Or, was it *just* the wind raging outside? I *have* to ignore it and continue."

(NO REVERB) 'And *Ethelred* uplifted his mace, and *struck* upon the *head* of the dragon, which *fell* before him, and gave up his *pesty* breath, with a *shriek* so horrid and harsh, and *withal* so piercing, that *Ethelred* had *fain* to close his ears with his hands *against* the dreadful *noise* of it, the like *whereof* was *never* before heard.'
(GHOSTLY SOUNDS GROW LOUDER. MOANING)

RODERICK
Stop! Victor…Listen. I know *you* hear it too. Don't deny it, Victor.

VICTOR
Hear *what?* Alright, I *do* hear it. Where is it coming from?

RODERICK
(Whispers) It's coming from *behind* that door.

VICTOR
Perhaps, one of the *servants* have left a hall window open and…
(GHOSTLY SCREAM)
EERIE MUSIC

What…is *that? Roderick? Roderick*, stop *staring* like that. *Snap* out of it, man. Come to your senses.

(REVERB) "But, his eyes are locked into *something* before him, his *body* has become as *rigid* as stone. When I *place* my hand on his shoulder, he *shudders* and a sickly smile *quivers* about his lips. His lips…they're *moving*…as if *talking* to someone. I must lean over to hear…"
MUSIC BUILDS

RODERICK
(Mumbling) Not *hear* it? Yes, I *hear* it and *have* heard it. Long…long …long…*many* minutes, many *hours,* many days, I've *heard* it. Yet, I

dared not...oh, *pity* me, miserable *coward* that I am! I dared not... I dared *not* speak! We have put *her* in the tomb...in the tomb...*still alive!* Didn't I *tell* you that my *senses* are *acute?* I have *heard* her...her first *feeble* movements in the *hollow* coffin. I heard them many, *many* days ago. Yet I *dared* not...I dared not *speak!* How can I *escape?* Don't you *understand? She* is coming! She is coming *here* to *curse* me, to *condemn* me for *locking* her in her coffin *before* her time. Haven't you *heard* her footsteps on the stairs? Don't you *hear* the *beating* of her heart? Don't you *know?* She's standing *outside that door!*

(THUNDER, WIND)

VICTOR
(REVERB) "At that instant, the great door *blows* open. And *there*...stands the *enshrouded* figure of the *Lady* Madeline of the House Of *Usher.* There is *blood* upon her *white* robes, and on her fingers *broken* and *bloody*...*evidence* of some bitter *struggle* as she had *fought* her way through the *wooden* coffin with her *emaciated* frame. For a moment she remains *trembling* and *reeling* back and forth in the doorway...

(LOW CRY)

"And, then she falls heavily *inward* upon her brother, and in her *violent* and now final *death*-agonies, *drags* him *down* to the floor... a *corpse,* and a *victim* to the *terrors* he had anticipated!
(VICTOR SCREAMS, THUNDER, FOOTSTEPS RUNNING)

"From that chamber, and from that mansion, *I flee*. The *storm* is still *raging* in all its *wrath* as I find myself *running* down the front path. *Suddenly,* a wild *burst* of lightning *illuminates* the night world and I turn to see the *vast* house and its *shadows* behind me. But, *that* isn't lightning...it's the house *itself*...*radiating* a glow. *Shining* from the inside, out. There's that *crack* in its façade, extending from the *roof* to the base and now *light* is *pouring* out of it and my brain *reels!*

(EXPLOSION)

"As I see the *mighty* walls tearing apart, collapsing, *exploding,* and a long, loud sound like *roaring* and *then*...

SILENCE

"...there is *silence* and the *dark* of night *falls* over the *fragments* of the House of Usher."

END

THE MASQUE OF THE RED DEATH

By Edgar Allan Poe
Adapted By Dan Bianchi

CAST – 2m
SYNOPSIS – A Renaissance Prince believes he and his friends can escape the dreaded plague by sealing themselves inside the castle.

MUSIC

NARRATOR
The *"Red Death"* had long devastated the country. *No* pestilence had *ever* been so fatal, or *so* hideous. *Blood* was its symbol *and* its seal…the *redness* and the *horror* of blood. There were sharp *pains*, and *sudden* dizziness, and then *profuse* bleeding at the pores, *ending* with *certain* death. The *scarlet* stains upon the body and *especially* upon the *face* of the victim, would chase *any* one away. The whole seizure, *progress* and *termination* of the disease, took place within a *half* hour. But, Prince *Prospero* did not despair. *He* was a happy and *wise* ruler. So, when he had lost *half* of his countrymen…

(GONG)
SILENCE

PRINCE
I want to summon a *thousand* healthy friends from among the *knights* and *dames* of my court. Then, we'll *retire* to a hidden room *deep* within one of my abbeys, one which *I* designed myself. I *know* that the high wall *surrounding* it is strong. And, the *gates* are made of iron.

MUSIC

Once we are *all* inside, I want the *blacksmith* to *hammer* and weld those gates *closed* with iron bolts, so that *no* one can get in *nor* out. We'll *stock* the abbey with *plenty* of provisions. Let the *outside* world take care of itself. We shall *not* feel any sorrow. We shall spend *our* days in pleasure. Send for the *dancers,* the *jesters* and musicians …*just* the *healthy* ones. And, be *sure* to stock *plenty* of wine. The Red Death won't be able to *find* us and even so, it *won't* be able to get in.

SILENCE

NARRATOR
Six months later…while the *pestilence* raged across the land, Prince

Prospero *entertained* his costumed friends at a *masked* ball.
(PARTY SOUNDS)
RENAISSANCE CHAMBER MUSIC

It was a *voluptuous* scene, that masquerade. All around the main room were *recessed* chambers and on the *walls* were stained glass windows. *These* were lit from behind, accordingly, to create a *mood* in each chamber. The *second* chamber was *purple* in its ornaments and tapestries, and *here* the stained glass *panes* were purple. The *third* was *green* throughout, and *so* were the curtains. The *fourth* was furnished and *lit* with orange, the *fifth* with white, the *sixth* with violet. The *seventh* chamber was *shrouded* in black *velvet* tapestries that hung *all* over the *ceiling* and *down* the walls, falling in *heavy* folds upon a carpet of the *same* color. But, in *this* chamber only, the color of the windows *failed* to correspond with the decorations. The panes *here* were *scarlet*…a deep *blood* red color.

SILENCE

Now, *all* of the rooms were lit by these windows *not* by daylight, but, by *huge* torches situated *behind* the panes. This caused a *multitude* of *gaudy* and fantastic effects. Only the *black* chamber with its *blood* red windows was *ghastly* in extreme. *Few* people cared to enter *that* room.
(BIG CLOCK TICKING)

It was in *this* chamber, also, that there stood against the wall, a *gigantic* ebony clock. Its pendulum *swung* back and forth with a *dull,* heavy, *monotonous* thud and when the hour *struck,* it produced a musical sound…

STRANGE TUNE

A strange, *weird* sound that caused even the *musicians* of the orchestra *and* the dancers on the floor to *stop* and listen to it. *Every* hour, the festivities would come to an *abrupt* stop when this happened.
STRANGE TUNE
(CROWD LAUGHTER)
CHAMBER MUSIC

When the echoes had *fully* ceased, an uneasy *laughter* at once *pervaded* the audience. The *musicians* looked at each other and smiled as if *they* hadn't been *annoyed* nor *mystified* at the interruption. But, in *spite* of these things, it was a gay and magnificent party.

PRINCE
Oh, I *know* my tastes are peculiar. But, you *must* admit, I have a *fine* eye for *colors* and effects. I don't care to follow the *latest* fashion. *My* plans are *bold* and fiery. *My* conceptions *glow* with *barbaric* luster. It was *my* idea for this *masquerade*...and I wanted the *costumes* to be *grotesque*. True, *some* of you *must* think I am mad.
(CROWD PROTESTS)

Now, now, there's *no* need to protest.
(APPLAUSE)

NARRATOR
Yes, there was a *lot* of *grotesquerie*. A great *deal* of glare and glitter. *Lots* of spice. *Some* of the participants were made to dress as *madmen*. The women were told to *dress* like whores. It was *very* bizarre and a *little* exciting and a *bit* disgusting, too. Everyone *roamed* in and out of the chambers. The orchestra played *wild* music.
(CLOCK TICKS, STRIKES)
STRANGE TUNE

And, as usual, the clock *struck* the hour and everyone would pause, standing *absolutely* still, *silently*, and then they were *right* back to having a *merry* time of it all.
(CROWD LAUGHTER, PARTY NOISE)
CHAMBER MUSIC

But, *no* one would *venture* into the *seventh* chamber...the *blackness* of the room, it's *blood* colored panes and *sable* drapery *scared* away the partygoers. The *other* chambers were *densely* crowded, and *in* them beat feverishly the *heart* of life. And, the *masquerade* went on, until the *sound* of midnight.
(CLOCK TICKS, STRIKES)
STRANGE TUNE

The music *ceased* and the *revolutions* of the dancers were quieted and *everyone* felt that *unease* once again.
OMINOUS MUSIC

And, *then* it happened...when *he* showed up...a *masked* figure who had *suddenly* caught the attention of *everyone* in the room.
(CROWD WHISPERS)

He just *stood* there as the partygoers *whispered* and murmured. *Who* could it be?

In *such* a crowd as I've described, it's *hard* to imagine that *any* individual's appearance could have *excited* such sensation. Even the *Prince* was surprised that *one* person could create *such* a stir among his guests.

Now, there are *some* things in life which *cannot* be touched without emotions. Even to *those* who don't mind *joking* about *life* and death, there are *some* subjects that *must* be considered *serious.*

SILENCE

So, it was *obvious* to *all* of these *festive* partygoers and *colorful* masqueraders ...that *this* strange figure was definitely *not* one of *them.*

OMINOUS MUSIC

No, *he* wasn't dressed to *join* in with the frolics. He was *tall* and gaunt and *dressed* in the *shroud* of the dead. His mask resembled the *skull* of a *corpse* and *try* as they might, *no* one could see a *real* person *under* the costume.

All of that *might* have been *accepted* by the audience, but, for the fact that his *shroud* and *face* was *dabbed* and *sprinkled* with fresh *blood,* the mark of the *Red Death.* He *walked* about the crowd with a *slow* and solemn movement.

SILENCE

The *Prince* was not amused.

(GONG)

PRINCE
Who *dares* insult us with this *blasphemous* mockery? *Seize* him and *unmask* him so we may know *whom* we have to *hang* at sunrise from the castle *walls!*

NARRATOR
Not a *sound* could be heard *throughout* the hall. The stranger *walked* closer to Prince *Prospero* who stood in the *blue* chamber with a group of *pale* courtiers by his side.

OMINOUS MUSIC

As *soon* as the Prince spoke, *some* of them *rushed* toward the intruder. But, they would go *no* further. They would *not* put a *hand* on the stranger. People *shrank* away from him as he walked *closer* to the Prince.   He *kept* on walking...*through* the blue chamber to the purple...through the *green* to the orange...to the *white* and *then* the *violet* chambers. *No* one attempted to *arrest* him.

It was *then,* however, that Prince Prospero, *maddened* with rage and the *shame* of his *own* momentary cowardice, rushed *hurriedly* through the *six* chambers. *No* one followed him on account of a *deadly* terror that had *seized* them. He drew a *sword* and approached within *three* feet of the figure when the *stranger* who had *reached* the *black* chamber, suddenly *turned* and *confronted* his *pursuer!*
(PRINCE SCREAMS, SWORD CLANGS TO FLOOR)

The sword dropped *gleaming* upon the *black* floor, upon which, *instantly* afterwards, fell *Prince* Prospero, *dead.*
(ANGRY CROWD)

Then, *summoning* their courage, a desperate *throng* of the revelers at once *threw* themselves into the *black* compartment, and, *seizing* the stranger, whose *tall* figure stood *erect* and motionless within the *shadow* of the *ebony* clock, *gasped* in *unutterable* horror at what they found...there was *no* tangible *form* beneath the *skull* and *shroud!*
SILENCE

And, now they *knew* the stranger's identity. They were *standing* in the *presence* of the *Red Death.* He had come like a *thief* in the night.
MUSIC

And, *one* by one, the *revelers* dropped in the *blood*-drenched hall, each *instantly* falling to the floor, *gasping* their last breath. As the *last* of them died, the *life* of the ebony *clock* stopped. The *flames* of the torches expired. And, *Darkness* and *Decay* and the *Red Death* held *never*-ending *dominion* over all.
END

THE SPHINX

By Edgar Allan Poe
Adapted By Dan Bianchi

CAST – 2w
SYNOPSIS – A woman visits her cousin in the country where she believes she has seen a gigantic monster...or she may be insane.

MUSIC

NARRATOR
(REVERB) "During the dreaded *Cholera* epidemic in New York, I had accepted the *invitation* of my cousin to spend *two* weeks with her in her cottage on the *banks* of the Hudson. It was summertime, so there was *plenty* of rambling in the woods, *sketching*, boating, *bathing,* music, and books. At first, all that seemed *very* pleasant, *except* that we would also receive the daily *report* about what was going on *back* in the city. Not a *day* passed without *sad* news of an *acquaintance* or distant *family* member *succumbing* to the disease. Eventually, we began to *fear* each day as the *numbers* of *deaths* mounted. There was *little* fun left to pass the time. I began to *obsess* over the approaching *wave* of death heading *North* toward us. But, my cousin, who was an *intellectual,* tried to keep a *level* head by *rationalizing* and discussing the problem from a *logical* viewpoint."

SILENCE

COUSIN
You *can't* be serious? You *really* believe in *omens?*

NARRATOR
Why *not?*

COUSIN
They are based on *nothing* but faith. Hollow, *insubstantial.*

NARRATOR
If they point to *truth,* why not *believe* in them?

COUSIN
If they *do* have an *ounce* of truth in them, it's *purely* coincidental. *Your* mind is given to *gross* imaginations. Anything you *can't* explain, *you*

believe it to be *supernatural.*

MUSIC

NARRATOR
(REVERB) "The fact is, that *soon* after my *arrival* at the cottage there had occurred an *incident* so entirely *inexplicable* that I don't know *what* else to call it but...an *omen.* It so *confounded* and *bewildered* me, that, I said *nothing* to my cousin about it for *many* days.

SILENCE

"Near the *end* of a hot day, I was sitting, *book* in hand, at an *open* window that looked out *over* the long river banks and a *view* of a distant hill. Occasionally, I'd *drift* off to think about the *gloom* and *desolation* happening back in the city.

EERIE MUSIC

"And, then...I looked *up* and *out* the window and *saw* something *just* over the hill. I saw...some *living* monster, *hideous,* gigantic, making its way *toward* me from the hill, *disappearing* into the forest nearby.

SILENCE

"Could that *be?* What *was* it? Was I *seeing* things? Or going *crazy?* Many minutes passed before I *succeeded* in *convincing* myself that I was *neither* mad *nor* in a dream. I *knew* I had seen it. Yes, I *know,* when I *hear* myself *describe* it, even *I* have difficulty in *believing* it truly occurred.

MUSIC

"I estimated that it was as *large* as the *biggest* ship at sea. There was a *mouth* and a *large* beak. It was some *sixty* or seventy *feet* in length, and about as *thick* as the body of an *ordinary* elephant. It had black *shaggy* hair. And, two *gleaming* tusks like a wild *boar,* but *much* larger. On each *side* of its head, was a *gigantic* staff, very shiny, *thirty* or forty feet in length...it *reflected* in the sun. *Two* pairs of *wings* outspread... *each* nearly *one* hundred yards in length. *One* pair being placed *above* the other, and *all* thickly covered with *metal* scales. And, *here* is the most *horrible* aspect of this monster...covering nearly the *whole* surface of its breast...the image of a *skull*...yes, a *Death's Head*...*glaring* white.

SILENCE

"While I *regarded* the gigantic monster, and more *especially* the *Death's Head* on its breast, with a feeling of *horror* and awe...

EERIE MUSIC

I felt a sense of *forthcoming* evil. *Coming* this way. The huge jaws *suddenly* opened and *from* them there proceeded a *sound* so *loud* and so *expressive* that it *struck* upon my nerves like a *church* bell *ringing!* As the monster *disappeared* at the foot of the hill, I *fainted* to the floor."

SILENCE

COUSIN
Cousin...what happened? Are you *alright?*

NARRATOR
(REVERB) "Upon recovering, my *first* impulse, of course, was to *inform* her of what I had *seen* and heard. But, I didn't. I didn't want to be thought *mad.* Nor the *butt* of ridicule.

MUSIC

"Three or four days later...we were *sitting* together in the room in which I had *seen* the apparition. I was in the *same* seat at the *same* window, and she was *lounging* on a sofa nearby. At that time, I told her *what* I had seen.   Well, she listened. She got up, *walked* about the room, thinking. Then...*suddenly*...I *looked* out through the window and *there* it was *again!*"

SILENCE

(NO REVERB) *Look! There it is!* I told you!

COUSIN
Where? *Where?* I don't *see* anything!

NARRATOR
Right *there*...coming *down* the hill. It's an *omen!* I'm going to *die!* It's *Death* itself coming for me! (SOBS)

COUSIN
Get up!

NARRATOR
I can't! I can't!

COUSIN
Get *up* I say! *Open* your eyes! *Look!* Do you see it *now?*

NARRATOR
What? *What?* It...it's *gone* now. Disappeared.

COUSIN
Listen, cousin...let me *explain* something to you...I shall *try* to keep it simple. The *principle* source of *error* in *all* human investigations lay in the *liability* of the *understanding* to *under* estimate or *over* value the *importance* of an object. *Understand?*

NARRATOR
No.

COUSIN
To *estimate* properly, for example, the *influence* to be *exercised* on mankind at *large* by the thorough *diffusion* of *Democracy*, the *distance* of the *epoch* at which *such* diffusion may *possibly* be *accomplished* should *not* fail to form an *item* in the estimate. Yet, can *you* tell me *one* writer on the *subject* of government who has *ever* thought this *particular* branch of the subject *worthy* of discussion at all?

NARRATOR
I have *no* idea of *what* you are talking about.

(REVERB) "She paused for a moment, *stepped* to a book-case, and *retrieved* a book on Natural History"

.
COUSIN
Let me sit *there* in the window light.   Here now...*look* over my shoulder...how is *that?*

NARRATOR
Alright.

COUSIN
But for your *exceeding* minuteness in *describing* the monster, I might *never* have had it in my power to *demonstrate* to *you* what it was. In the *first* place, let me *read* to you a *schoolboy* account of the *genus Sphinx,* of the family *Crepuscularia* of the order *Lepidoptera,* of the class of *Insecta*...or *insects.*

(READS) "Four *membranous* wings covered with *little* colored scales of *metallic* appearance...mouth forming a *rolled* proboscis, produced by an *elongation* of the *jaws,* upon the *sides* of which are found the *rudiments* of *mandibles* and downy *palpi*...the *inferior* wings *retained* to the *superior* by a *stiff* hair... *antennae* in the form of an *elongated* club, prismatic... *abdomen* pointed, The *Death's–headed* Sphinx   has occasioned *much* terror, at times, by the *melancholy* kind of *cry* which it *utters,* and the *insignia* of *death* which it *wears* upon its *breast."*

MUSIC

NARRATOR
(REVERB) "She closed the book and leaned forward in the chair, placing herself *exactly* in the position where *I* had seen the *monster".*

COUSIN
Ah, *here* it is now…the *monster* as *you* call it is *climbing* the face of the *hill,* and a *very* remarkable looking *creature* I must admit it to be.

NARRATOR
You see it too?

COUSIN
Still, it is by *no* means *so* large or *so* distant as *you* imagined it…for the *fact* is that, as it *wriggles* its way *up* this thread, which some *spider* has *wrought* along the *window*-sash, *I* find it to be about a *sixteenth* of an inch in its *extreme* length, and also about a *sixteenth* of an inch *distant* from the *pupil* of my eye.

NARRATOR
No!

COUSIN
Yes.

NARRATOR
You mean to *say…?*

COUSIN
Yes.

NARRATOR
But, that *can't* be…

COUSIN
Yes it *can* be. And, it is. *Your* mind, as usual, is given to the *supernatural.* And, your *imagination,* I am afraid, *and* your *state* of *depression* and your *great* fear of *death* has created for *you*…from the *smallest* of creatures…a *monster* of *gigantic* proportions. In short, you are *seeing* things.

NARRATOR
Cousin…am I going *insane?*

COUSIN
Of *that*…I cannot be *too* certain.

END

LIGEIA

By Edgar Allan Poe
Adapted By Dan Bianchi

CAST - 1m/2w
SYNOPSIS - A man is haunted by his dead wife.

MUSIC
(TRAIN WHISTLE, TRAIN CAR INTERIOR)

EDGAR
(REVERB) "I cannot *remember* how I *first* became *acquainted* with the lady *Ligeia*. It was a *long* time ago. A lot of *water* has passed under the bridge. A *great* deal of suffering. *Ligeia!* She was as *intelligent* as she *was* beautiful. But, *now* she is gone.

"There are *some* things I *do* remember quite clearly. Ligeia was *tall*, somewhat *slender*, and, *near* the end, she was *even* emaciated. She was *so* light on her feet, I would *never* hear her *floating* down the hall. She'd come and *go* like a shadow. Her *voice* was like music. Oh, and her *beauty?* In that category, I have *never* seen *any* woman who could *equal* her.

EERIE MUSIC

"Yet, there was a *strangeness* about her. Her *skin* was *pure* white and *smooth* as silk. Perfect. Maybe, *too* perfect. Her *hair* was *raven* black and *hung* in curls. Her sweet *mouth*, soft *and* voluptuous. Such a *radiant* smile. And, then, there were her *eyes*. *I* was *not* the *only* one *captivated* by those eyes. Men have almost violently, *passionately* fallen in love with her. All *she* had to do was to *look* at them with those *eyes* of hers. Yet, again, there *was* something *else* behind those black, *wild* eyes. Something *I* could not grasp. But, I *desired* to find out.

MUSIC

"Ligeia was well educated. She spoke several languages and knew many modern dialects, as well. I have never known her at fault. She knew more about more subjects than any man I had known, certainly. She could converse about anything from *morality* and philosophy to *physical* and mathematical science.

SILENCE

"I was *shocked* with *grief* when she left me. *My* Ligeia. I missed her readings, her *revelations*, the radiant *luster* of her eyes.

SAD MUSIC

"As she had grown *sicklier,* those *eyes* shone less and less. I *knew* she was dying but, I struggled *desperately* to keep my *own* spirit alive.   At first, I thought that her stern nature would *face* death *without* terror. But, not so. It tore me *up* inside to watch her *wrestle* with Death itself each day.

SILENCE

LIGEIA
(Coughs) You know I love you, Edgar.

EDGAR
Ligeia...don't talk. Please, save your strength.

LIGEIA
Truly, I do.

EDGAR
I don't *deserve* someone like you. Your love...

LIGEIA
I don't have much longer. *Oh God!* Oh God! Is there *no* other way? Can't *Death* be conquered? God Almighty in Heaven above...are we *not* your children? Are we not *part* of you? *You* know all the *mysteries* of life. *You* are the Almighty *One!*

EDGAR
Ligeia! Please...please calm yourself. Get back in bed, *please!*

LIGEIA
Come...come near me.

EDGAR
What is it?

LIGEIA
You know all the mysteries of life. *You* are the Almighty.

EDGAR
Ligeia!

(REVERB) "But...she was dead. Died in my arms. I felt...as if the *life* in me had been sucked out. All that was left was a vacuum. *Crushed* to dust with sorrow. I cared for nothing else.

MUSIC
(TRAIN BELL, TRAVELING TRAIN INTERIOR)

(REVERB) "Months passed. I *wandered* the Earth, from city to city. *Anything* to pass the time. All the while I *grieved* like a child who had lost its mother. No, *Ligeia* was *more* to me than that. The pain, the *pain* was so great. Would I *ever* get over it? Did I *want* to? I needed to *escape* this pain. So, I turned to *opium* for that. I am a worthless *mongrel,* now. *Worthless* to this world.

SILENCE

"And, to *prove* it even more so...I married *again.* The fair-haired and *blue*-eyed Rowena.

MUSIC

"I'd even brought her to my *home* which I filled with *enough* material *objects* and works of art to *satisfy* a museum. Sculptures, *carved* furniture, *woven* tapestries, velvet ottomans. *All* that I offered to Rowena. Yet, I *could* not, *would* not, *forget* my *Ligeia.*

SILENCE

"Did Rowena *love* me? I doubted it. *Why?* Because, I was, I *am* a moody, *temperamental* son of a...! I became *prone* to outbursts. I *frightened* her. So, she *shunned* me. I had begun to *dislike* her...very much. No, in truth, I believe, I *loathed* her.

MUSIC

"Yes, the *only* solace I found at that time was when I remembered my *Ligeia.* My beloved, the beautiful, *wise* Ligeia who had *truly* loved me... but, *she* lay *entombed* in her crypt.

EERIE MUSIC

"No *wonder* I had turned to *opium* to *block* such visions...I had become a hopeless *slave* to it, *drowning* myself in *drug*-induced dreams on a *daily* basis. *Ligeia!* I called her name during the *silence* of the night, or, when I took long *walks* into the forest during the day. If only I could have *restored* our lives to carry out the *life* we had planned together on this *Earth!*

SILENCE

"But...merely *two* months into my marriage to Rowena...and *suddenly,* she came down with a terrible illness."

ROWENA
The doctor says...

EDGAR
The *doctor?* What does *he* know? Country hack. *What?* What are you pointing at now?

ROWENA
There's something *there*...in the *corner* of the room.   I'm sure of it. *Look!*

EDGAR
There is *nothing* there, my dear.   Now lie back...you're delirious. Trembling. Under the covers now.

ROWENA
What's wrong with me, Edgar?

EDGAR
You're getting excited.

ROWENA
Edgar...I hear...I *hear* things. And, the tapestries...on the wall...I'm *sure* they're moving.

EDGAR
You're *hallucinating,* Rowena. I know all about that.

ROWENA
And, the *figures* in the paintings, too.

EDGAR
Yes, yes, my dear.

ROWENA
Look at me. I'm withering *away,* Edgar. Tossing and turning all night. (Whispers) It's that *sound*...it keeps me awake. Mustn't let it hear me *talking* about it...*spying* on us...*shush!*

EDGAR
Rowena, my dear, what you *hear* is probably the *wind* rushing through the hall outside. It *lifts* the tapestries from the wall. They're *rippling*, you see, in the *drafts* and it *appears* as if they are moving on their own, that's all.

ROWENA
No...no...it's *not* the wind. Oh, I feel so *light* headed, Edgar, you *will* stay with me tonight?

EDGAR
Of course. But, first, let me get you some *warm* milk from the kitchen. That should do the trick.

MUSIC

(REVERB) *"Ha!* On the way there, I planned to get a bottle of *whiskey* for myself. So, I went to the kitchen and heated and *poured* her milk and as I was *heading* for the liquor cabinet...

(WIND)
EERIE MUSIC

"What was *that?* Something...something had just *touched* me. I was *sure* of it. It went right by me. Something *invisible*...now, I was starting to...*aaah!* What *was* that? *There!* Outlined *against* the wall...a *shadow?* A shadow *almost* imperceptible...a shadow of a *figure*...a *person,* I was certain of it. Then, I told myself...Hold on, you fool! You had just inhaled *opium* thirty minutes earlier...had you *forgotten* already? Come now, you'd seen *worst* visions than *that* before. But...oh...my...*God!* Right *there,* in front of me...the carpet...someone, some*thing*...it was as if an invisible *being* was *walking* across the carpet, leaving indented footprints. And, oh! A *ruby* colored liquid... *dropping out of thin air* into the glass of milk! What *magic* was this? I would have to *cut* down on my *opium* intake if I was going to start *seeing* things like *that!"*

SILENCE
(DOOR CLOSES)

(NO REVERB) Here Rowena, dear...here's your milk. Drink it down now.

(REVERB) *"Seeing* things, Edgar? It's the *opium,* you fool? Seeing things. Ridiculous."

ROWENA
Thank you...love...

MUSIC

EDGAR
"That was *three* days before Rowena's condition had grown worse. No, that is when she died. Yes, of course. You remember? Her corpse lay there in that empty room, while I ingested my *opium* to release *me* from reality. The whole house reeked of its fumes.

EERIE MUSIC

"*Wild* visions, shadows, *weird* angles of the room, the figures in the paintings *moving,* the *flames* in the fireplace *dancing.* In the *middle* of it all, the *shrouded* body of Rowena. I awoke from that nightmare only to realize that, somehow, I had transported her body down into the crypt. I must have laid her in her coffin...and I'd been *gazing* at her *still* and rigid figure...staring, for *hours,* I suppose. So, then, I closed her coffin....

(STONE SLAB CLOSED)

"And, I turned...and just as I had left the crypt...

(WOMAN SOBBING ECHOES)

"*What? That* came from her *coffin,* no? I was sure...yes, I could *hear* it clearer. I had never been a *superstitious* man, but, that *sound*...it was *terrifying.* I was *quaking* from within.

(IRON GATE CREAKS, STONE SLAB MOVED)

"I rushed back to that room to see for myself...sliding away the *stone* lid of her coffin and I looked... looked *hard* at the body...it wasn't moving, was it? No. Certainly not. It's a *corpse,* Edgar, you fool. It's that *damned* opium. Give it up.

(LOUDER SOBBING)

"No, it *not* the opium! This was not delirium...this was real! *Real"*

SILENCE

(NO REVERB) *Rowena?* Is that *you,* my dear? Here, let me lift that *veil.* Let me see your face. *Oh!* Your face...am I *seeing* things? It's slight, *barely* noticeable...but, yes, I do perceive a definite *tinge* of color in your *cheeks* and eyelids.

MUSIC

(REVERB) "Listen to yourself, Edgar, you *buffoon* ...talking to a *corpse!*

You've gotten yourself worked up...you can barely *hear* your heart beating. Your arms, legs, they are *frozen* from fear. I *know!* But, can it be....Rowena *still* lives? I don't want to leave her...suppose she *is* alive?

CHAOTIC MUSIC

"No...look...her *face*...it's *no* longer got color in it...turning *gray* now. *Lips* shriveling ...oh, Lord, such a *ghastly* expression of death and rigor mortis and...this poor girl. I should be *ashamed* of myself. *God* forgive me. No matter *how* I try, I feel *nothing* for poor Rowena. I can't *stop* envisioning my Ligeia.

SILENCE

"And, so, I was about to leave...

(WOMAN'S SIGH ECHOES)

"What is *that?* Did I *hear* her just...? *Look!* Her lips are *quivering!* Am I losing my mind? Am I *seeing* things?

(NO REVERB) *Stop,* let's be *reasonable* here, now, Edgar.

(REVERB) *"No,* her forehead ...there's *color* there again. *And* the cheeks, *and* the throat....feel her skin? It's *warm*...yes, it is. Listen to the heart! I will. Oh...oh....oh, *yes,* it's beating...she's *alive! Alive!*

MUSIC

"Well, now, I felt *obligated* to restore her to life. I had to! I must! So, I rubbed and *bathed* her temples and hands. The doctor had gone. I was all alone. What *else* was I to do? But ...my work was in vain.

SILENCE

"Suddenly, the color disappeared, the pulsation *ceased,* the lips *resumed* the expression of the dead, and, in an instant afterward, the whole *body* became icy cold. And, again... I thought *not* of Rowena, but, of *Ligeia.* Why was this happening? Why, why, *why?*

(SOBBING ECHOES)
MUSIC
(INTERIOR TRAIN)

"It didn't end then and there. All night long, until the dawn, Rowena seemed to *revive* again...only to *die* again. It was horrible. Every *collapse* seemed to be *more* severe than the last. It was as *if* she was *struggling* some *invisible* enemy and *losing* each time. Who *knew* what the *next* struggle might bring? I remember that last time she twitched and stirred back to life...

EERIE MUSIC

"Appearing to be *more* vigorous than before. Her *limbs* relaxed, the color of life *returned* to her skin...she hadn't opened her eyes, but, I could see them *moving* under her their lids. Over and over, I remember that night... *reliving* it, there in that tomb...

"Yes, I believed, this time that...she *may* just make it. And then ...*Ohhhh!* She was *rising!* Rising up...*standing...* I couldn't think! I couldn't *breathe!* Tottering on her feet. *Rocking* back and forth. *Walking* now...with the *shroud* covering her eyes and her whole head... sleepwalking...Should I *speak* to her? *Wake* her?

MUSIC BUILDS

"No, I *dared* not. Besides, I was *paralyzed* where I stood. Either that, or I was *mad,* surely. How could this be happening? How could she *still* be alive? But, *there* she stood...that *shroud* still covering her entire *head* and body...it was a *ghost* standing before me.

(BREATHING)

"Her eyes...even from *beneath* the shroud, her *eyes* were *staring* at me! And, I could hear her *breathing*. And, then...that ghastly shroud began to slip down...*off* from her head...and, at once, in the dim light of the tomb...I saw those *cheeks...rosy* red...but, wait...*are* those *her* cheeks? *Her* eyes? And...she *seemed* to have *grown* taller ...

(TRAIN WHISTLE, TRAIN STOPS,
STEAM, CONDUCTOR YELLS
"FINAL STOP! EVERYONE OUT!"

"Wait...wait...I have to get off...I don't want to remember all this! But, you must, Edgar, you *must* ...you *had* to see for yourself, remember? You had to *thrust* that candle *closer* to her face...and...*ahhh!*

CHAOTIC MUSIC

"That *hair!* It *streamed* forth in *huge* masses, long and *disheveled! Blacker* than a *raven's* wing at midnight! And then...*Jesus!* She was opening her *eyes* and I *knew! I knew! I knew!* Those *eyes*...they could *never* be mistaken...those *full,* black, *wild* eyes! There *standing* before me was...my *lost* love...*Ligeia!"*

END

THE MURDERS IN THE RUE MORGUE

By Edgar Allan Poe
Adapted By Dan Bianchi

CAST - 3m/1w

SYNOPSIS - Auguste Dupin and Detective Burton must solve two mysterious and brutal murders.

(QUICK DOOR KNOCKS)

DUPIN
Hold on! I am on my way…

(DOOR OPENS)

Detective *Burton!*

BURTON
Dupin!

DUPIN
Detective, what brings *you* here at this hour? The sun isn't even up, yet.

BURTON
Sorry about that, Dupin. But, there's been a horrible murder… *murders,* I should say…in Rue Morgue. About *three* A.M. this morning. It's a *mystery* I tell you…a *baffling* mystery.

DUPIN
Well, then, come in and *tell* me what you know….

(DOOR CLOSES)

BURTON
It happened at *19* Rue Morgue…the *sole* occupancy of one *Marie* L'Espanaye, and her *daughter,* Camille. Bloody *screaming* was heard all over the neighborhood. I dare say, all of *N'Orleans* might have heard it.

DUPIN
Have a seat. Well, have *you* been there…to the murder scene?

BURTON
I arrived there within minutes. It so happens, I *live* but a block away from that house.

DUPIN
Tell me what you saw...as *concise* as you can remember it....

BURTON
Well...I can still hear those screams from my home...howls...
MUSIC
(DISTANT WOMEN SCREAMING, ECHO)

...echoing in the night. I rush to where a crowd has gathered in Rue Morgue...some neighbors and I break down the front door...
(CROWD MURMURS, DOOR BROKEN)

By this time, the *cries* have ceased...but, as we enter...
(DISTANT ARGUING)

I can hear two or more voices *arguing* upstairs. Soon, everything is quiet. *"Hello!"* I yell. No answer. And, again I yell, *"Hello!* The police are here!"* ...but, again, no answer. So, up we go.
(FOOTSTEPS ASCENDING)

Upon arriving at a *back* bedroom on the *fourth* floor, I find the door *locked,* with the *key* inside.
SILENCE

DUPIN
Aha!

BURTON
Again, we force this door open...
(MEN GRUNT, DOOR BROKEN)
MUSIC

And, and...it's *horrible,* just *astonishingly* horrible. The apartment is in the *wildest* disorder...the furniture *broken* and thrown about in all directions. There is only *one* bed...the *linens* are thrown on the floor. On a chair lay a *razor*...smeared with blood. On the *floor* are *two* or three long and *thick* clumps of *grey* human hair, *also* soaked in blood, and *seeming* to have been *pulled* out by the roots.

DUPIN
Belonging to the *victim,* no doubt.

BURTON
Yes. Upon the floor…assorted *silverware* and jewelry. And…hard to believe…*four- thousand* dollars!

SILENCE

DUPIN
Four-thousand dollars!

BURTON
That's what I said. Four-*thousand* dollars. The *bureau* drawers have been *rifled,* but, *many* articles remain. Then, I discover a small *iron* safe under the bed, *locked.* One of my *officers* finds the key and I open it…nothing much, *old* letters and papers.

DUPIN
Doesn't *sound* like a *robbery,* does it? Hmmm…and, the *victims?* The old woman? The *daughter?*

EERIE MUSIC

BURTON
No *sign* of them…at first. But, then I notice…there is an *unusual* quantity of *soot* in the fire-place. I look up the chimney and…*sure* enough, *there* is the daughter…her body *stuffed* up there.

DUPIN
Stuffed up the chimney?

BURTON
Why, it takes *two* men to free the body…which is still *quite* warm. Many *lacerations,* some from the chimney bricks, I *imagine*…but, upon the *face* are many *severe* scratches, and, *upon* the throat, *dark* bruises, and *deep* indentations of finger nails…

DUPIN
Strangled to death?

BURTON
Looks that way. The face is…well, *discolored*…black and blue and purple…and the *eye*-balls protruding. The *tongue* has been *partially* bitten through. There's a large *bruise* upon the *pit* of the stomach…

DUPIN
Produced, probably, by the *pressure* of a knee.

BURTON
Next. we make a *thorough* investigation of the *whole* house...there is a
trap door on the roof, but, so old, it is *rusted* shut. But, when we search
the *yard*...we find the *corpse* of the old woman...with *her* throat *so*
entirely cut, that, when we *try* to raise her...the *head* falls off.

DUPIN
No!

BURTON
She's *terribly* mutilated, I swear, Dupin...it's *hard* to tell she's a human
being. All the bones of the *right* leg and arm are more or less *shattered*.
The left *tibia* splintered, as well as *all* the ribs of the *left* side. The whole
body is *dreadfully* bruised and discolored.

DUPIN
Hmmm....And, the *murder* weapon?

BURTON
None to be found. I'd guess a heavy wooden *club* or an iron *bar?* A
chair? Whatever was used, the killer is *very* powerful. No *woman* could
have *inflicted* those blows with *any* weapon. The *head* of the deceased
is *entirely* separated from the body, and her skull is also *greatly*
shattered. The *throat* has evidently been *cut* with some very *sharp*
instrument...probably, with a razor.

SILENCE

You *know?* It *sounds* like the work of *Jack* The Ripper. They never *did*
find him back in London. Do you think *he* might have come *here* to
N'Orleans?

DUPIN
Perhaps. Or, at least, it is someone who is *duplicating* those terrible
murders.

BURTON
Wonderful.

DUPIN
Although, his work was a *bit* more refined...some thought him to be a surgeon. *These* crimes you describe...sound *savage* beyond belief.

BURTON
I agree. So, *that* is where I have left it, my friend. Dupin, *you* have the greatest mind for *deduction* I know of in our city. I wonder if *you* might be able to *help* me solve this mystery?

DUPIN
I'll get my hat.

MUSIC
SILENCE

BURTON
Auguste Dupin...This is Mrs. Duffy...a neighbor of the victims.

MRS.DUFFY
As I've told the police, I've known *both* of the deceased for *six* years. The old lady and her daughter seemed on good terms...very *affectionate* towards each other. *Both* told *fortunes*, for a living. They made a pretty penny, I can tell you.

DUPIN
Did they have many visitors? Any *relatives?*

MRS.DUFFY
Not that *I'd* seen. *And,* no servants. No, no visitors...the *two* of them always went to their *clients'* houses to tell their fortunes. I *will* say, it was *strange* that they *lived* in that big old house in the dark...

DUPIN
What do you mean?

MRS.DUFFY
Well, the window shutters...they were *never* opened. Both front *and* rear. *Appalling* way to live, no?

DUPIN
And, you *heard* them shouting...before Detective *Burton* arrived on the scene?

MRS.DUFFY
Definitely. And, I can tell you, *one* voice was *not* a woman's voice... He was *shouting* something...*"Devil! Beast!"* he said. There was another *shrill* voice...sounded like a foreigner...but, I couldn't tell if it was *male* or female...sounded *Spanish*...maybe *I-talian*. But, I knew the old lady and her daughter. I'm *sure* that the *shrill* voice was *not* either of theirs.

DUPIN
How *long* did the screaming last?

MRS.DUFFY
Oh, I'd say, a good *ten* minutes or so. Long and loud... *awful*. Just awful. Then, I heard a *scraping* or a scuffling sound.

BURTON
Yes, *I* heard that, as well.

DUPIN
And, when was the *last* time you had actually *seen* Mrs. *L'Espanaye?*

MRS.DUFFY
Let's see...oh, yes, I saw her earlier *yesterday*...in the afternoon, at the bank. She was *withdrawing* a good deal of money...I saw the cashier *put* it in her leather bag. I *know* she had *property* investments. I spoke to her last *spring,* was it? Yes. That's when she began making *frequent* deposits in small sums.

DUPIN
Really? And, then, she withdrew *four* thousand on the day she was murdered? *Hmmm....*

MUSIC
SILENCE

BURTON
Well, *Dupin*, do you have *any* idea how the *perpetrator* got into *and* out of that *locked* room? The door was *bolted* from the inside...we had to *smash* it in. And, the *windows* were shuttered and *locked* as well.

DUPIN
What about the *chimneys?*

BURTON
The chimneys are too *narrow* to freely admit a human being. The body

of the daughter was...

DUPIN
Yes, I know.

BURTON
Baffling, isn't it?

DUPIN
We shall see.

                                        MUSIC
                                       SILENCE
                (PERIOD PHONE RINGS, PICKED UP)

DUPIN
Dupin speaking...

BURTON ON PHONE
Dupin! Have you heard? We have a *suspect!* His name is Adolph
Steinheimer...

DUPIN
You have *evidence* to tie him to the killings?

BURTON ON PHONE
Well...he...*confessed.*

DUPIN
You've *questioned* him thoroughly...he can actually *describe* the
murders in detail...?

BURTON ON PHONE
We're working on it.

DUPIN
You're grasping at *straws,* Detective! *Confessed!* The man is probably
mentally disturbed. Meanwhile, the *real* criminal is free.

BURTON ON PHONE
Well...we need *something* to quiet the people, the newspapers...the
Mayor!

DUPIN
What you *need* is a *proper* method of detection. You can't just *deal* with *whatever* is there at the moment. With no *foresight*, no *hindsight.* Yes, the police department has the *diligence* to *plow* ahead, but... without a *map,* you shall fail. One must *look* at the whole picture, not just a *few* facts of a crime before you. *Truth* isn't just *found* at the bottom of a well, you know... it is *up* on the mountain tops, too.

BURTON ON PHONE
Well, we are *doing* the best we can... given the circumstances...

DUPIN
You say you *have* the murderer? He's *confessed?* Well then, what has been his *motive* for this bloody crime? *Robbery?* He'd left *four-thousand* dollars on the floor. *Revenge?* Did he even *know* the victims?

BURTON ON PHONE
Not that we've determined.

DUPIN
Did he *sexually* force himself upon the females?

BURTON ON PHONE
There is no sign of that.

DUPIN
Bah!

BURTON ON PHONE
Well, maybe I've overlooked something. Shall we *inspect* the premises once again?

DUPIN
I already have.

BURTON ON PHONE
And?

DUPIN
And, in approximately *thirty* minutes from now... *you* shall meet the person who, *although* not the *perpetrator* of these butcheries, *must* have been in *some* measure *implicated* in their perpetration.

BURTON ON PHONE
What?

MUSIC
SILENCE

DUPIN
It is true that he may not arrive... but, highly *probable* that he will. Should he come, it will be *necessary* to detain him. You have your *pistol?*

BURTON
Of course. Who *is* this person, Dupin?

DUPIN
All in good time, Detective.   Now...I have ruled *out* that the old lady *might* have destroyed her daughter and *then* committed suicide.

BURTON
How could she have *stuffed* the daughter's corpse up the flue?

DUPIN
Exactly. And, the *wounds* upon her *own* body were not *self*-inflicted. *Murder,* then, had been committed by some *third* party whose *voice* had been heard by *others* including yourself.   Did you observe anything *peculiar* about the *testimony* stated concerning the voices?

BURTON
Only that the *voice* was *strange* enough to confuse *several* listeners, including me. But, there was *no* disagreement about the *other* voice...it sounded *shrill,* or harsh. We all *agree* to its *sound,* but, we couldn't distinguish any words.

DUPIN
Now, what about the *bedroom?*   The means of *exit* used by the murderers?

BURTON
You think there were more than *one?*

DUPIN
It is not *too* extreme to say that *neither* of us *believe* in the supernatural, *correct?*

BURTON
Well...yes, I suppose...

DUPIN
Madame and *Mademoiselle* L' Espanaye were *not* destroyed by spirits.

BURTON
No, I agree. The murderer was *indeed* a material being.

DUPIN
Then, *how* did he escape? Let us examine the possible *means* of exit.
It is *clear* that the *assassins* were in the room where the daughter
Camille was found, when *you* ascended the stairs.

BURTON
We've laid bare the floors, the ceilings, *and* the masonry of the walls, in
every direction. There are *no* secret passages. The door *leading* from
the room into the hall was *securely* locked, with the keys *inside.*
                                                              MUSIC

DUPIN
Now, we *know* that the *chimneys* are *too* narrow to allow access for a
human being. Alright, what about the *windows?* Anyone *escaping*
through the *front* windows would have been seen by the crowd. What
about the *rear* windows?

BURTON
There are *two* windows in the bedroom. They were found *securely*
fastened from within. *Nailed* shut. The windows were *not* used as exits.

DUPIN
Do you think *so?*

BURTON
What do you mean?

DUPIN
I have found that the *sash* in each is *spring* loaded. The window can
move on its own. The *one* window won't budge. But, the other? If I
remove the nail, which is *old* and broken... the window *pops* open. Try
closing it, the *spring* is very strong. A person passing *out* through this
window *might* have *reclosed* it, and the spring would have *closed* the
window with such force...*Driving* a nail into the woodwork. Making it

appear to be *nailed* shut. *Pressing* the spring, I gently *raised* the sash but a few inches… the nail went up with it. When *closed*, the old *nail* found its *hole* and it *appeared* to be nailed shut.

BURTON
You mean the nail sits *loose* in its hole…and when the window is *raised* it goes up with it…and when it comes down hard, it *re-enters* the hole…?

DUPIN
Precisely.

SILENCE

BURTON
Well, I'll be….

DUPIN
Your men missed that. And so, the *whole* mode of escape was *missed* as well.

BURTON
But, how did the murderer *descend* down *four* floors on the outside?

DUPIN
There is a *lightning* rod that runs from the ground to the roof, no?

BURTON
Yes, but, if someone climbed it, it's *impossible* for anyone to reach the *window* itself, to say *nothing* of entering it.

DUPIN
However, the *shutters* of the *fourth* story are of the *peculiar* kind rarely used these days, but, *frequently* seen upon very old mansions.

BURTON
The *shutters?*

MUSIC

DUPIN
They are in the form of an ordinary *farmers* door, where the *top* half opens *separately* from the bottom…and so offers an *excellent* hold for the hands. Again, *individually,* each shutter *might* not amount to much. But, *together,* if you *look* at the *entire* rear wall of the building, they create a *ladder* of sorts for the intruder *straight* up and down to the fourth

floor bedroom window, *or* down from the roof, *suspended* by a rope *tied* to the lightning rod.

BURTON
But, for *anyone* to manage all that...

DUPIN
Of course, they would need to be an acrobat.

SILENCE

BURTON
I'm beginning to *wonder* if it *was* a ghost after all.   So, that *may* be the means of escape. But, *how* did the murderer enter?

DUPIN
Probably, the same method.

MUSIC

And, once inside, he *rifled* through the bureau, although *much* of the clothing and articles remained in the drawers. If the thief was to take *anything*, why *hadn't* he taken the best?   Why not take *all?* He *did* abandon *four* thousand dollars...for *what* reason?

BURTON
Obviously, the motive was *not* to rob the women.

DUPIN
But, Detective Burton, *you* have a man *locked* up who has *confessed* to the crime. Yet, *you* have *no* idea *why* he had committed that crime.   *If* the perpetrator had gone *through* such an *elaborate* break-in to *steal* the money, he is an *idiot to* have left it all behind.

SILENCE

BURTON
Alright...so...*there* is the peculiar voice.   The unusual *agility.*   The *absence* of motive. The *atrocious* murders.

DUPIN
Let's look at the *butchery* itself.

MUSIC

A woman *strangled* to death by manual strength. *Thrust* up a chimney.

BURTON
Head downward.

DUPIN
Is *that* the work of an *ordinary* assassin? I think not. Who would try to hide a *full* grown adult *up* inside a chimney?

BURTON
Yes, that *is* strange, isn't it?

DUPIN
Even if the person is the most *depraved* of men, he'd *have* to have the strength of *five* men.

BURTON
Even *five* men had difficulty *retracting* the body.

DUPIN
And what about the long thick *tresses* of *gray* hair, *torn* out by the roots, *found* on the floor? It takes a *lot* of force to tear even *twenty* or thirty *hairs* at the same time. *You* saw the roots with *fragments* of the scalp. *And,* the *throat* of the old lady was *not* merely cut, but the *head* absolutely *severed* from the body...

                                                                    SILENCE

BURTON
The instrument *could* have been a mere *razor.*

DUPIN
That's pretty *brutal* in itself.

BURTON
The killer *must* have been ferocious. Those bruises on the body had to be *inflicted* by a *blunt* instrument.

DUPIN
I agree.

                                                                    MUSIC

But, *I* believe that instrument was the *stone* pavement below where the *thrown* body had landed. So, let's now add...the *odd* disorder of the room, the *astounding* agility, *superhuman* strength, a *brutal* ferocity, butchery *without* motive, a grotesque *horror* absolutely *alien* from humanity, and a voice *foreign* to men of *many* nations and *devoid* of all distinct language. What *then* do you think we are *dealing* with here?

BURTON
Sounds like…a *madman* is on the loose. Some raving *maniac*, escaped from a nearby asylum.

DUPIN
You *may* be right, but, I think not.

SILENCE

BURTON
No?

DUPIN
The *voices* of madmen, even at their *wildest* can be understood. Madmen speak *languages* and *dialects*, however *incoherent* the words may be. Besides, the *hair* of a madman is *not* such as I *now* hold in my hand. Look at *this*…

BURTON
What is that?

DUPIN
I disentangled this little *tuft* from the *rigidly* clutched fingers of *Mrs.* L' Espanaye. Tell me what *you* can make of it.

BURTON
Dupin! This hair is *most* unusual…this is no *human* hair.

DUPIN
I didn't say it *was.*

MUSIC

But, *before* we decide this point, *please* look at this little *sketch* I've actually *traced* of the dark bruises, the *finger* indentations *left* on the neck of the daughter, Camille. There is a firm and *fixed* hold. Each finger *imbedded* into the *skin* of the victim's neck. Attempt, now, to place *all* your fingers, at the *same* time, in the *respective* impressions as you see them.

BURTON
There's no way…I can't fit them *exactly*…even if I *fold* it into a *cylinder*

and *wrap* my fingers around it...no, it won't work. The hand print is *too* large. It *can't* be human. What on *Earth* are we *dealing* with here, Dupin?

SILENCE

DUPIN
Have you ever heard of the *orangutang* of the East Indian Islands? They have a *gigantic* stature, *prodigious* strength, *wild* ferocity...*and* they *are* known to *imitate* humans when *trained* in circus side shows.

BURTON
You don't *mean* to say...?

DUPIN
And, *their* digits are *exactly* in accordance with this tracing. The *tuft* of reddish hair, *too*, is *identical* with this here.

BURTON
But...are you *forgetting* that there were *two* voices heard, one possibly an Italian or Frenchman? And the words... *"Devil! Beast!"*

DUPIN
It *could* be that the beast had *escaped* from its owner. He *may* have followed it to the house...*yelled* at it...but, did he *recapture* the animal? Is it *still* at large?

BURTON
What should we do?

DUPIN
Here...read *this* in tonight's paper...

BURTON
"Caught...in *Cornwall* Street, late last night, a very large, *tawny* Orangutang of the Bornese species. The *owner* may have the animal again, upon *identifying* it satisfactorily, and paying a *few* charges arising from its *capture* and keeping." *What?* This is *your* address, Dupin!

MUSIC

DUPIN
I have taken the *liberty* of setting a *trap* for our murderer. If I am wrong, he won't show himself. But, if I am *right,* the owner of the *murderer* will appear. He will say that *he* is innocent. He is poor. The *beast* is of

great value. Perhaps, he will think we are *ignorant* of the crime in the Rue Morgue. After all, we have *allegedly* found the creature in *Cornwall Street*, a good mile from the crime. The owner thinks he will get the *orangutang* back and keep it hidden until it is safe to sell it.

(DISTANT DOOR CREAKS)

BURTON
What's that?

DUPIN
(Whispers) I've left the *front* door open. *You* hide in the closet. Be *ready* with your pistols, but *don't* fire them until I give you the signal. I've left the *front* door open.

(ASCENDING FOOTSTEPS)

He's coming up the staircase now.

(KNOCKING)

DUPIN
Come in!

(DOOR OPENS)

SAILOR
Good evening.

SILENCE

DUPIN
Sit down, my friend. I suppose *you* have called about the orangutang? Upon my word, I almost *envy* you the possession of him... a remarkably *fine,* and no doubt a *very* valuable animal. How *old* do you suppose him to be?

SAILOR
I have no way of telling... but he *can't* be more than *four* or five years old. Have you got him here?

DUPIN
Oh no... we have *no* conveniences for keeping him here. He is at a *livery* stable in Rue *Depardieu,* nearby. You can get him in the morning. Of course, you are prepared to *identify* the property?

SAILOR
To be sure I am, sir.

DUPIN
I shall be sorry to part with him.

SAILOR
I don't want to put you through any more trouble. Couldn't expect it. I'm *very* willing to pay a *reward* for the finding of the animal... that is to say, anything in reason.

DUPIN
Well, that is all very *fair,* to be sure. Let me *think!* What shall I have? *Oh!* I know. *My* reward shall be this. *You* shall give me *all* the information in your power about the *murders* in the Rue Morgue.

SAILOR
What the...? Say, mister, what are you *playing* at? Why, I *ought to...!*

DUPIN
Detective Burton!

BURTON
Put that *cane* down, sir, or you're *dead* where you stand! Now...sit *down!*

DUPIN
That's better. My friend, you are *alarming* yourself unnecessarily. *We* mean you no harm. I *know* that you are *innocent* of the atrocities in the Rue Morgue. However, you cannot *deny* that you are implicated in them. You are not *guilty,* not even of robbery. You *couldn't* have avoided the *terrible* deaths. You have *nothing* to conceal. But, you are *bound* by honor to *confess* all you know. A man is now imprisoned, *charged* with the crime of which *you* know he is innocent.

SAILOR
So help me God, I *will* tell you all I know about it. But, I do *not* expect you to believe *one* half of my story. I would be a fool *indeed* if I did. *Still,* I *am* innocent, and I *will* make a *clean* breast before I die for it. I have been a *sailor* for nearly *thirty* years. On my *last* voyage to the Indian Islands, we landed at Borneo...

MUSIC
(JUNGLE SOUNDS)

...and we traveled into the interior on an *expedition* where we *captured* the *Orangutang* in question. It was *near* death and *I* nursed it back to health. But, the *long* voyage back on board ship proved difficult.

(ROARS)

The beast was often *wild* and fierce. When we *docked* here in New Orleans, I kept it *carefully* secluded. I intended to *sell* it. Returning home two nights ago, I found that the beast had *broken* out of its cage and was *free* in my bedroom.

(GROWL)

So, I walked in…and *there* he is, *holding* my shaving razor and *staring* at me. I'm terrified. I don't know *what* to do! I take out my whip. It had *worked* in the past.

(WHIP SNAP)

But, as soon as he sees it, he's *down* the stairs and out the window.

(WINDOW CRASH)

I try my best to follow it. He *knows* I am right behind him. And, then he stops to *look* at me and he *waves* the razor. Pulls it right across in front of his throat as if threatening me. I tell ya, my *heart* stopped beating just then. It was as if…he *knew* what to do with that razor alright. I wasn't about to approach him, I tell ya.

BURTON
Well, so?

SAILOR
Well, so, then, he's *off* again. Thank God the streets are *quiet* at that time of night. Well, I *trot* behind him, see? *Trying* to keep him within eyesight. When he comes to the *rear* alley of the Rue Morgue…he's *attracted* by a light *gleaming* from an open window in the *fourth* story of the house. He *climbs* up there in a flash…and *throws* open the window and he's in. It only takes a minute.

(WINDOW SLAM)

Well, here I'm thinking, he's *contained,* at least.   But, how can *I* recapture the beast…*alone?* And, what's it *doing* inside that house …*and* to the *people* in there?   So…*I* climb up the same way…only it takes some time…I *barely* reach the open window and look inside…and what I see…*it's monstrous!*

(ROARS, SCREAMS, FURNITURE CRASH)

All those *shrieks* of terror! *Blood* everywhere. The ladies must have been sitting with their *backs* to the window and didn't *see* him come in...

DUPIN
What do you see?

SAILOR
I see...the gigantic animal *seize* the old lady by the hair and he starts to *slash* at her face with the razor. I think he had *watched* me shave *each* morning from his cage...and there *he* is...*imitating* the same motion on *her!* The daughter, *she* faints.
                    (WOMAN SCREECHING, ANIMAL GRUNTS, ROAR)

Now, he starts to pull out the old lady's *hair*. She *screams* like the devil. *That* makes him even madder. With one big *swoop* of his arm, he nearly *cuts* off her head.
                    (ORANGUTANG SCREECHING, FURNITURE CRASHES)
                                                    MUSIC BUILDS

The sight of blood...he goes *crazy!* I tell you, he goes *crazy*. *Gnashing* his teeth, *flashing* fire from its eyes. He *jumps* on the daughter and starts to *tear* at her throat until she's dead. Then, he turns...and he *sees* me at the window...*staring* in horror at him. I think he's afraid I'll *whip* him...he suddenly gets *real* scared. So, he tries to *hide* the body.
                                        (FURNITURE CRASHES)

He *drags* it all over the room, upsetting all the furniture... he finds the chimney and *sticks* her up there. He takes the old lady and *heaves* her corpse out the window. I *yell* at him...that *devil*...that damned *beast*. He just keeps jabbering.
                                                        SILENCE
BURTON
So, what do *you* do?

SAILOR
Do? There's nothing *I* could do...I needed to get *out* of there. I guess he *escaped* out the window again...the window must have closed behind him.
                                                        MUSIC
                                        (DOOR KNOCKS, OPENS)

DUPIN
Detective *Burton!* What brings you here? Come in...
                                            (DOOR CLOSES)

SILENCE

BURTON
Hello, Auguste.

DUPIN
Ah, you call me by my *first* name. Something must be up. I've heard that the *original* suspect was *instantly* released, yes? But, the article says that the *real* murderer is *still* at large and has *fled* the city...

BURTON
Yes. Yes. They've even alluded to the *possibility* of him being *Jack* The Ripper. Can you imagine *that?* I mean, who would ever *suggest* such a thing?

DUPIN
Yes, I wonder. But, what of the *orangutang?*

BURTON
It has been quietly *donated* to the zoo.

DUPIN
And, its owner, the *sailor?* I do not read in the papers that *he's* been brought to justice. After all, it *is* illegal to *own* such a dangerous animal in our city and...because of that, *two* women are dead.

BURTON
And, you will *not* read such a thing. The Mayor *and* The Commissioner of Police will have *none* of it. The Sailor is *long* gone and won't be returning.

DUPIN
But, *why?*

BURTON
It *seems* that the Mayor's *brother* is the *Harbor* Master who *should* have inspected the live *cargo* removed from the ship. In fact, the Harbor Master was *paid* by the *ship* owner to look the *other* way. *I've* discovered that he's grown *rich* accepting *bribes* on the waterfront.

DUPIN
Aha! Well, *such* is the politics in our fair city. *Corrupt* to the core...*present* company excluded, Detective.

MUSIC

BURTON
And, so ends the case of the *Murders In The Rue Morgue*...although, there will be *no* reward for solving the case, my friend. Not even an *iota* of recognition, *nor* thanks. At least, I have had the *pleasure* of working with you once again. Your astounding *powers* of observation and *deduction* always amaze me. In fact, I would venture to say that they *surpass* that English fellow who's getting *quite* a reputation across the pond for solving crimes...what's his name? I can't think of it...it's a *silly* name...oh, you *must* know it...

DUPIN
On the contrary, Detective, I do not have *any* idea to *whom* you are referring.

END

THE CASK OF AMONTILLADO
By Edgar Allan Poe
Adapted By Dan Bianchi

CAST – 2m
SYNOPSIS – A man who has been insulted by another carries out his revenge.

MUSIC

MONTRESSOR
(REVERB) "I've been insulted a *thousand* times, no, *more*, by that *Fortunato*. Always, I've *kept* my tongue. *Now,* I want *revenge*. This is no *mere* threat. Oh no. He *deserves* punishment. But, not just *any* punishment. Now, you may say that *revenge* is wrong. Alright, I *know* that *another* wrong *cannot* make something right. But, is it *right* for me to *allow* the wrongdoer to get *away* with his *wrongdoing? Hmmm?* I *knew* you'd see things *my* way.

"It *must* be understood that *I've* done *nothing* wrong in *word* nor *deed* to make Fortunato *doubt* my good will. *He's* a man to be respected *and* feared. *But,* he has a *weak* point. He *prides* himself on being a *wine* connoisseur. A *true* virtuoso. He advises British *and* Austrian *millionaires* when they are *constructing* and *stocking* their wine cellars. Alright, I have to admit, *Fortunato* knows his wines. *I* am skilled in this field, *myself*, so, I am *qualified* to make this claim.
(CARNIVAL SOUNDS, FESTIVE CROWD)
CARNIVAL MUSIC

"This evening, during *carnival* season, I *ran* into Fortunato in the streets. He was drinking and *carousing* and *costumed* as a harlequin. He shook my hand, *wringing* it, as if *I* was the *one* person on Earth he had *prayed* to meet tonight."

FORTUNATO
Montressor! My friend! Come, *drink* and be merry! Do you *like* my bells on my hat?
(JINGLE BELLS)

MONTRESSOR
Fortunato, it's *luck* I ran into you. You're looking *remarkably* well.

FORTUNATO
What can I say? I am *blessed* with good health.

NARRATOR
That's good because *I* need *your* help.

FORTUNATO
Help? Why *certainly*...what is it that *I* can help you with...?

MONTRESSOR
I've just received a *barrel* of what *passes* for *Amontillado*. But, I have my doubts.

FORTUNATO
Amontillado? A *whole* barrel? *Impossible!* And, in the *middle* of carnival time!

MONTRESSOR
I purchased it at auction. Now, I *have* my doubts and I was *silly* enough to pay *quite* a lot for it...though it *is* still a bargain... without consulting *you* in the matter. You weren't available and I was *fearful* of losing a bargain, so...

FORTUNATO
Amontillado!

MONTRESSOR
I do have my doubts.

FORTUNATO
Amontillado!

MONTRESSOR
I *wish* I could get a *definitive* answer.

FORTUNATO
Amontillado!

MONTRESSOR
That's *quite* alright. If you're *too* busy, I can *always* ask *Luchresi. He's* got good taste. He'll tell me...

FORTUNATO
Luchresi cannot tell A*montillado* from a pail of beer. He's a *buffoon.*

MONTRESSOR
Really? Well, *some* fools still think *his* taste is a match for your own.

FORTUNATO
Ha! I *scoff* at that. See how I scoff? *Ha!* Come, let's go.

MONTRESSOR
Where?

FORTUNATO
To your *vaults!* (Coughs)

MONTRESSOR
No, you're *much* too busy. I can get Luchresi...

FORTUNATO
I'm *not* too busy. Let's go. (Sneeze)

MONTRESSOR
But...you *sound* as if you have a cold.

FORTUNATO
It doesn't matter.

MONTRESSOR
The vaults are *insufferably* damp. They are *encrusted* with *nitre.*

FORTUNATO
Nitre? Oh, we *don't* like nitre. *Nasty* stuff...I think. Fact is, I'm not certain I know what nitre is, exactly.   Ah...well, nevertheless, we shall go!

MONTRESSOR
But, obviously, you've had a great deal to drink already and...

FORTUNATO
Obviously...I just have a head cold. Now...*Amontillado!* Let's make sure you have *not* been swindled. And, as for *Luchresi,* he's got a nose like a *hound* dog...*not* made for the *delicate* art of *wine* tasting. Come, there's not a moment to lose...let's go right now!

MUSIC

MONTRESSOR
(REVERB) "So, he takes me by the arm and we are *off* down the crowded street of carnival goers. Did I tell you that *I* am wearing a *mask* of black silk and a *red* velvet cape? Rather *fetching* don't you think?"
                    (IRON DOOR CREAKS, VAULT, DRIPPING ECHOES)

FORTUNATO
Where are your servants?

MONTRESSOR
Oh, they're *all* out at the carnival. They won't be back until morning. This way to the vaults, sir.

FORTUNATO
Thank you, *kind* sir.
                                        (FOOTSTEPS ECHO)

MONTRESSOR
Be careful. It's *dark* down here. It is long and winding. We are entering the *catacombs* where my family the *Montressors* have been *burying* their dead for centuries.

FORTUNATO
Where's the barrel? Just show me to the *Amontillado!*

MONTRESSOR
We're getting there. Meanwhile, *observe* how the *white* walls *gleam* like bright light when the *torch* light hits them.

FORTUNATO
Ah...that's the *nitre* you were speaking about. (Coughs)

MONTRESSOR
Correct, *nitre*. How *long* have you had that cough?

FORTUNATO
It is nothing. (Coughs)

MONTRESSOR
Maybe, we should go back. Your *health* is precious. You are rich, *respected,* admired, *beloved. You* are happy. *I* used to be happy. *You* are a man to be *missed.* For me, *my* life, it doesn't matter. We will go back. You are going to get sick and *I* don't want to be held responsible.

Besides, there is always *Luchresi*...

MONTRESSOR
Enough. The *cough* is nothing. It's *not* going to kill me. I'm not going to *die* from a cough.

FORTUNATO

MONTRESSOR
Very true.

FORTUNATO
What's that you say?

MONTRESSOR
Still, you *should* be careful. You know what *might* help? A *draft* of this *Medoc* will *defend* us from the *damp* air down here. *Before* we get to the Amontillado. Here we go...a *fine* year too...*Drink,* my friend....

FORTUNATO
Let's *drink* to the dead who are *buried* around us.

MONTRESSOR
And, to your *long* life.

FORTUNATO
Now, can we *proceed?*   These vaults are extensive.

MONTRESSOR
The Montressors were a *great* and numerous family.

FORTUNATO
Onward to the Amontillado.

MUSIC

MONTRESSOR
(REVERB) "The wine *sparkles* in his eyes and those silly bells on his hat and costume jingle. He enjoys his *swig* of Medoc. Gets him in the mood. We pass through *long* walls of piled *skeletons*, with casks and *caskets* intermingling, into the *innermost* recesses of the catacombs. I pause again, and *this* time I *seize* Fortunato by his arm."

SILENCE

(NO REVERB) The *nitre!* See, it increases. It *hangs* like moss upon the vaults. We are below the river's bed. The drops of moisture *trickle* among the bones. Come, let's go *back* before it is too late. Your cough....

FORTUNATO
It's nothing. Let's keep going. But first, another swig of the Medoc.

MONTRESSOR
Of course.

MUSIC

(REVERB) "This time he *empties* the bottle with one *long* swig. His eyes *flash* with a *fierce* light. He *laughs* and throws the bottle *upwards* with a *gesticulation* I do not understand. I look at him in surprise. He *repeats* the movement."

SILENCE

FORTUNATO
You do not *comprehend?*

MONTRESSOR
No.

FORTUNATO
Then you are *not* of the brotherhood. The *masons?*

MONTRESSOR
Yes, I *am.*

FORTUNATO
You? Impossible! A mason?

MONTRESSOR
A mason.

FORTUNATO
Then, give me a sign. A *sign...*

MONTRESSOR
How about *this?*

(REVERB) "Smiling, I produce from *beneath* the folds of my cape a *trowel."*

FORTUNATO
Now you jest. Come on, where's this *Amontillado?*

MUSIC

MONTRESSOR
(REVERB) "I replace the tool *beneath* the cloak and again offer him my arm. After *so* much drinking, he *leans* upon it heavily. We continue our route in *search* of the Amontillado. We pass through a range of low arches, *descending* and descending again, arriving at a *deep* crypt, in which the *foulness* of the air nearly extinguishes our torches.

"At the *farthest* end of the crypt there appears *another* less spacious crypt. *Its* walls are *lined* with human remains, *piled* to the vault overhead, in the fashion of the *great* catacombs of Paris. Three sides of this *interior* crypt are *ornamented* in this manner. From the *fourth* side the bones have been *taken* down, and lay *scattered* on the earth, exposing the bare wall...*there* is a *hole* in that wall. The bricks have been *removed*. There is an *interior* crypt or *recess* about four feet by *six* feet. Why is it *there?* I hold my torch up to it."

SILENCE

FORTUNATO
Why are we stopping? Is the Amontillado inside? Shall we go in? It's dark in there.

(IRON DOOR CREAKS)

MONTRESSOR
I'm right behind you.

FORTUNATO
Well...it *seems* to end here. A dead end. What are you...*doing?*

MUSIC
(CHAINS RATTLE, LOCKS)

MONTRESSOR
(REVERB) "I am taking his hand and *locking* it to the iron *cuffs* on the wall. First *one,* then the *other.* In his stupor, he does *little* to object. I take my *key* and lock each cuff with chains about his wrists. And, then, I step back."

(NO REVERB) If you pass your *hand* over the wall, you can't *help* feeling the nitre. It *is* damp isn't it?

FORTUNATO
The *Amontillado!*

MONTRESSOR
Ah, yes, the Amontillado.

(REVERB) "As I say these words I *busy* myself among the pile of bones on the earthen floor.   Throwing them *aside*, I soon uncover a quantity of *building* stone and mortar. With *these* materials and with the *aid* of my trowel, I begin *vigorously* to *wall* up the *entrance* of that *recessed* area.
                    (TROWEL, BRICKS, CEMENT)

"I have *scarcely* laid the *first* row of bricks when I *discover* that the *intoxication* of Fortunato has begun to wear off.
                        (FORTUNATO MOANS)

"That is *not* the cry of a drunken man. Now, he's silent. I will lay the *second* row, and the *third*, and the *fourth*.
                (CHAINS RATTLE, FORTUNATO ROARS)

"I stop working and listen."
                                    SILENCE

FORTUNATO
What are you doing?

MONTRESSOR
What does it look like I am doing? I am building a wall.

FORTUNATO
Are you *crazy?* Let me *out* of here! I'll have the *law* on you! You won't be able to live *or* work in this city ever again!

MONTRESSOR
Ah, *now* you've made me see the light.

FORTUNATO
I should *hope* so! You *maniac!*
                                    MUSIC

MONTRESSOR
(REVERB) "I *resume* my work with the trowel, and *finish* without

interruption the *fifth,* the sixth, *and* the seventh row"

FORTUNATO
Wait! What are you doing? *Stop! Help! Someone help me!*

MONTRESSOR
(REVERB) "The wall is now nearly *level* with my breast. I again pause, and holding the *torch* over the *new* wall, throw a few feeble *rays* upon the figure within."

FORTUNATO
You're out of your mind! No…wait, please, Montressor, I *apologize!* I'll do anything! *Ahhhhh….*

(CHAINS RATTLE)

MONTRESSOR
(REVERB) "He *lunges* at me. Luckily, the *chains* on his cuffs only go so far. For a brief moment I hesitate, I *tremble.* I have brought a *knife* with me just in case. But, I don't need that. I place my hand upon the solid wall and feel satisfied."

SILENCE

FORTUNATO
Help me, *somebody!*

MONTRESSOR
Help me, *somebody!*

FORTUNATO
Get me out of *here!*

MONTRESSOR
Get me out of *here!*

FORTUNATO
I'm being held prisoner by a *madman!*

MONTRESSOR
I'm being held prisoner by a *madman!*

FORTUNATO
Ahhhhhhh!

MONTRESSOR
Ahhhhhhh!

MUSIC

(REVERB) "At last, he falls silent. It is now *midnight*, and *my* task is drawing to a close. I have completed the eighth, the ninth *and* the *tenth* row of bricks. There remains but a *single* stone to be fitted and plastered in. I weigh it in my hand. But now…

FORTUNATO
Hahahahah! A very good *joke!* An excellent jest! It's *carnival* time, of course. We shall have *many* laughs over this for years to come, no? Over our *wine?*

MONTRESSOR
The *Amontillado?*

FORTUNATO
Yes, the *Amontillado!* Isn't it getting late? Shouldn't we be *returning* to the party? Let's go…

MONTRESSOR
Yes…let's *go.*

FORTUNATO
For the love of *God, Montressor! Ahhhhhh!*

SILENCE

MONTRESSOR
(REVERB) "And next there is silence…"

(NO REVERB) Fortunato! *Fortunato?*

(REVERB) "No answer. I thrust a torch through the remaining aperture and let it fall within.

(BELLS JINGLING)

"What's that? *Bells?*

MUSIC
(LAYING BRICKS, PLASTERING)

"My heart grows sick. It must be the dampness, the *nitre* of the catacombs that causes it. I hurry to finish my task. I force the *last* stone into its position... I plaster it up. Against the *new* masonry I re-erect the *old* wall of bones. For centuries, *no* mortal has *disturbed* them until now. Rest in peace, Fortunato."

END

THE SYSTEM OF DOCTOR TARR AND PROFESSOR FETHER
By Edgar Allan Poe
Adapted By Dan Bianchi

CAST – 4m/1w
SYNOPSIS – A man makes an unexpected visit to an insane asylum.

MUSIC
(CAR DRIVING, INTERIOR)

NARRATOR
(REVERB) "I had been traveling down South when my route led me within a few miles of *St. Mary's* asylum, a *private* madhouse, of which *I* had heard about from my *medical* friends. I had never *been* to a *mental* hospital before, so, I thought I'd stop to take a *look* and, perhaps, I'd write an *article* about it for my newspaper.

(CAR PULLS UP, STOPS)

"The building, *itself,* was secluded…about *two* miles off the main road and set in a *dank* and gloomy forest. It was an old *plantation* house which looked *dilapidated* to me, *hardly* fit for tenants, much less *patients*. *And,* it looked rather scary. I *almost* turned my car around, *but,* gathered my courage and proceeded up to the *gateway* where a face *peered* out at me from behind the bars."

MAILLARD
What do you want?

NARRATOR
I'd like to see Dr. *Maillard.*

MAILLARD
I am Dr. *Maillard.*

NARRATOR
We have a mutual *friend*, Doctor.

(REVERB) "I mentioned a few names until he recognized one, or, *pretended* to… and, only *then* did…

(IRON GATE OPENS)

"…he allow me in through the gate. I followed him into the house where there was a neat parlor containing many books, drawings, pots of flowers and musical instruments.

SAD PIANO MUSIC
(CRACKLING FIREPLACE)

"A cheerful fire blazed in the fireplace. A young and very beautiful woman played a mournful tune on the piano."

(NO REVERB) Doctor, I've heard from my *medical* friends that you employ a *unique* treatment here...the system of *soothing*...and that *all* punishments are *avoided,* yes?

MAILLARD
That's true. Even our *patients* are *not* confined to cells or rooms. They are allowed to roam *freely*, but, of course, are *watched* by our staff.

NARRATOR
(REVERB) "I wasn't sure if the *pianist* was a lunatic, so I was cautious in what I said before the young lady. She nodded and smiled and *appeared* to be quite sane...but, I know that one can never be *too* sure about such people."

MAILLARD
Sir, this is my niece. A most accomplished pianist don't you think?

NARRATOR
Niece? Oh? Yes, she plays *marvelously!*

MAILLARD
I am happy to invite *young* people such as *yourself* into our home to *witness* our achievements. As long, as you view all of this with an *open* mind. Unfortunately, *most* people still retain a rather *dim* view upon our system here when it was in operation.

NARRATOR
You mean, it is no *longer* used?

MAILLARD
It has been *some* time since we last used it. I have *renounced* it forever.

NARRATOR
Is that *so?*

MAILLARD
We found it absolutely *necessary* to return to the *old* methods. There was *danger* in the soothing system. Its advantages have been *much* overrated. Well, *I* believe we gave it a *fair* trial. We did *everything* that *rational* humanity could suggest. I am sorry that you could not have paid us a visit at an *earlier* period, that you might have judged for yourself. But, I *presume* you are aware of the *details* in the *soothing* practice?

NARRATOR
Not altogether. I've heard it explained by fellow medical students at college.

MAILLARD
Well, simply, we *humored* our patients. That is, we did not attempt to turn them *away* from *any* fantasies they may have had. We *indulged* and *encouraged* them to continue. To *some* patients, *such* treatment seemed *absurd,* as if they were here to *argue* their case…and when they *realized* that they received *no* conflict, their *own* sense of logic made them come to their senses. *One* man thought he was a *chicken.* When we treated him *as* a chicken, feeding him *corn* and *allowing* him to *sleep* in the shed, he awakened one day to *realize* that *he* is a man. And, so, he was cured.

NARRATOR
I find that to be an *amazing* treatment.

MAILLARD
We put much *faith* in *amusements* of a simple kind, such as *music,* dancing, *gymnastic* exercises generally, cards, *certain* classes of books, and so forth. We treated *each* individual as if for some *ordinary* physical disorder, and the word *'lunacy'* was never employed. We'd even appoint *certain* patients to watch *other* patients, to give them *confidence* and *responsibility.* The body *and* soul must be treated. It also allowed us to *dispense* with the *expense* of *hired* guardians.

NARRATOR
And, you utilized *no* punishments of *any* kind?

MAILLARD
None.

NARRATOR
And, you never *confined* your patients?

MAILLARD
Very rarely. Now and then, if someone was *violent,* we locked him in a cell *separated* from the others. Actually, we don't *welcome* such cases, so we *return* them to their families or to public hospitals.

NARRATOR
But, now you have *changed* all this... for the *better?*

MAILLARD
Absolutely. The system had its *disadvantages,* and even its *dangers.* I believe that our findings have *ended* this treatment *throughout* the country.

NARRATOR
That surprises me. I didn't *know* that they used the system elsewhere.

MAILLARD
Ah, don't always put *faith* in what *others* tell you. Believe *nothing* you hear, and only one-*half* of what you see. After dinner, when you have *sufficiently* recovered from the *fatigue* of your ride, I will be *happy* to show you the house, and *introduce* to you a system which, in *my* opinion, and in the opinion of everyone who has *witnessed* its operation, is *incomparably* the *most* effectual as yet devised.

NARRATOR
Your *own?* Is it of your *own* invention?

MAILLARD
I am *proud* to acknowledge that it is... at least in *some* measure. Come this way. I'll show you the gardens and conservatories. I *cannot* let you see my patients at the moment. I wouldn't want to *shock* you. And, I do not wish to *spoil* your appetite for dinner.
                              SILENCE
              (DINNER BELL, DINING SOUNDS, DISHES,
                  SILVERWARE, PATIENTS CHATTER)
              78 RPM RECORD PLAYING 1920s ORCHESTRA

NARRATOR
(REVERB) "At six, dinner was announced and my host conducted me into a *large* dining room where there were about *twenty-five* or thirty people... *apparently,* some of them were of *high* society by the way they were dressed, perhaps, a little *over*-dressed for such an establishment. At least two-*thirds* of them were *females* bedecked with jewelry, *rings,*

bracelets, *plunging* necklines, *bare* arms.   But, I noticed that *some* of the dresses were *not* well made and were *ill* fitting.   And there was Maillard's niece *now* dressed in *high-heeled* shoes, a short tight dress, fishnet stocking and a long blonde wig. In fact, *everyone* looked rather odd...as if, at a *masquerade* party? Perhaps, the *soothing* system was not *completely* extinguished? Perhaps, the good doctor did not *want* me to be *put* off from dining with *lunatics?*

"The table was *loaded* with plates of delicacies. *Too* many. Meats and pastries, *so* much it seemed *lavish* and wasteful. And, where was that *music* coming from?   Ah, an old Victrola in the corner of the room. Instead of a regular evening meal, it *appeared* that I was at a royal *banquet* that had *suddenly* gone *awkward*.   It was *truly* bizarre. But, the world is made up of *all* kinds of people, *no?* Who am *I* to judge? I took my seat and *participated* as best I could."

MAILLARD
Are you having a good time, sir?

NARRATOR
Excellent!

MAILLARD
We had a fellow here *once* who fancied himself to be a *tea-pot*. Nothing *rare* about that. *Every* asylum in the country has one of *those*. Our gentleman believed himself to be made of *fine* china, so he *polished* himself every morning.

NARRATOR
Was he *cured?*

MAILLARD
And, then, *not* long ago, we had a person who had taken it into his *head* that *he* was a donkey. But, *he* was a *troublesome* patient. We couldn't keep him within *bounds*, you understand. He would *eat* nothing but *thistles*. So, *we* insisted he eat nothing *else*. *That* cured him. But, he *did* kick a lot.

LADY
Mr. *De Kock!* I will *thank* you to *behave* yourself!

MAILLARD
What's wrong *now,* Mrs. Oliphant?

LADY
Please tell Mr. *De Kock* to keep his *feet* to *himself!* He has *spoiled* my *brocade!*

DE KOCK
A thousand pardons! I had *no* intention of *offending* the good woman. I, *Mr. De Kock,* will do *himself* the honor of partaking *wine* with you.

MAILLARD
Go sit down, Mr. De Kock. Have you had any of the *veal,* sir? It's quite good.

NARRATOR
Yes, I *will* have some, thank you.

MAILLARD
Ah, here it comes *now!*

NARRATOR
(REVERB) "At that instant three *sturdy* waiters *deposited* on the table an *enormous* platter containing a *small* calf roasted *whole* with an *apple* in its mouth."

MAILLARD
Ah, *that* looks *scrumptious,* doesn't it? If you don't *like* that, we *do* have some *rabbit,* as well...? *Peter*...please bring out the *rabbit*...and the *ham*....with a side dish of cat...

NARRATOR
Excuse me...did you say *cat?*

MAILLARD
Cooked in a *special* sauce. It's a *local* tradition.

NARRATOR
No, thank you, I'll just have a piece of this *cheese.*

MAILLARD
You know...*that* reminds me...we *did* have a patient once who believed *he* was a *Gruyere* cheese. He went about with a *knife* in his hand, asking his friends to try a small *slice* from the *middle* of his leg.

DE KOCK
What about the man who thought he was a *champagne* bottle?

(POPS HIS CHEEK)

Always going about *popping* his cork and *hissing* and fizzing.

LADY
And then there was an *ignoramus* who mistook *himself* for a *frog,*

DE KOCK
Which, *by* the way, he *resembled.*

LADY
I wish you could have *seen* him, sir, oh, the natural *airs* that he put on.
Sir, if *that* man was *not* a frog, it's a pity.

DE KOCK
He'd croak... *o-o-o-o-o-gh–o-o-o-o-gh!*

LADY
Then he'd put his *elbows* upon the table after taking a *glass* or two of
wine and *opened* his mouth like this and *rolled* up his eyes, and *wink*
them just so. You'd *think* you were in the *presence* of a frog. *He* was a
genius, he was.

NARRATOR
I have no doubt about it.

DE KOCK
And, what about Little *Andrew?*

LADY
He was a pumpkin. He *persecuted* the cook to make him up into pies.
The cook *refused* of course. But, I *don't* know why. It *might* have tasted
just fine. *You* look fine *yourself*, sir.

NARRATOR
Doctor...?

MAILLARD
Ha! ha! ha! Very *fine* indeed! *Don't* be frightened, my friend. *She* won't
bite!

(CHATTER, DINING SOUNDS GROW LOUDER)

DE KOCK
Remember Mr. *Bouffon*? Now, *he* was crazy. Thought he had *two* heads. A *real* lunatic...

MAILLARD
Mr. De Kock...you *know* we don't use such language here.

DE KOCK
He thought *both* heads were *Greek* philosophers discussing the *world* each day. He *loved* to orate. Do you know *that* word, sir? To *orate?*

LADY
I can *dance* if you so desire to see me dance...do you *desire* to see me dance? Mrs. *Jocelyn* used to dance like a *rooster. Cock a doodle do! Cock a doodle do!*

MAILLARD
Mrs. Toady *behave* yourself! If you *cannot* conduct yourself at the table like a lady...

NARRATOR
But, *I* thought *she* was Mrs. *Oliphant?*
          (SCENE GROWS LOUDER, SHOUTING IN BACKGROUND)

MAILLARD
Miss *Salsafette,* please do *not* remove your *clothing!* Put that back on...

NARRATOR
But...isn't *she* your *niece?*

MAILLARD
Everyone sit down, *please* be quiet, *eat* your meals! Miss *Salsafette,* you may *stop* undressing *now!* Oh, nevermind...
                    (YELLS, SCREAMS, CHAOS)

NARRATOR
(REVERB)   "The whole place had suddenly turned into...well, a *madhouse!* My *own* nerves were affected. Many of the patients were *frightened* by the *few* who had gone *wild.* I felt *sorry* for them, *shrinking* within their seats, *quivering* and *jabbering* in terror. Then...a *strange* loud noise...
                    (BANGING, HOWLING)

"And after a while ...

SILENCE

"...all was *quiet* and as before."

(NO REVERB) What on *Earth* was that *sound?*

MAILLARD
Oh nothing. *We* are *used* to these things, and care really *very* little about them. The *lunatics*, every now and then, get a bit *wild* and like to *howl* like *dogs* in the night. Especially when there is a full moon. You should have *heard* it when we had a *packed* house here. *Now*, things are *so* different.

DE KOCK
Yes, *so* different here now.

LADY
Indeed, *very* different!

(BANGING ON TABLE, LAUGHTER)

MAILLARD
Hold your *tongues*, every *one* of you! Turn that *music* off, *now!*

(RECORD SCRATCHES)
SILENCE

NARRATOR
So... *all* of these people... *you* conclude that they are *quite* harmless?

MAILLARD
What? Do you think *they* are *insane?* Nonsense. They are as *sane* as *I* am. *These* are *not* patients. All of *these* people are my *friends.* And, staff.

EERIE MUSIC

NARRATOR
What? All of them?

MAILLARD
Oh, *you* think they behave a bit *odd?* Is *that* it?

NARRATOR
Odd? I should think so!

MAILLARD
It *may* be you had *too* much *wine?*

NARRATOR
Doctor, if you *have* done away with the *soothing* system...what *exactly* have you *replaced* it with?

MAILLARD
What? Why, the system invented by Doctor *Tarr,* of *course!* You *must* have heard of *him,* no? *And,* Professor *Fether*...he has added a *few* adjustments, as well.

NARRATOR
I've *never* heard of them.

MAILLARD
Good Heavens! Did *you* say that you have *never* heard of the *learned* Doctor *Tarr* and the *celebrated* Professor *Fether?*

NARRATOR
No. I apologize. But, I am not so *educated* in this field of study. Believe me, I will *seek* out their writings and *acquaint* myself with their works.

MAILLARD
Say no more, my young friend. Have another glass of *brandy?*
(DINNER PARTY SOUNDS RESUME)
1920s JAZZ RECORD IN BACKGROUND

NARRATOR
(REVERB) "We *drank* along with the rest into the late hours. *Everyone* chatted and *joked* and laughed...
(CHAOTIC NOISE, SCREAMS, CRAZY LAUGHTER)

"...the *music* played on and *once* again, the whole scene turned into a *chaotic* mess. We had to *shout* over the din!"

(NO REVERB) *Doctor!*...You mentioned something *before* dinner about the *danger* incurred in the *old* system of soothing! How is *that?*

MAILLARD
Yes, there was, *occasionally,* very *great* danger indeed. There is *no* accounting for the *caprices* of *madmen!* And, in *my* opinion, as well as, in that of Doctor *Tarr* and Professor *Fether,* it is *never* safe to *permit*

them to *run* at large unattended! A *lunatic* may be *soothed,* as it is called, for a *time,* but, in the end, he is *very* apt to become *hostile.* He is *cunning* too. *If* he has a *plan* in mind, he can *hide* it by playing *dumb* and docile. When a madman *appears* thoroughly *sane,* it is time to put *him* in a strait *jacket!*

NARRATOR
But, the *danger*…have you *had* any *terrible* cases in your experience, Doctor?

MAILLARD
Of *course!* Right *here* in this house. The *soothing* system, you know, was *then* in operation, and the patients were *free* to roam. They behaved *remarkably* well…so much so, a *keen* mind might have *sensed* that *something* was brewing. Sure enough, *one* morning, the *keepers* found themselves *tied* up and *thrown* into cells by the lunatics who had *taken* over, *posing* as the staff *itself!*

NARRATOR
No! How did *that* happen? What did you do?

MAILLARD
A *stupid* fellow…a *lunatic* had taken it into his *head* that *he* had invented a *better* system of government than *any* ever heard of before…a *lunatic* government! *He* wished to give *his* invention a trial, I suppose, and *so* he *persuaded* the *rest* of the patients to *join* him in a *conspiracy* for the *overthrow* of the reigning *powers!*

NARRATOR
And, he *really* succeeded?

MAILLARD
Absolutely! The keepers were *soon* made to exchange *places* with the lunatics. The *real* keepers were *not* treated very well, I must say.

NARRATOR
But, I *presume* this situation could *not* have lasted very long? Visitors coming to see the *establishment* would have given the alarm*, no?*

MAILLARD
Ah, but you are *wrong* there. The *leader* was *too* cunning for that. He admitted *no* visitors at all…with the *exception,* one day, of a *very* stupid-looking *young* gentleman of whom he had *no* reason to be afraid. He let

him in to *see* the place...just to have a little *fun* with him. As soon as he had *fooled* him sufficiently, he let him out, and *sent* him about his business.
(SCREAMS, GLASS BREAKS, RECORD SCRATCHES OFF)

NARRATOR
So how *long*, then, did the *madmen* control the place?

MAILLARD
Oh, a *very* long time....a *month* certainly...how much longer I *can't* precisely say. In the *meantime,* the *lunatics* had a *jolly* time of it...*believe* me. They got *rid* of their *own* shabby clothes, and *broke* into the family *wardrobe* and jewels. *And,* the *wine* cellar. They lived *well,* I can tell you.
MUSIC BUILDS

NARRATOR
And, the *treatment*...what was the *particular* method of treatment which the *leader* put into operation?

MAILLARD
Oh, a *much* better treatment than before. It was a *very* capital system indeed...simple... *neat*...*no* trouble at all...in fact it was...
(OTHERS YELLING, FIGHTING, DISHES BREAKING)

NARRATOR
Doctor, it appears as if things are getting *out of hand!* The *lunatics* must have *broken* into the room...they're coming *closer!*

MAILLARD
You're *right, sir*! They *are* out of control!
(DOOR BROKEN, WINDOWS SMASHED, CHAOS)

NARRATOR
Doctor! Come back! Where are you *going?*

(REVERB) "*Maillard,* to my *excessive* astonishment *hid* under the table. I had expected *more* resolution at his hands.
(RIOT)
ODD LIVE PIANO MUSIC

"Meanwhile, upon the main *dining*-table, among the *bottles* and glasses, *leaped* Mr. De Kock who began to *orate*"

DE KOCK
Four score and seven years ago...

LADY
Look at *me*...I'm the dying swan! See me *dying?*

MAN
And, *I* am a *glorious* bottle of champagne...*Pop! Fizzzzz!*

MAN 2
Burrrpppppp.....burrppppp....cricket, *cricket...*

LADY
Catch that frog!

MAN
And, now I am an absolute *ass! He haw! He haw! He haw!*

LADY
Cock a doodle do!

                                        (CHAOS CONTINUES)

NARRATOR
(REVERB) "I shall *never* forget the *emotions* of *wonder* and *horror* in me when I saw *leaping* through these windows, and *down* among us, fighting, *stamping*, scratching, and *howling*, there rushed a perfect *army* of *madness!* I received a *terrible* beating after which I *rolled* under a sofa and lay still. After lying there some *fifteen* minutes, during which time I *listened* with both ears to what was going on in the room, I came to a conclusion that...

                                        SILENCE
                                    EERIE MUSIC

"It was the good Doctor *Maillard* who was the *lunatic* who had *excited* his fellows to rebellion. *He* had been merely relating his *own* exploits. This gentleman *had,* indeed, some *two* or three years before, been the *superintendent* of the establishment, but grew crazy *himself,* and *so* became a patient.

                        (CAR ENGINE STARTS, SPEEDS OFF)

"My *medical* friends back home, of course, had *no* knowledge of this. The *keepers* at the asylum had been *overpowered, tarred* and then *feathered* and then kept *locked* in the *cells* underground! They had been *imprisoned* for over a *month* down there and given some *bread* and water.   Eventually, *one* escaped through a sewer and *freed* the rest.

"The *soothing* system, with *important* modifications, has been *resumed* at the asylum. Although I have searched *every* library in Europe for the works of Doctor *Tarr* and Professor *Fether,* I have, up to the *present* day, utterly *failed* in my endeavors at *procuring* a volume of their philosophy."

END

THE PIT AND THE PENDULUM
By Edgar Allan Poe
Adapted By Dan Bianchi

CAST – 1m or 2m
SYNOPSIS – A prisoner is tortured in a fiendishly devised chamber.
NOTE - The role of VOICE may be a separate actor...or, the lines
may be recorded as timed cues in the PRISONER's own voice and
perceived as conversing with his inner self.

MILITARY DRUM
(IRON JAIL CELL DOOR CLANGS)
MUSIC

VOICE
(REVERB) "You're *sick*..."

PRISONER
I *am* sick...sick to *death* from this *long* agony.

VOICE
(REVERB) "Well, at least, they've finally *untied* you."

PRISONER
Yes, I can sit and rest awhile.

VOICE
(REVERB) "You're exhausted."

PRISONER
That sentence...

VOICE
(REVERB) "That *dreaded* sentence of death..."

PRISONER
I can *still* hear them, the last of their words, the *sound* of their voices...

VOICE
(REVERB) "The *judges*..."

PRISONER
I can *still* see the *white* lips of those *black*-robed judges.

VOICE
(REVERB) "Those thin, thin lips."

PRISONER
As if they were *locked,* immovable...

VOICE
(REVERB) "Resolute, in contempt..."

PRISONER
Yet, quite *capable* of *approving* human torture.

VOICE
(REVERB) *"Capable* of declaring *your* Fate."
                                                  (GAVEL STRIKES, ECHOES)

PRISONER
I still see those lips *squirming* as they *pronounced* my sentence.

VOICE
(REVERB) "The way they *fashioned* the *syllables* of your name."

PRISONER
Makes me *shudder...*after *that,* I *heard* nothing else.

VOICE
(REVERB) "The seven white *candles* on the table?"

PRISONER
At first, they had *appeared* to offer comfort.

VOICE
(REVERB) "Like slender *angels* come to save you."

PRISONER
But, all at once, I grew *sick,* nauseous. I felt every *fibcr* in me *shocked*
as if I had put my *hand* into *burning* oil...

VOICE
(REVERB)   "While the *angels* transformed into *ghosts,* with flaming

heads."

PRISONER
No, I'd get no *help* from them.

MUSIC BUILDS

VOICE
(REVERB) "But, think...what about the *comfort,* the sweet *rest* there must be in the grave?"

PRISONER
I thought of that...and *just* as I began to get *used* to it, to *appreciate* it fully, those *judges* vanished...*and* the seven white candles *shrunk* into nothingness...and their *flames* went out.

VOICE
(REVERB) "And, the blackness *swallowed* you up in a mad *rushing* descent into *Hell.*"

SILENCE

PRISONER
Then, *silence...*

VOICE
(REVERB) "And, *stillness...*"

PRISONER
And, *night* became my universe.

VOICE
(REVERB) "When you fainted...unconscious."

MUSIC

PRISONER
Well, I still haven't given up on *sleeping* at last in my grave. *Unconscious* forever. There *is* no immortality for man. As I awakened, I remember my slow return to my senses.   First, my *mental* or *spiritual* condition...and, secondly, my *physical* existence. Unconsciousness...it is a *weird* sensation...that *momentarily* offers *escape* from reality. It certainly affects one's impressions.

VOICE
(REVERB) "A momentary escape...to a place where *strange* palaces

and *wildly* familiar faces *glow* like hot coals."

EERIE MUSIC

PRISONER
I've seen *sad* visions that are *forbidden* to view...

VOICE
(REVERB) "Smelled the *perfume* of some *unknown* flower...

PRISONER
Listened to the *sounds* of a weird music never heard before...

VOICE
(REVERB) "The brain is *bewildered* by it all."

PRISONER
Now, at this moment, after *all* of that, I must admit...I *still* imagine I might *successfully* escape from my current predicament.   But, then I remember...

(FOOTSTEPS DESCENDING ECHO)

...those figures *lifting* me up and *carrying* me in silence, taking me *down* here, somewhere.

SILENCE

VOICE
(REVERB) "Your heart nearly stopped *beating* when *they* stopped."

PRISONER
I seemed to *float* in nothingness. After that, I remember a *flatness*, a dampness. Listen...

(DULL THUMPING GROWS LOUDER)

VOICE
(REVERB) "It is the *beating* of your heart. Pulsing,"

PRISONER
Thumping.

VOICE
(REVERB) *"Louder!"*

PRISONER
Louder!

SILENCE

VOICE
(REVERB) "Shush…are you sure you are even awake?"

PRISONER
Am I *sure* I am *alive?* I *am* thinking…talking to myself…I must *be alive.*

VOICE
(REVERB) "You are afraid."

PRISONER
Terrified.

VOICE
(REVERB) "Trying *desperately* to *comprehend* what is happening to you."

PRISONER
Where *am* I?

MUSIC

VOICE
(REVERB) "If only you can *delve* back into unconsciousness."

PRISONER
No…no escape that way.

VOICE
(REVERB) "Then, you *must* revive your *soul* and *then* your body."

PRISONER
Right! I must move. Must think. *Must* remember!

VOICE
(REVERB)   "Remember…the trial, the *judges,* the black-hooded robes…"

PRISONER
The sentence…

VOICE
(REVERB) "The sickness, the fainting..."

PRISONER
And, then a *whole* day of *forgetfulness* I can't recall. I mean, I haven't even *opened* my eyes, yet. I feel that I'm *lying* upon my back, *untied* now.

SILENCE

VOICE
(REVERB) "Go on, *reach* out your hand...can you *feel* anything?"

PRISONER
Where can I be? I am *afraid* to open my eyes...*not* afraid of what I might see, but...suppose I see *nothing?*

VOICE
(REVERB) "Go on, *open* your eyes."

MUSIC

PRISONER
Aaah! Just as I *feared!* The blackness...*unending* darkness. *Ugh!* It's so hard to *breathe* here.

VOICE
(REVERB) "Such *darkness* is oppressive, in itself."

PRISONER
Stifling. The air is so... close, heavy.

VOICE
(REVERB) "Just lie quietly. Try to think...go back to the beginning ...the trial, the proceedings..."

PRISONER
My *sentence* seems *eons* ago. Am I *dead?* But, I *can't* be dead.

VOICE
(REVERB) *"That's* the stuff of fiction."

PRISONER
This is real. *Now.* Alright, so...*that* doesn't help me to define what *state* I am in.

VOICE
(REVERB) "Those condemned to death...are *usually* destroyed by fire."

PRISONER
Everyone knows that.   Well, *I* haven't been destroyed...by fire *or* otherwise...*yet.*

VOICE
(REVERB) "You've been *remanded* to this dungeon to *await* your punishment."

PRISONER
Which might be *months* from now.

VOICE
(REVERB) "Well, that *is* the *usual* routine for *condemned* prisoners"

PRISONER
I *must* be in a *cell,* no?

VOICE
(REVERB) "Try to stand...that's it...get on your feet."

                                                            SILENCE

PRISONER
Total darkness...I can't *see* a thing.

VOICE
(REVERB) "Reach out...do you *feel* anything? Go on, *reach!*"

PRISONER
I'm *reaching*...I feel *nothing*...in *any* direction. I am *terrified* to move a step. Where are the *walls* of this place? Wait a minute... can this place be my *tomb?*

VOICE
(REVERB) "A *humorous* thought."

PRISONER
This is *torturous!* I'm *drenched* in my own sweat. A *cold* sweat...

VOICE
(REVERB) "Every *pore* forming cold *beads* upon your forehead."

PRISONER
I can't *stand this*! I don't know what's happening…this is *intolerable*.

VOICE
(REVERB) "Try to move forward…just a bit."
(FOOTSTEPS SHUFFLING)

PRISONER
I'm straining my eyes…if *only* I could *see* a *faint* ray of light. *Something!*
It's so dark…

VOICE
(REVERB) "Go on, go on…there, *that's* not *so* bad now, is it?"

PRISONER
It's a *bit* better over here…yes…a *bit* cooler…but, if I *am* in a dungeon
then…I've *heard* people *whispering* about places like this…

VOICE
Rumors *too* ghastly, too *strange* to believe.
MUSIC

PRISONER
Am I going to die of *starvation* in this darkness?   Or, is there something
worse hiding out *there* for me?   I *know* that at the *end* of it all will be
death.

VOICE
(REVERB) "The rumors *are* true about that."

PRISONER
But, *how* and *when* will it happen? *Oh! Oh, wait!* Finally, my hands feel
something solid. A wall, a *stone* wall. Very smooth, slimy, and cold.

VOICE
(REVERB) "That's it…now follow it up and down, stepping *carefully* to
the right and left."

PRISONER
I still have *no* idea how *big* my dungeon might be. If *only* I had my knife.
I could *force* it into the crevices between the bricks and…

VOICE
(REVERB) "And do *what?*"

PRISONER
Well, I...I could tear the *hem* of my shirt...*what?*

SILENCE

VOICE
(REVERB) "Haven't you noticed...? They have taken your clothes."

PRISONER
What is *this* I am wearing? It's coarse, feels like a *burlap* robe of some sort. Well, alright...I can tear the *robe* and put a piece on the floor at my feet *against* the wall...then I'll move *about* the space, hands on the wall, until I return *back* to the piece of fabric.

VOICE
(REVERB) "Yes, but...you have not counted upon the *size* of the dungeon. It may be *vast.* An underground cavern that goes on for miles. And, *you* are weak. The ground is *moist* and slippery. You can *stagger* about...but, *if* you stumble...and fall? Perhaps, you should *stay* where you are?"

PRISONER
I am so tired. I just want to lie down.

VOICE
(REVERB) "Sleep...sleep..."

MUSIC

PRISONER
(Stretches) Ahhhh....how long have I been asleep? What...what is this? Feels like...a loaf of bread...and *here* is a pitcher with *water.*
(EATING, DRINKING SOUNDS)

VOICE
(REVERB) *"Eat! Drink!"*

PRISONER
Oh...I never thought it could taste this good...

SILENCE

VOICE
(REVERB) "Are you ready to resume your exploration of this ..."

PRISONER
Tomb?

VOICE
(REVERB) "But, they don't expect you to *die* here...surely. They've given you provisions."

PRISONER
That's true. I *suppose* I *am* a prisoner. But, how long *before* my sentence is fully carried out?

MUSIC

Fifty-one, fifty-two, fifty-three....*fifty-four* paces. Well, I am *back* to the piece of fabric. A hundred and *fifty-four* paces...about *fifty* yards in perimeter. I have met with more than a few *angles* in the wall, so, I can't be sure.

VOICE
(REVERB) "Aren't you curious to explore *further?* Next time, don't stay near the wall. Try to go *across* the space."

PRISONER
The stone floor...It's very slimy. I'll have to be careful and...*whoa!*
(HE FALLS, STRUGGLES)
MUSIC BUILDS

Ohhh...that hurt! Took my breath away. *Phew!* Something *smells* in here. Like decaying fungus. I'll just...*oh no!*

VOICE
(REVERB) *"Watch out"*

PRISONER
Oh my God, there's a *precipice* here! I'm lying on the *brink* of it...the very *edge!*

SILENCE

VOICE
(REVERB) "Another step or two and you *might* have fallen right over it!"

PRISONER
This is maddening! I'm in a gigantic pit...a *circular* pit...

VOICE
(REVERB) "How large is this pit? Where does it end? Why don't you drop a *pebble* over the side? Into the abyss…?"

PRISONER
Here, I've got one here. Well, here goes…
                                        (PAUSE, DISTANT SPLASH)

VOICE
(REVERB) *"Water!"*
                                        (TRAP DOOR CREAKS OPEN)

PRISONER
What is that?

VOICE
(REVERB) "A door overhead…it's *opening*! See! A faint *gleam* of light flashing suddenly through the gloom…"

PRISONER
…and *just* as suddenly fades away.
                                        (DOOR SLAMS SHUT)

VOICE
(REVERB) "They are watching…listening…"
                                        MUSIC

PRISONER
They *thought* I had *fallen* to my death below. So, *this* is the fate my judges…those *fiends*…have devised for me.

VOICE
(REVERB) "Who *knows* what sort of *death* hides out *there* in the darkness?"

PRISONER
My nerves…how much *longer* can I go on?

VOICE
(REVERB) "Your voice is trembling…you're losing it."

PRISONER
Of course, I am! This place…this *pit*…a *torture* chamber.

VOICE
(REVERB) "You're shaking like a leaf in a storm. Why don't you try to *grope* your way back to the wall? Easy now...
(FOOTSTEPS SHUFFLING)

PRISONER
I'd rather die right *here* on this spot than risk the *terrors* of that pit.
SILENCE

VOICE
(REVERB) "Your imagination... it's conjuring up all *kinds* of torture down here, isn't it?"

PRISONER
Maybe, I *am* a coward for not taking *control* of my own life *and* death. Maybe, I should run and *plunge* right over the side into the abyss.

VOICE
(REVERB) "Maybe... maybe...
MUSIC

"You've been asleep. Reach out, that's right... another loaf and pitcher of water. Drink... drink... so thirsty... but..."

PRISONER
But...?
SILENCE

VOICE
(REVERB) "What if... the food and drink have been drugged?"

PRISONER
Yes... it must have been. (Yawns) I am *already* tired... again.
MUSIC

How long has it lasted *this* time? Hours? *Unconscious?* Wait... hold on... I can *see*... just barely.

VOICE
(REVERB) "Yes, there is a dim light now. *Glowing,* coming from somewhere."

PRISONER
I see...something...*objects* around me.   And...and...I can see the *extent* of my prison.

VOICE
(REVERB) "Looks like you were *greatly* mistaken about its *size*."

PRISONER
It can't be more than *twenty*-five yards in circumference.

VOICE
(REVERB) "Not that it matters. You are *still* a prisoner."

SILENCE

PRISONER
I have to occupy my mind with *something,* no matter *how* important or not. I can't give in to...

EERIE MUSIC

VOICE
(REVERB) "Look, there...the walls are *painted* with monstrous forms ...menacing *fiends,* skeletons..."

PRISONER
I've never seen such frightful images...who *made* these things? They must be very old.. The colors seem faded and blurred...

VOICE
(REVERB) There, in the center of the room...a circular pit."

SILENCE

PRISONER
But, I *can't* see properly...*can't* move...*uhhn...I...*

VOICE
(REVERB) *"You're tied down!"*

PRISONER
(Struggling) *What is... this now? Unhh...!*

VOICE
(REVERB) "On your back...it appears you're *stretched* out on a low *wooden* framework."

PRISONER
They must have done this to me when I was drugged…unconscious! Cowards!

VOICE
(REVERB) "Your limbs, wrists, ankles…all tied with leather straps…"

PRISONER
Can just about move my head…a bit. (Yells) Aaaaaah! Let me go you sick, demented…! Why are you doing this to me? Get it over with!

VOICE
(REVERB) "They've left your left arm free…"

PRISONER
Why? So that I can still feed myself from that dish?

VOICE
(REVERB) "The water pitcher is gone."

PRISONER
Of course! Now, when I am still consumed with thirst. That's part of my punishment, isn't it?

VOICE
(REVERB) "And, to make matters worse…"

PRISONER
The meat in the dish has been seasoned with salt and dried herbs. (Yells) Fiends! You no good…!

VOICE
(REVERB) "Look up there… It is some thirty or forty feet overhead. Painted on the ceiling…the figure of Father Time…he usually carries a scythe, but, in this case…"

PRISONER
What is…that thing?

VOICE
(REVERB) "Looks like a huge pendulum…like those in antique clocks. And, it is not a painting. Unfortunately…it is very real."

MUSIC

PRISONER
It's...moving, I think it's moving.

(GEARS CHURN, PENDULUM
SWINGS RHYTHMICALLY, GAINING MOMENTUM)

Oh my God! It's *swinging*...back and forth...and that...*that...*

VOICE
(REVERB) "It's got a monstrous, *crescent* shaped *blade* on the end of it! *Sharp as a razor!*"

PRISONER
They mean to *cut me in two!*

(RATS SQUEAKING)

VOICE
(REVERB) "And, they hope to get every *minute* of *enjoyment* out of it, too! Look at that glistening steel *gleaming* in the dim light...as it *swings* back and forth, back and forth..."

PRISONER
What's *that* now? *That's* not the machine...something else... *squeaking* noise...in the darkness there...*damn it! I can't see over there!*

VOICE
(REVERB) "Do you really want to *see? Rats! Enormous, ravenous rats! And they're coming this way!*"

PRISONER
Of *course* they are...and *I* am their *dinner!*

VOICE
(REVERB) "They're *pouring* out of holes in the wall! Forty...*fifty...*"

PRISONER
Jesus Christ! A hundred of them!

VOICE
(REVERB) *"Two hundred!* Probably attracted by the *scent* of that greasy *meat* in that *dish!*"

PRISONER
And, when they *finish* eating *that*...? *Oh Jesus!* How can I scare them

away?

(PENDULUM SWINGING FASTER)
MUSIC BUILDS

The pendulum! It's dropped nearly a *yard* already! And, it's swinging even *faster* now!

VOICE
Listen! It seems to *hiss* as it *cuts* through the air!

PRISONER
(Yells) *You! I know what you're doing! Ha! You can't destroy me! My spirit! I know!*

VOICE
(REVERB) *"Down* it comes...*relentlessly* down! *Vibrating!* The next swing will be within *three* inches of your *chest"!*

PRISONER
Let me go! Let me go!

VOICE
(REVERB) "You *must* struggle, no matter what...*try* to *free* your right arm!"

PRISONER
How can I? Wait...*uhhh*...there...it's *free!* Well, from the *elbow* to the hand! If I can *only* break the *knots* above the elbow...I can seize the pendulum, *stop* it somehow!

VOICE
(REVERB) "You might as well attempt to *stop* an avalanche"

(PENDULUM SWOOPS)

PRISONER
It's getting closer!

VOICE
(REVERB) "Try to *shrink* your body."

PRISONER
Every time it *ascends* I watch it...*mesmerized*....but, when it *sweeps* back down toward me...

VOICE
(REVERB) *"Close* your eyes, you *fool! Don't watch it!"*

PRISONER
(Yells) *Go ahead! Kill me now!* It will bring me relief.

VOICE
(REVERB) "Oh, yes, how *brave* you are to *welcome* death. Yet, you *quiver* in every nerve…just *thinking* how *slight* the blade might *sink* into you, *slicing* away at you…the first time it *touches* your flesh…then the second…and so on…"

PRISONER
I give it another *ten* or twelve passes before *that* will happen. I *have* to be calm. Collect myself.

VOICE
(REVERB) "That's right. Now, *think!* The *knot* on your chest…the way it is *tied*….if it *should* be broken, *sliced* through by that blade…the *rest* of your bonds would *slacken* and…"

PRISONER
I'd be set free.

VOICE
(REVERB) "You *might* be able to *quickly* unwind yourself from the bonds."

PRISONER
But, *if* I am too slow…?

VOICE
(REVERB) "That deadly blade will *descend* on its return swing and…"

PRISONER
But, *how* can this be? How can they have *tied* me this way? *One* knot untied can *free* me?

VOICE
(REVERB) "Is it part of their *plan?"*

(RATS SQUEALING LOUDER)

PRISONER
I don't care. I *have* to try it.

VOICE
(REVERB) "The floor beneath you...it's *swarming* with rats! Their red eyes... *glaring* at you!"

PRISONER
(Struggling) *Waiting to eat! Unhh...Unhhh...come on...*

VOICE
(REVERB) "Waiting to *eat* the freshly killed food they have been *accustomed* to eating in the past...waiting....watching..."

PRISONER
Get away you bastards!

VOICE
(REVERB) "You can *wave* all you want at them! It's not working. *Wasting* time on these vermin."

PRISONER
Owww! They bit my fingers!
                    (SWISHING BLADE SWOOPS LOWER)

VOICE
(REVERB) "They're *backing up!* They're *afraid* of the blade..."

PRISONER
Look! I've *smeared* some of the *fatty* meat from the dish upon the *knots* on my chest! The creatures...they're *nibbling* at it...

VOICE
(REVERB) "You've done *it now!* They're *all* jumping up on you! *Hundreds* of them! And, *these* don't seem *frightened* by the pendulum at all..."

PRISONER
Gnaw away, you bastards! Hungry, are you? *Chew* that knot...that's right!

VOICE
(REVERB) "They're *swarming* all over you now...your *throat...*"

PRISONER
Aaaaah! I can *feel* their cold lips on me! Can't breathe! Getting *smothered*...so *many* of them. *Please,* let it be over quickly! *Please,* God, *loosen* this knot! This is *unbelievable!*

VOICE
(REVERB) "It must *already* be loosened in several places. Just lie *still* if you can."

PRISONER
I think I have it now...wait...*Aha! That did it! Look! I'm free! I'm free!*

VOICE
(REVERB) "The *knot,* the *rope,* they've torn it to *ribbons!*"
(RATS SQUEAL)

PRISONER
Aaaaah! Get off me, you bastards!
(PENDULUM SWOOPS BY)
MUSIC BUILDS

The pendulum! Nearly got me that time!

VOICE
(REVERB) *"It's cut through your robe!"*

PRISONER
Ahhhh! The blade got me. Slightly cut into *my chest*...the pain ...*shooting* through every nerve.

VOICE
Never mind that! The moment of escape has arrived. *Now! Jump up!*
(RATS SQUEAL)

PRISONER
Get out of here, you stinking beasts! Eat me, will you!

VOICE
Forget *them!* Stay out of the path of the *blade!* Careful now...move sideways...*slide* out of those bonds...*beyond* the reach of the blade!
SILENCE

PRISONER
I am free! God in Heaven, I am free! Phew…

VOICE
For the *moment*, at least.

PRISONER
Free! (Sobs)

VOICE
(REVERB) "No time for self-pity.   You're *still* in the grasp of your *captors!*"

    (PENDULUM MACHINERY STOPS, CHAINS PULL IT UP)
                SILENCE

PRISONER
The *pendulum!* It's stopped… it's being pulled back upward. Now what? (Yells) *Now, what?* This is just a game, isn't it? You're watching me every minute, aren't you? Free? *Hahaha! Free?* I've escaped death in one form of agony… only to be delivered into something *worse* than death!

VOICE
(REVERB) "They don't *want* to kill you… not yet."

PRISONER
Of course not! They're not *done* with me. (Coughs)

VOICE
(REVERB)   *"Sulphur*… something… is happening… changing.   See… that *gas* …coming through the *fissures* in the wall.   And, down below there… *under* the walls…"

PRISONER
The walls are not *connected* to the *floor!*

                EERIE MUSIC

VOICE
(REVERB) *"Images* on the wall…:

PRISONER
Yes, I can *see* them now… more *distinctly*… they're growing brighter… Glowing…

VOICE
(REVERB) "Are those the eyes of a *demon*?"

PRISONER
Glaring at me. Many, *too* many to count. *Staring* at me. I hadn't seen them before now.

(LOW RUMBLE)

VOICE
(REVERB) "Getting *hotter* in here."

TENSE MUSIC

PRISONER
As if the walls...*are on fire!*   And that smell...(Coughs)   That odor...*suffocating*...the walls...

VOICE
(REVERB) "The *iron* walls are being *heated* from the other side..."

PRISONER
That light pouring in from *under* the walls...*redder* and redder...and... (Coughs) I can't breathe...*No air, no air!*

VOICE
(REVERB) *"More* torture from them!"

PRISONER
(Yells) *Tormentors!* Hiding up there, watching me *squirm* like a worm on a hot griddle...

VOICE
(REVERB) *"Gasping* for every little breath."

PRISONER
Look at those walls...*glowing* with heat! Unbearable...

VOICE
(REVERB) "The whole room is like a *giant* kettle being *heated* on a stove"

PRISONER
Wait...I know...*the pit?* The pit of *water* below?

VOICE
(REVERB) "Yes. The *coolness* of water?"

PRISONER
Relief...maybe, *rescue?*

VOICE
(REVERB) "Or, a certain *death?*"

MUSIC BUILDS

PRISONER
To die with the *sin* of *suicide* on my soul. That's what *they want!* (Yells)
Why are you doing this to me! *Kill me* now and get it over with! (Coughs)
Kill... me...now....

VOICE
(REVERB) "Getting hotter."

PRISONER
This must be the end...they'll *cook* me alive.

(MACHINERY GRINDS)

Not the *pendulum* again? No...that's a *different* sound...

VOICE
(REVERB) "The walls...the room is changing form. It *was* square
...now, rectangular."

PRISONER
The walls of burning *iron*...*they're moving!* Closing in on me!

(RUMBLING)

(Yells) Is *this* the way you're going to kill me? *Crush* me? Is this *finally*
the end? Well, I *welcome* death, *any* death! But, *you* are going to have
to kill me! I *won't* jump into the *pit!* *Hahahaha!*

VOICE
(REVERB) *"Fool!* The moving walls will just *push* you into the pit
anyway."

PRISONER
Can I *resist* its heat? The *pressure?*

VOICE
(REVERB) "It's closing in."

PRISONER
There's no time to think. I can *shrink* back no more. They're *pressing* upon me. My *toes* are near the edge of the pit...

VOICE
(REVERB) "No matter if your *seared* and tortured body is *hanging* on, *inches* from the pit's edge...you must fight them...save your *soul,* man!
                                                                    SILENCE

PRISONER
I *can't* struggle anymore. If *this* is to be my end, so be it.

VOICE
(REVERB) "Close your eyes..."
                              (ALARM. GUNFIRE, CROWD VOICES,
                                  DISTANT SCREAMS, RUMBLING)

"What on *Earth?* The walls...they're *retracting!* Listen to it *rumble!* Like a *thousand* thunders! The *fiery* walls...*they're pulling back*"!

PRISONER
Too late...my knees are buckling...I cannot *stand* a second longer...the *end* is here...

VOICE
(REVERB*)* *"No! No!* There is an arm...a hand...*reaching* down to you...*catch it! Catch it, you fool..."*

PRISONER
Who? Who...*is it?*

VOICE
(REVERB) "Does it *matter?* You are saved."
                                                              END

THE PURLOINED LETTER
By Edgar Allan Poe
Adapted By Dan Bianchi

CAST – 2m
SYNOPSIS – The famous detective Dupin describes how he solved the mystery of a harmful letter stolen from a famous politician.

MUSIC
(THUNDER, DOOR KNOCKS, DOOR OPENS)
SILENCE

DUPIN
Ah, it's Detective Burton.

BURTON
Dupin…

DUPIN
Well, Detective…come in, come in out of the rain. It's been a long time since we've seen each other. What brings you here at this hour of the night?

(DOOR CLOSES)

BURTON
Ah, Auguste…

DUPIN
Don't tell me! Whenever you call me by my first name, I know that you are in the midst of a *baffling* case and you have come here to ask if *I* may help?

BURTON
I guess you don't have to be a detective to figure that out, hey? Why, yes, I've come because…well, to put it plainly…I've been baffled *before,* Auguste, but…*this* affair…it is so *simple* and yet…

DUPIN
Perhaps, it is the very *simplicity* of the thing which has you puzzled. The mystery is a little *too* plain…a little *too* self-evident. So, tell me, what is

this case that *stumps* you and the whole police department?

BURTON
Well, to begin with... this case does not concern the *whole* police department. *Only* me. I will tell you in a few words... but, *before* I begin, let me *caution* you that this is an affair demanding the *greatest* secrecy. I should most probably *lose* my job were it known that I *confided* it to anyone.

DUPIN
Of course. Proceed.

MUSIC

BURTON
Well, then... I have received *personal* information, from a very high office... that a certain *document* of *great* importance, has been *purloined* from his personal property. Oddly enough, the *individual* who *purloined* it is known... in fact, he was *seen* taking it. And, he *still* has it in *his* possession.

DUPIN
How do you know that?

BURTON
Well, because of the *content* of the letter. You see, if it *were* to be *released* from the thief's possession... we would *know* that *he* no longer owned it.

DUPIN
Can you be a little *more* forthcoming?

BURTON
Well, I may venture so far as to say that this *letter* gives its holder a certain *power* in a *certain* area where *such* power is immensely valuable.

DUPIN
You'll have to be clearer than *that,* Detective.

BURTON
Ah, well... the *disclosure* of the letter to the public... would bring into question the *honor* of a great and *much* admired dignitary in our state government... and this fact gives the *holder* of the letter a certain *power*

over the *illustrious* person whose *honor* and peace are so jeopardized.

DUPIN
You mean that, with this letter, the *thief* could *blackmail* the person in power?

BURTON
Exactly!

SILENCE

DUPIN
How was this letter *stolen* in the first place?

BURTON
Oh, the *method* of the theft was ingenious...*and* bold, let me tell you! The letter in question is of a highly *personal* nature...*if* you *know* what I *mean?*

DUPIN
Highly *personal,* you say? *Embarrassing,* more likely...*if* anyone else *should* read it, that is?

BURTON
Embarrassing is right. *Ahem!* Yes, well...*I* wouldn't know the details of its content...only that it *is* rather *explicit...if* you know what I mean?

DUPIN
Well, to begin with, who sent this letter?

BURTON
An old flame...raking up dead ashes. But, she is not part of any blackmail scheme. I checked on her. She has no idea this *letter* of hers has been *purloined.*

DUPIN
Again...*how* was it stolen?

MUSIC

BURTON
As *I* understand it...just as *our* man, the *politician,* was *reading* the letter in question in his office...he was *suddenly* interrupted by *another* state official and he had *no* time to conceal it, so he quickly placed it on *top* of other letters on his desk. Now, during a *conversation* in the office,

our man is called away by his *secretary* for just a moment…leaving this *other* state official *alone* in his office. Well, this *other* man, a *rival* politician…*spies* the letter on *top* of the pile, *recognizes* the handwriting of the *address* and *quickly* reads its content. When *our* man returns to the room…this official *pretends* to read *another* document of no *real* importance and casually places it on the desk…*next* to the *private* letter in question. After a *short* conversation, during which *our* man turns away to speak to yet a *third* person who had entered the room…the *thief* hastily retrieves his document on the desk…*along* with the *private* letter in question and *hurries* out the door.

SILENCE

DUPIN
And, the *rightful* owner saw none of this?

BURTON
Ah, but, he *had!* Of course, he dared not call *attention* to the act, in front of the *third* person who was present.

DUPIN
And, this *third* person was…?

BURTON
A man from the press. A reporter. You see, *our* man couldn't confront the *thief,* now, could he? Not in front of a *reporter,* certainly.

DUPIN
And, risk *exposing* such a *delicate* matter to a *news* hound? By morning, whatever is in that letter would be all over the headlines.

MUSIC

BURTON
Exactly! So, Dupin…you see? The one who has been *robbed* …knows *precisely* who has robbed him. And, *why?* It can only mean that the thief plans to *blackmail* our man. You see, the thief has been an *arch* rival of *our* man for some time…*he* wants the office for himself. What *better* way than to bring public *shame* to our *married* man in office?

DUPIN
Ah, so…it is *that* sort of letter, is it?

BURTON
So, I am *led* to understand. Its content is rather…*well, s*ome may call it *sordid.* Distasteful. Disgusting. Even, *filthy?*

DUPIN
I *understand,* Detective.

BURTON
Which is why *I* was ordered to be *above* discretion in sorting all this out. Well... *our* man is beside himself. He *insists* that the letter in question is about something that happened a *long* time ago... it has *little* bearing upon his *current* status... both, in politics *and* at home... yet, it would *still* cast a *bad* light upon him... *enough* that it would cause him the *upcoming* election.

DUPIN
Ah, so *our* man, as you have put it... is the *Governor?*

BURTON
Now I've put my foot into it! And, here I was *trying* to be discreet and...

DUPIN
Don't worry, Detective Burton, I have surmised it all along. As you have said... *if* the letter had been *utilized* by now... we would have heard about it. No doubt it would be the *talk* of the town... on the front pages of every newspaper in the city.

BURTON
Our man... the Governor... he cannot take it upon *himself* to retrieve this letter... in *any* manner... so, he has asked *me* to do it for him... *tactfully,* of course. The *thing* is... it's *not* as if the thief is *blackmailing* him for *financial* gain. He wants *power* over our man... *that's* what he wants. Power to *make* him *bow* to any demand... or lose his *honor,* his career... his office ... perhaps, his *family,* as well.

                                                                SILENCE

DUPIN
Let me think a moment. Here, have a burgundy. It's a rare vintage.

BURTON
Thanks. I can use it. Hmmm...

DUPIN
So, have you begun your search for this letter?

                                                                MUSIC

BURTON
Yes. My first move was to make a *thorough* search of the hotel where the thief is *currently* staying. He is only *visiting* this city for a convention. He *lives* elsewhere...a hundred miles upstate. *Naturally,* I had to enter his hotel suite without his knowledge...and without bringing *attention* to the hotel staff that a *policeman* is doing such a thing. If the thief *ever* found out...if he should *suspect* I am on to him...*that* might cause him to make the letter *known,* immediately.

SILENCE

DUPIN
So, Detective...you are *not* working here in an *official* capacity...but, rather, as an *undercover* agent for the Governor? If you pardon me for asking...why were *you* chosen for this job?

BURTON
Don't ask me. The Commissioner chose me. In the department, only *he* and I know of this theft. He said that I was the most *trustworthy* officer in the whole police department.

DUPIN
He is *correct*...for once.

BURTON
How could such a crime be made *known* to the whole department? Surely, it would get out to the press and the whole *city* might be thrown into chaos.

DUPIN
Well, *that* is debatable. It wouldn't be the *first* time a politician was caught with his...never mind, why have you come to me?

MUSIC

BURTON
Well...needless to say, after a *thorough* search of his rooms...*twice*...I have *not* found the letter. I've looked *everywhere,* every *nook* and cranny...under his desk, his *bed,* every *shelf* in his wardrobe. His clothes, every *pocket.* I looked under *cushions* in the sofa. Between the *mattresses* of his bed. As a detective, I know about *secret* drawers and panels too...oh, I searched for *those,* believe me.

SILENCE

DUPIN
Well, there are *always* the *bedposts!* Why, *I* once found a *confession* written by a *murderer* who had rolled the *note* into a tight tube and *inserted* it into the cavity within the bed post and *screwed* the top knob back onto it and...never mind...did you check the *rest* of the furniture?
MUSIC

BURTON
Every *rung* of every chair. *And*, under the rugs. It did not appear that *anything* had been *recently* tampered with...I checked *behind* the mirrors, the *pictures* on the wall, under *dishes* in the cabinet and *behind* the curtains, too. I went over *everything* with a fine tooth comb, short of using a *microscope* to scrutinize every *inch* of that place. Why, his suite even adjoins *another* suite occupied by *another* party...and I went so far as to sneak into *that* place as well.

DUPIN
Really, Detective! How did you *manage* that?

BURTON
It wasn't easy.

DUPIN
Perhaps, you've lost your calling as a government *spy?*

BURTON
Perhaps. For the last *two* days, I have done *nothing* but worked on this case. The man is a *prodigious* reader...he has *many* books...I went through *every* page of all of them, shaking them, *hoping* the letter would fall out.
SILENCE

DUPIN
Then, I *suppose* the letter is not upon the premises.

BURTON
Exactly! But, Auguste...where do I go from here?

DUPIN
We shall see. Return a *week* from today...

BURTON
What? But, *time* is of the essence and...

DUPIN
A *week* from today.

BURTON
Oh...alright...

MUSIC
(QUICK KNOCKS, DOOR OPENS)
SILENCE

DUPIN
Detective! Right on time...

BURTON
Well, well? What do you have to tell me? Have you *solved* the problem? I've gone *half* insane over it, Dupin.

DUPIN
Come in, come in. First of all...the Governor...is he offering a monetary *reward* to you and your Commissioner...for the *return* of this *damaging* letter? Or, is it strictly a code of *honor* causing you to work so *diligently* to *release* him from this blackmail? I hope this has nothing to do with *party* ties?

BURTON
What party ties? Don't be ridiculous! I didn't even *vote* for him!

DUPIN
You are *not* rescuing him from this dire difficulty *purely* out of friendship?

BURTON
Of course not...I don't even *know* the man, personally, that is.

DUPIN
And, as *you* have admitted...this *delicate* problem was *not* handed to the *department* to solve as an *official* case.

BURTON
No...

DUPIN
Well, *then?*

BURTON
Now that you mention it...the victim *did* offer *five-thousand* dollars for the *return* of the letter...

DUPIN
Excellent! Now, get out your checkbook, Detective...and write me a check for *five-thousand* dollars. Do not despair, I will not cash it until I am certain you have deposited the reward in the bank. Don't look so dumbstruck. *I* am doing *you* a service. I am saving your career. Perhaps, you may even *garner* a promotion.

BURTON
What? Are you *crazy?*

DUPIN
You want *me* to solve *your* dilemma? You don't want to *risk* your career over *failure* to deliver the goods? If *I* am to save *you* from such disgrace, *I* must eat, too, and...

BURTON
Yes, yes! Alright! Give me a pen! This is an *outrage!* I come to you as a *friend* in need and...and...*there!* There is my signature...now ...have you a solution?

DUPIN
Oh, much better than that...*I* have the letter.

BURTON
You...? What? Where? *How?*
                              (UNLOCKS CABINET DOOR)

DUPIN
It's right here in my wine cabinet. Here you are.

BURTON
Oh my God! This is it...*the letter!* I can't believe it! *How?* How did you do it?

DUPIN
Sit down, catch your breath and I shall tell you.

BURTON
This...I have to hear.

MUSIC

DUPIN
You have your ways and *I* have mine.   True, *you* are persevering, ingenious, *cunning,* and *thoroughly* versed in the knowledge of crime detection.   I felt entirely *confident* in your having made a *satisfactory* investigation of the thief's hotel room.   I am *certain,* if the letter *had* been hidden in that room, *you* would have found it.

BURTON
Exactly! So, then, *where...?* Please, go on.

DUPIN
However...*that* sort of detection was *inapplicable* to this case.   It allows for one to *err* by being *too* deep or *too* shallow, for the matter in hand. Why, even a *schoolboy* might see that.

BURTON
A school boy? *Why, I...!*

DUPIN
Detective, had the *purloined* letter been hidden *anywhere* within the limits of *your* examination, its *discovery* would have been a matter altogether *beyond* question.   But, one must take into account the *nature* of the man, the *thief* in question...and if you *know* the man, you will *know* that he is *well* schooled in the art of detection and the *methods* of police work here in this city.   He would *never* have hid the letter in his rooms...even *under* the floorboards, or cleverly *secreted* in the bed post, or *taped* under a desk drawer.   A *common* criminal thinking he was *clever* might have done such things, but, *not* this man.   No...he would not head for the *ordinary* nooks and crannies, to hide the evidence of his crime.   Do you remember...I said that this mystery *troubled* you because it is so *very* self-evident?   Did you ever *think* it probable, *or* possible, that the thief had *deposited* the letter immediately beneath the *nose* of the whole world...by way of best *preventing* any portion of that world from *perceiving* it?

BURTON
I don't understand.

DUPIN
The more I *reflected* upon the daring, dashing, *and* discriminating *ingenuity* of this man...and *guessing* that the document must *always* have been at hand, *if* he intended to *use* it to *wield* his power...the more

satisfied I became that, to *conceal* this letter, he *must* have resorted to *not* concealing it at all.

BURTON
What! Did he post it on a *billboard* for all to read?

DUPIN
One fine morning, on *Wednesday* this week...I *found* the perpetrator in the *lobby* of the Grand Hotel...yawning, lounging, and *perusing* the daily newspaper. He does not know me. He took *me* to be a fellow *resident* of the hotel. I sat across from him in a leather arm chair and *pretended* to read a periodical. Occasionally, I *noticed* that he would look up from his paper toward the lobby *desk* where the clerk stood. He looked in *that* direction, oh, I would say, at least, *seven* times while I was there. And, *each* time he looked...I discerned a *smile* on his face.

BURTON
The *clerk?* What has *he* to do with *this?*

DUPIN
Nothing. But...*behind* the clerk, Detective Burton...stands the *mail* cabinet...containing small but *open* compartments which *hold* the mail for *each* resident of the hotel. Nearly *all* of the compartments were empty, since *most* residents pick up their mail on a daily basis. Yet, I noticed that there was *one* compartment...that was nearly *filled* with mail from days past. So, I entered a nearby phone booth and called the lobby desk...

BURTON
What on Earth *for*, Dupin?

DUPIN
I said that I am a *florist* who has been asked to send a *bouquet* to the man in question...may I have his *suite* number?

BURTON
And?

DUPIN
I was given his suite number...*201*. Next, I *wandered* over to the lobby desk and took a *look* at the compartment numbers and, *sure* enough, the compartment jammed with *unopened* mail belonged to none other than...

BURTON
No!

DUPIN
Yes. And, *yet*...here *he* is sitting in the lobby just a few *yards* from his *unopened* mail. A politician who *neglects* to read his mail? For *what* reason? Well, now I had *all* I could do to keep my *own* eyes off of that compartment of his. I *knew* I should have to look through that mail, myself. But, *how?* The clerk would *never* allow that. And, *he* knew that the *owner* of *that* mail was sitting there before him.

BURTON
What did you do?

DUPIN
I waited until the lobby was rather crowded. I had noticed that *one* of the maids had left a *lunch* wagon *unattended* near the elevators. When no one was looking, I...*lit* the napkins with a match and...yelled, *Fire!*

BURTON
Are you mad?

DUPIN
Oh, there was no danger of burning down the hotel, I *assure* you...but, it was a *sufficient* diversion in order for the clerk to leave his place behind the lobby desk and *run* to help put out the fire. During which time, *I* sneaked *behind* the lobby counter and *grabbed* the mail in compartment 201. It was rather *easy*, actually. All eyes, including the thief's...was upon the fire.

BURTON
You are a *danger* to us all! I had *no* idea you would *stoop* to such a level as this, Dupin. Lying...setting fires...stealing mail...

DUPIN
Once I was *safely* out onto the street...and taking *refuge* in a nearby alley where I was alone...I went through the mail and...lo *and* behold, *there* was a sealed, but plain, *unaddressed* envelope. I wonder where *that* came from? Upon opening it...*there* was the letter you sought. It had been *hid* amongst all his mail, yet, in *plain* sight in the *lobby* of the Grand Hotel.

BURTON
You are *incorrigible,* Dupin!

DUPIN
And, yet, *successful*…which is why you had come to me in the first place! Now, Detective…I know I will be able to *cash* this check once you have placed the reward of *five*-thousand dollars in your bank account?

BURTON
Why, *yes,* of course! But, uhm, how do you *know* that I won't *cancel* that check once I place the money in the bank?

DUPIN
Well, as *you* have admitted time and again…*I,* Auguste Dupin, am the greatest detective in the city, perhaps, in the whole country …and…*because* of that fact…it should be quite clear to *you,* that, *I* would *not* have made such a *financial* arrangement concerning the reward had I *not* been working for the most *trustworthy* officer in the whole police department!

END

KING PEST

By Edgar Allan Poe
Adapted By Dan Bianchi

CAST – 4m
SYNOPSIS – Two drunken sailors wander into a haunted house in the midst of a deadly epidemic.

(CROWDED TAVERN)
PERIOD LIVELY ACCORDIAN MUSIC

NARRATOR
One night in the month of October, two seamen belonging to the crew of the *Free and Easy*, a trading schooner…now at *anchor* in the Hudson River…found themselves seated in the tap-room of an ale-house on the lower West Side of New York City. *The Jolly Tar,* it was called.

Now, *Legs* was the much taller of the two, about six feet six. Stooped at the shoulders. *Exceedingly* thin, high cheek-bones, a *large* hawk-nose, retreating chin and *huge* protruding white eyes. Always looked as if he *couldn't* care less about the world around him. Solemn. Totally indifferent.

Hugh was the *younger* of them. The very *opposite* of his companion. *Unusually* short…four feet *four* in his stocking feet. A pair of *stumpy* bow-legs. Squat, *unwieldy* figure. *Thick* arms *dangling* from his sides like the *fins* of a sea-turtle. Small eyes of no *particular* color…but, let us be kind and say, *twinkling.* His *nose* remained buried in the *mass* of flesh which *enveloped* his round, *full,* and purple face. His thick *upper*-lip rested upon the *still* thicker one beneath it. He *always* appeared self-satisfied. And, evidently, he got along with his tall shipmate. *Unfortunately*, this night, they had been visiting *other* taverns and both inebriated men had come to *this* tavern with empty pockets.

There they are now, *each* sitting with their elbows resting upon the *large* oaken table in the middle of the floor…*both* staring at the empty pitcher of beer before them…which, at *this* point, has not *yet* been purchased.

HUGH
What say, on the count of three, we make a *bolt* for the door, Legs?

NARRATOR
Legs nods.

HUGH
One, two...*three!*

NARRATOR
Both leap up and quickly make a path *through* the crowd toward the door.

HUGH
Make way! Coming through! My friend is going to be *sick!*
                              (FOOTSTEPS RUNNING IN STREET)
                                                          MUSIC

NARRATOR
Although, the *intoxicated* Legs mistakes the *fireplace* for the door...*both* make it to the street and *high*-tail it in the direction of the dock *hotly* pursued by the *landlord* of *The Jolly Tar* screaming, "*Hey! You sonsabitches!* Get *back* here and pay for your ale!"
                                                    SAD MUSIC

Now, at the time of this *eventful* story...America is *still* under British rule and, even *more* unfortunate for Americans...the city has been *depopulated* by the terrible *yellow* fever epidemic. And, in the vicinities down by the *waterfront* on both the East *and* West side, amid the dark, narrow, and *filthy* lanes and alleys...the *Demon* of Disease strikes awe, *terror,* and *superstition* amongst the lowest of the low.

By authority of the English King, himself, *some* districts have been placed under ban, and *all* persons forbidden to *intrude* into these areas. But, does everyone *obey* such a law? No, neither the *mandate* of the monarch...nor the *huge* barriers erected at the *entrances* of the streets...nor the *prospect* of that *loathsome* death which, with almost *absolute* certainty, will *overtake* anyone who enters...can *prevent* the unfurnished and *untenanted* dwellings from being *stripped* bare by *looters!* That means every article, such as *iron*, brass, or lead-work...*anything* that can be turned to a *profitable* account. Locks, *bolts,* and secret closets *and* cellars...nothing works to protect *rich* stores of wines and liquors which, when sold by *looters*, will supply many of the local taverns.
                                                    EERIE MUSIC

However…there are very *few* of the terror-stricken people who attribute these *disappearances* of goods to human beings. *Old* world superstitions run *rampant* at such times and so, the *blame* is put upon *pest*-spirits, *plague*-goblins, and *fever*-demons…all popular *imps* of mischief. *Blood*-chilling tales are told, so much so, the *quarantined* area becomes *enveloped* in terror as *if* in a shroud…and the *superstitious* plunderer *himself* is often *scared* away by *imagined* horrors. After a while, the entire *prohibited* district is cast in gloom, *silence*, pestilence, and *death*.

> (FOOTSTEPS RUNNING)
> *SILENCE*

Now, it is *into* one of these *terrible* areas that Legs and Hugh have ended their *flight* from the tavern.

LEGS
(Breathless) Where do we go from here, Hugh?

HUGH
Well, we cannot go back. They'll be looking for us.
> (WIND HOWLS, DISTANT CHURCH BELLS TOLLS)

LEGS
Where the *hell* are we? It's cold and…the *fog* here is…

HUGH
Yeah.

LEGS
The houses round here…looks like they're falling down.

HUGH
And, the weeds…coming up everywhere through the cobblestones. *Phew!* Stinks unbearably, as well.

LEGS
It's the *sickness*. Death.

HUGH
I know.

LEGS
It's so dark. No light in any windows…those buildings that still *have*

windows. Is everyone...?

HUGH
Yeah. Look *there!* A *body!*

LEGS
Looks like he's been here a long time. A sack next to him...

HUGH
What's in it?

LEGS
Candlesticks...a clock...forks, knives. Hugh, this man is...*was...*

HUGH
A *thief.* Aye. A looter...struck down by the *same* plague that did away with the *owners* of that loot.

LEGS
Then...what are *we* doing here? We have to get out of here!

HUGH
Quiet! Would you rather face a long stint on the work-ships, chained to an *oar* for the next twenty years...or, take our chances *hiding* out here for a while?

LEGS
Well, when you put it that way...

HUGH
Come on...

                                                            EERIE MUSIC

NARRATOR
Onward, they continue into the darkness...every *step* echoing in the silent streets...becoming *more* frightening. Steep buildings cast *black* shadows across the narrow streets *clogged* with decaying wagons and *overgrown* weeds... and *skeletons* of those who had just *dropped* once caught in the *jaws* of death.

                                                               SILENCE
                                                            (COLD WIND)

HUGH
In here...let's get of the cold.

(DOOR CREAKS OPEN)

LEGS
It sure is dark in here.

HUGH
Come on...

(FLOORBOARDS CREAK)

LEGS
Can't see my hand in front of me...hold on, Hugh...where are you...?
Aaaaaahh!

(THUMPS, FALLING DOWNSTAIRS)

HUGH
Legs! Where did you go?

LEGS
I'm down *here!* Fell down an open trap door...*ow!* My ankle...

HUGH
What's down there?

LEGS
How should *I* know? I can't see a damned thing.

HUGH
Well...*strike* a flint! Ya got a *tinder* box, don't ya?

LEGS
Yeah, yeah...hold on...now, where is it...ah....

(CLICK, CLICK, CLICK)

HUGH
Hurry up!

LEGS
I *am* hurrying! Ya think I *want* to be down here in the dark?

(CLICK, CLICK, FLASH)

That did it!

HUGH
Here! Here's a bit of a candle! *Catch!*

LEGS
Alright...there it is...

HUGH
Well, can you *see* anything...maybe something *valuable* left down there?

LEGS
Nothing but a lot of *wine* barrels. And, bottles...all *filled.*

HUGH
Wine barrels? *Filled,* ya say? Oh my *God!* Are you *fooling* me, Legs?

LEGS
And, in the *middle* of the room is a table...and a big bowl...very big... filled with rum *punch,* it looks like to me. Hmmm...*tastes* like it, too!
                                                            MUSIC

NARRATOR
True. A very big punch bowl on the table. And, all around him are bottles of various wines and cordials... jugs, pitchers, *and* flagons of every shape and quality. But, *now,* right before his *eyes*...there appears as if out of *thin* air...*seated* around the table...a company of *six!*

LEGS
And, there are *people* down here!

HUGH
People, ya say?

NARRATOR
At the head of the table sits a gentleman who *appears* to be the leader of the group. He's tall, *emaciated*, gaunt, not *unlike* Legs himself...with eyes *glazed* over with the *fumes* of intoxication...no different than the *rest* seated at the table. *He's* wearing a cloak of *richly*-embroidered black silk-velvet...and a *hat* full of feathers which he *nods* to and fro with a *jaunty* and knowing air. In his right hand, he holds a *huge* human *thigh*-bone...with which he just knocked *one* of his companions in the head for *some* reason. *Opposite* him is a lady who is *definitely* not emaciated by *any* description. Her face is *exceedingly* round, red, and

full. Now, her *mouth* is remarkable since it begins at her *right* ear and *sweeps* with a terrific *chasm* to the left. In fact, her pearl earrings keep *bobbing* into that *crack* called a mouth. She's trying her *best* to keep her mouth closed and look dignified...*despite* being dressed in a newly starched and ironed *shroud* coming up close under her chin, with a crimpled *ruffle* around the neck.

At her right hand, sits a *diminutive* young lady, a *delicate* little creature, with *trembling* bony fingers...and her *livid* lips quivering...a white, *leaden* complexion...*consumptive*, most likely. She wears a large and *beautiful* winding-sheet of the *finest* India linen. Her hair hangs in *ringlets* over her neck... a soft smile *plays* about her mouth... but her nose, *extremely* long, thin, sinuous, flexible *and* pimpled...bends down *far* below her under lip...and in spite of the *delicate* manner in which she now and then *moves* it to one side or the other with her *tongue*...well, it's gives her a *confused* expression...hard to *know* what she's thinking.

Next to her is seated a little puffy, *wheezing* old man, whose cheeks hang like *two* huge bladders of *Greek* wine. Resembles a *blood* hound. His arms are folded but his one *bandaged* leg rests upon the table. *His* shroud is rather *gaudy,* must have cost him a pretty penny. Fashioned from one of those *fancy* silks embroidered in England, no doubt. *Aristocratic,* perhaps. Or, at least, it is *supposed* to look as if he is...*aristocratic,* that is.

And, *here's* a gentleman in long white stockings and cotton drawers. *His* jaws are tightly *tied* up by a bandage of muslin...his arms being *fastened* in a similar way at the wrist. *Unfortunately*, this prevents him from helping *himself* to the *liquors* upon the table...while the *rest* of them drink freely. His *prodigious* ears cannot *help* but listen to the *sloppy* imbibing going on and whenever a *cork* pops...

(CORK POPS)

...to him it sounds like a *cannon* blast.

As for the *sixth* person at the table, *he* appears to be afflicted with a *serious* paralysis. Perhaps, a stroke victim. Mute. He sits, or, rather *lays* upright, *uniquely,* in a new and handsome mahogany coffin. Interesting. There are *arm*-holes cut in its sides so that the man is actually *wearing* the coffin...but, of course, he cannot sit *erect* as his associates. He must *lay* there at a 45 degree angle...and roll his *goggle* eyes each time someone belches.

(MAN BELCHES)

And... *before* each of the party lay a portion of a *skull*, which is used as a drinking cup. Overhead... is suspended a human *skeleton*, by means of a *rope* tied round one of the legs and fastened to a *ring* in the ceiling. The *other* limb hangs free. The whole *dangling* thing rattles *loosely* at the slightest draft that has found its way down here into the cellar. And, to make things even *spookier*... in the *cranium* of this *hideous* thing lay a small quantity of *ignited* charcoal... which throws a *flickering* but *vivid* reddish light over the entire, *ghoulish* scene!

HUGH
So? What do you see down there? Legs? Are ya *listening* to me?

NARRATOR
In the middle of this *extraordinary* assembly... down here in this *bizarre* environment... Legs stands with jaws *wide* open in horror... eyes *bulging* to their fullest.

HUGH
Stay there! I'll try to find a ladder or a rope or something to get down there! Just don't you drink all that *wine* now, hear me!
(GROUP CHATTER)

NARRATOR
The *leader* of the group smiles at Legs and *graciously* invites him to sit at the table. Legs offers not the *slightest* resistance, but sits down. The leader pours out a *skull* of red wine. The *fat* lady laughs. The *consumptive* is distressed. The gentleman in the *coffin* seems perturbed. But, the leader will hear no objections.
(BANGS GAVEL THREE TIMES)
SILENCE

KING PEST
Ahem! It becomes our *duty* upon the present *happy* occasion...

LEGS
Wait! Wait now, I say... and tell us who the *devil* ye all are, and *what* business ye have here... *dressed* like foul fiends, and *swilling* this wine and rum punch!
(THE OTHERS ARE AGHAST!
ANGRY MUTTERING)

NARRATOR
The others are *aghast* at this *unpardonable* piece of *ill*-breeding. Half

rising to their feet, and *uttering* wild accusations...
(GAVEL BANGS THREE TIMES)
SILENCE

KING PEST
Ahem! Most *willingly* will we *gratify* any *reasonable* curiosity on the part of our *illustrious* guest...even though he be *naïve* and ignorant. Know Sir...that in *these* dominions *I* am monarch, and *here* rule with *undivided* empire under the title of *King Pest the First.* You may not have noticed when you first *entered* this abode...but, *this* was once cellar under the shop of an undertaker...

LEGS
What?

KING PEST
Look around you, Sir.

EERIE MUSIC

NARRATOR
It's true...Legs had *not* noticed...but, now, as he turns his eyes to *peer* into the deep darkness...on *all* sides, he can just barely see the *stacks* of *coffins* lining the walls.

KING PEST
Currently, I have chosen this place to be the *Royal* Chamber of our Palace, *devoted* to the councils of our kingdom, and to *other* sacred and *lofty* purposes. The noble *lady* who sits opposite is *Queen* Pest, our *Serene* Consort. The other *exalted* personages whom you behold are *all* of our family, and wear the *insignia* of the *blood* royal under the *respective* titles of ...His *Grace* the Arch Duke *Pest*iferous...His *Grace* the Duke *Pest*ilential...His *Grace* the Duke Tem*pest*...and Her *Serene* Highness the *Arch* Duchess Ana*pest.*

As regards, your *demand* of the business upon which we sit here in council...we *might* be pardoned for *replying* that it concerns our *own* private and *regal* interest... and is in *no* manner *important* to *any* other than ourselves. But, in *consideration* of *those* rights to which as a *guest* and a *stranger* you may feel *yourself* entitled...we will *furthermore* explain that *we* are here this night...to examine, analyze, *and* thoroughly *determine* the indefinable *spirit*...the *incomprehensible* qualities *and* nature...of those *inestimable* treasures of the palate...the *wines*, ales, *and* liqueurs of this *goodly* metropolis...by so doing to advance *not* ourselves, but, the *true* welfare of that *unearthly* sovereign whose *reign* is over us all...whose *dominions* are unlimited, and whose *name* is *Death*.

SILENCE

LEGS
Are you *insane*, Sir? Because if you are...
(THE OTHERS ARE AGHAST, AGAIN!
ANGRY MUTTERING, BANGS GAVEL)

KING PEST
Profane varlet! Profane and *execrable* wretch! We have *said,* that in *consideration* of those rights which, even in thy *filthy* person, we feel *no* inclination to *violate*... we have *condescended* to make reply to thy *rude* and *unseasonable* inquiries. We, *nevertheless*, for your *unhallowed* intrusion upon our councils... believe it our *duty* to *drown* thee and *thy* companion in each a *gallon* of rum...toasting *first* to the prosperity of our kingdom...
(OTHERS BECOME RAUCOUS)

...in a single *draft*...and upon your *bended* knees...ye shall be forthwith *free* either to *proceed* upon your way...or *remain* and be admitted to the *privileges* of our table...according to your respective *and* individual *pleasures!*
(BANGS GAVEL THREE TIMES)
SILENCE

LEGS
Oh yeah, you're *insane* alright. Look, your *majesty*...It would be a matter of *utter* impossibility to *imbibe* even one-*fourth* of all the liquor in this place. First of all, my *friend* and I have *already* partaken *enough* liquor *this* night to sink a ship. I cannot *swallow* another drop...least of all that *bilge* water *you* call rum!

KING PEST
The sentence *cannot* be altered *or* recalled. The conditions we have imposed *must* be fulfilled *to* the letter, and *that* without a *moment's* hesitation...in failure of which *fulfilment* we decree that *you* do here be *tied* neck and *heels* together, and duly *drowned* as a rebel in yon *cask* of October *beer!*
(THE OTHERS SCREAM... *"A sentence! A righteous and just sentence! Here, here! A glorious decree! A most worthy and upright, and holy condemnation!"*)

MUSIC

NARRATOR
Well, now, the *whole* Pest family are shouting and carrying on as if *they* are about to break *free* from invisible chains!   King Pest *raises* his eyebrows and the little old man *puffs* out his chest and the fat lady *waves* her fists and the *emaciated* lady sticks out her *nose* and the gentleman in the cotton drawers *pricks* up his ears and *she* of the shroud *gasps* like a dying fish and *he* of the coffin *rolls* up his eyes!

LEGS
Where the *hell* am I? *You!* Mr. King *Pest!* Are you *asking* me to drink to the *Devil* himself? I mean, I *know* I am a sinner...but, what *you're* asking...it's quite *another* sort of a thing, and *utterly* and *altogether* past *my* comprehension!
                    (CROWD UPROAR EVEN LOUDER)

NARRATOR
He is not allowed to *finish* this speech...the whole assembly has *leaped* from their seats!
                    (THE OTHERS SCREAM *"Treason! Treason!"*)
                              MUSIC BUILDS

And, *just* as Legs commences to *pour* for himself a skull of liquor...the *fat* lady *takes* him by his collar and *lifts* him *high* into the air...

LEGS
Whoa!

NARRATOR
...and *heaves* him without *ceremony* into the *huge* bowl of punch!
                              (SPLASH!)

LEGS
Glub...glub...glub! Help!

NARRATOR
Bobbing up and down, for a few seconds, like an *apple* in a wash tub at Halloween time...he *finally* disappears.

LEGS
Aaaahhh!

                              SILENCE

NARRATOR
...amid a *whirlpool* of foam! Then, as *all* stand about *staring* in silence at the *bubbling* foam...

MUSIC

Suddenly, Legs *bursts* out of the bowl...*ready* for combat!

LEGS
Aaaaahhhh!

(SCREAMS, CHAOS, FURNITURE
CRASHES, GLASS SMASHES)

NARRATOR
King Pest *turns* to run, but, Legs *grabs* him by his cloak and *slams* him *down* to the floor...*cursing* loudly...and *strides* to the center of the room where he *tears* down the *skeleton* which *swings* over the table...*rips* the leg bones free and *bounces* one off the *noggin* of the little *gentleman!* As the others *charge* at him, Legs *overturns* the cask *full* of October ale, *rolls* it over and over and in an *instant*...

(FLOOD SOUNDS, GURGLING, BUBBLING)

Out bursts a *deluge* of liquor *so* fierce...*so* impetuous...so *overwhelming*...that the room is *flooded* from wall to wall...the *table* is overturned...the coffins floating, *tumbling* in the foam...the tub of punch *flies* into the fireplace...and the ladies *fly* into hysterics! Jugs, pitchers, *and* casks mingle *promiscuously* in the melee...wicker flagons *crash* with bottles and junk. The trembling man *drowns* on the spot...the little stiff *gentleman* floats *off* in his coffin...and the victorious Legs, *seizing* by the waist the *fat* lady in the shroud...clambers and climbs *atop* her shoulders so that he can *easily* reach to the trap door *overhead* and *haul* himself up and *out* of the cellar from *Hell!*

SILENCE

HUGH
Ah, *there* you are now! How did *you* get back up here? I've just found ourselves a *ladder* and I was just about to...

LEGS
Never mind with that! Get *out* of here now! *Follow me!*

HUGH
I am not following *you!* I thought you said the cellar was *full* of liquor!

LEGS
Forget *that!* I never want to even *see* another *drink* again!

HUGH
Are you *mad?* But, you *can't* go out into the *streets* again! You'll be *caught!*

LEGS
Then, I'll take my chances with the *law!* Twenty years of *rowing* ain't *nothing* compared to what I just seen! Stay if you like, I'm leaving!

HUGH
Wait!

LEGS
(Distant) *Goodbye Hugh!*

HUGH
Goodbye Legs! Gone, just like that. Breaks my heart. Leaving me here alone. And, on top of that, swearing off *drinking?* In *which* case, I might be better off without him. Now...where's that *cellar* full of booze?
MUSIC

NARRATOR
As far as we know...*Legs* was *indeed* caught and sentenced to only *ten* years of hard labor for having *stiffed* the landlady of *The Jolly Tar.* It is *believed* that his friend *Hugh*, having stayed behind to join the *others* at the table, *succumbed* to yellow fever.
END

THE MAN THAT WAS USED UP

By Edgar Allan Poe
Adapted By Dan Bianchi

CAST – 1m/2w
SYNOPSIS – A southern belle recounts the time when she met a legendary war hero.

NARRATOR
(REVERB) "Do I remember when *and* where I first made the *acquaintance* of that *truly* fine-looking fellow, Brigadier General John A. B. C. *Smith?* I most certainly *do* remember. My cousin *Tabitha* introduced me to the gentleman...at the 17th Annual Beaverbrook *Military* Cotillion. How could I *forget* that fateful night?
PERIOD WALTZ MUSIC
(CROWDED BALLROOM)

"Ah, Brigadier General John A. B. C. *Smith*...he stood, perhaps, a whole six *feet* in height...and, certainly, he *exhibited,* what you might call, a *commanding* presence. A distinguished *air* about him. High breeding. Jet black *flowing* hair. A great beard *and* moustache. In fact...and I am *not* exaggerating when I say, they were the *handsomest* pair of whiskers under the sun! And, *beneath* that face hair, his *unequalled* mouth...well, it was *filled* with the *most* entirely even, and the *most* brilliantly *white* of *all* conceivable teeth. From between them issued a voice of *unadulterated* clearness, melody, *and* strength. As for his *eyes*...they were of a deep *hazel*...exceedingly *large* and lustrous. I'd say, *extraordinary* orbs that offered *great* expression. Yes, indeed.

"The *rest* of him might be described as *that* belonging to the *Greek* God, Apollo. A *fine* set of limbs surrounding a fit, *sculptured* torso. There was neither *too* much flesh *nor* too little... neither *rudeness* nor *fragility*. Very *properly* proportioned. And, I could not *imagine* a more graceful *curve* than that of his...the, uhm, yes, ahem, well...

"Now, as you know, men so absolutely *fine*-looking are *not* plentiful in this region. But, the General's attributes do *not,* altogether, rest in the *supreme* excellence of his *bodily* endowments. As for his *manner* ...there was a *primness*, not to say *stiffness*, in the way he presented himself. His movements, *too* precise, if I may use this description. *Dignified.* Not that there was anything *wrong* with that!

"My dear cousin *Tabitha,* who knows more about *anyone* than anyone *else* wants to know, *whispered* in my ear some few words of *comment* upon the man."

TABITHA
He is a *remarkable* man...a *very* remarkable man... indeed one of the *most* remarkable men of the age. He is a special *favorite,* too, with the ladies...*chiefly* on account of his high *reputation* for courage. In that point he is *unrivalled*...indeed he is a perfect *desperado*...a downright *fire-eater,* no mistaking *that*...if you *know* what I mean?

NARRATOR
No, Cousin Tabitha, I do *not* know what you mean.

TABITHA
Well, he was the *finest* definition of bravery in the late *tremendous* swamp-fight, out West, with the *Bugaboo* and *Kickapoo* Indians. Bless my soul! *Blood* and thunder, and all that! *That* man is a *real* prodigy of valor!

NARRATOR
Oh, Tabitha!

TABITHA
Don't take *my* word for it! *That* is what the papers called him. You know he is the man who...why *here* he is now! Why, how do you *do,* General Smith?

NARRATOR
(REVERB) "Here we were interrupted by the General *himself*...and my cousin Tabitha *seized* me by the hand as he drew near, and bowing *stiffly* but profoundly...*I* was presented. I remember thinking...I have never *heard* a clearer nor a *stronger* voice, nor beheld a *finer* set of teeth!
                                                                                    SILENCE

"And, when my cousin had to *leave* us...well, I *must* say that the General and I partook in a *delightfully* luminous conversation and I was *not* only pleased but *really* educated. I never heard a more *fluent* talker, or a man of *greater* general information. With becoming *modesty,* he mentioned only briefly of the *mysterious* circumstances attending the *Bugaboo* war... as well as, *other* topics of *philosophical* interest. He delighted, *especially,* in commenting upon the rapid *march* of *mechanical*

invention."
MUSIC

GENERAL
There is nothing at *all* like it. We are a *wonderful* people, and live in a *wonderful* age. Parachutes and railroads...*mantraps* and *spring*-guns! Our *steam*-boats are upon *every* sea... and the Nassau *balloon* is about to run *regular* trips...fare either way only *five* dollars...between *here* and Timbuktu! Ha! Can you imagine that?   And, *who* shall calculate the *immense* influence upon social life...upon *arts*...upon *commerce*...upon *literature*...which will be the *immediate* result of the great principles of *electro*-magnetics! Nor, is this *all*, let me assure you! There is really *no* end to the *march* of invention. The most wonderful...the most *ingenious*...and let me add, the most *useful*...the most *truly* useful ...*mechanical* contrivances are daily *springing* up like *mushrooms,* like grasshoppers...*figuratively* speaking ...like *grasshoppers!*
SILENCE

NARRATOR
(REVERB) "I left General Smith with a *heightened* interest in the man... with an *exalted* opinion of his *conversational* powers...and, yes, with a *deep* sense of the *valuable* privileges we enjoy while *living* in this age of *mechanical* invention.
(APPLAUSE IN THEATER, DISTANT
ACTOR ACTS "IAGO")

"However, my *curiosity*, had not been *altogether* satisfied and, the following evening while Tabitha and I sat in a *box* at the *Rantipole* Theater...where the fine tragedian, *Climax*, was doing *Iago* to a *very* crowded house... I resolved to inquire *further* regarding the *tremendous* events of the Bugaboo *and* Kickapoo campaigns out West."

TABITHA
(Whispers)   *Horrid* affair that!   A bloody set of *wretches*, those Kickapoos! The General *fought* like a hero...a *prodigy* of valor...that's what the *papers* called him...an *immortal* renown. *Smith!* Brigadier General John A. B. C.! Why, you know *he's* the man who...?
(APPLAUSE)

And, did you *ever* behold a finer figure? Or, so *inimitable* grace?

NARRATOR
But, what about the *Bugaboos?*

TABITHA
What? Oh, yes, great *wretches*, those Bugaboos…*savage* and so on…
(DISTANT ACTOR ROARS OTHELLO)

NARRATOR
(REVERB) "At that moment, *Othello* roared in my ear…our box was *right* above stage right…and shaking his *fist* in my face *all* the time, I could not hear a *word* Tabitha had said thereafter.
PERIOD CHAMBER MUSIC

"At the soiree of the lovely widow, Mrs. Kathleen O' *Trump*, I was *confident* that I should meet with *no* similar disappointment. Accordingly, I was no sooner *seated* at the card-table, with my pretty *hostess* for a face to face, than I *propounded* those questions… the solution of which had become a matter so *essential* to my peace.

"How do you think she replied? Well, with the same *exact* descriptions I've heard repeated *time* and again, not *only* by Tabitha, but, by *any* young woman who carries on and on about our *hero,* that *prodigy* of *valor*… Brigadier General John A.B.C. *Smith!*
SILENCE

"For the next week…I could not find an answer to my *query* regarding the *brave* General and the Bugaboos. Well, I would *not* be thwarted in my goal.   There *was* one resource left to me yet. I would go to the *fountain* head. I would call *forthwith* upon the General *himself,* and *demand,* in explicit terms, a *solution* to this *missing* piece of mystery. Here, at *least,* there should be *no* chance for equivocation.
MUSIC
(DOOR KNOCKS, DOOR OPENS)

"It was early when I called and was shown at *once* into his library by an *old* servant, who remained in *attendance* during my visit. As I entered the room, I looked about, of course, for the occupant, but did *not* immediately perceive him. There was a large and *exceedingly* odd looking *bundle* of something which lay close by my feet on the floor…and, as I was *not* in the best humor in the world, I gave it a *kick* out of the way."

(THUD, OOMPH!)
SILENCE

BUNDLE
Ahem! Ahem! That's *not* very nice, I *should* say!

NARRATOR
(REVERB) "Said the bundle, in the smallest, *and* altogether the *funniest* little voice that I had *ever* heard in *all* the days of my existence."

BUNDLE
Ahem! Not very civil at *all!*

NARRATOR
(REVERB) "I didn't have *time* to tremble...I fairly *screamed* with terror..."

(NO REVERB) *Aaaahhhhh!*

(REVERB) "I suppose I *should* have *fainted* on the spot! Instead, I *ran* to the far corner of the room and *hid* behind a large armchair."

BUNDLE
Now, now, that'll be *enough* of that! Why, what *is* the matter with you? I really *believe* you don't *know* me at all.
                                                              MUSIC

NARRATOR
(REVERB) "What could I say to all this? I *staggered* into the armchair, and, with *staring* eyes and open mouth, *awaited* an answer to my astonishment. As if *that* wasn't enough to cause *heart* failure to even the most *physically* fit human being...a second *later*...a *leg*...yes, a *leg...popped* out of the bundle and, literally, *flew* across the room, knocking over a *vase!*"

                                                              (CRASH!)

BUNDLE
Strange you shouldn't *know* me though, isn't it? *Benedict!* Bring me that *leg!* It's made of *cork,* you know? Strange, you shouldn't know me.

NARRATOR
(REVERB) "And, as the servant did so, the bundle *took* the leg and *screwed* it onto itself...and then, *stood* upright before my eyes. Luckily, he had a *second* leg to stand upon, as well."

BUNDLE
And, a *bloody* action it was...

NARRATOR
(REVERB) "Meanwhile, he continued muttering and talking...as if in the

midst of delivering a soliloquy!"

BUNDLE
But, then... one mustn't *fight* with the Bugaboos and Kickapoos and expect to come *off* with a mere *scratch. Benedict!* I'll *thank* you now for that *arm.* There is a *craftsman* in the village, a Mr. *Cumberbatch,* who is *decidedly* the *best* hand at *fashioning* a cork leg... but, if you *should* ever want an *arm* I must recommend Mr. *Bishop* in the city.

NARRATOR
(REVERB) "I was *dumbfounded,* staring *dumbfoundedly* as the *servant,* screwed an *arm* onto the bundle!"

BUNDLE
We had rather *hot* work of it! Oh yes, *that* is no exaggeration. Those Bugaboos, they know how to *tear* into a man and... Now, Benedict, you *dog,* will you slip on my *shoulders* and *bosom? Ah!* Mr. Elias *Spector,* now, there's a *real* artist...he makes the *best* shoulders, but for a *bosom* you will have to go to the *Bosom* Shop on Main Street.

NARRATOR
(REVERB) "As it was, I could not believe my *eyes*...but, now I could not believe my *ears.* Had he...*it*...just mentioned...the *Bosom* Shop...on *Main* Street?"

BUNDLE
Benedict, will you *never* be ready with that *wig? Real* hair is the *only* way to go with a wig. But, *scalping* is a *rough* process, after all. True, the Bugaboos are rather well skilled when it comes to *scalping,* but...*I* prefer *L'Orme's*...authentic *European* artistry when it comes to hair. Now, Benedict...my *teeth!* For a *good* set of *these* you had best go to *Baldini's*...yes, I know, *high* prices, but *excellent* work. These here are *real* teeth, you know? They're not *mine,* of course, but, *real,* nonetheless. *I* swallowed most of my *original* teeth when a Bugaboo warrior *rammed* me in my mouth with the *butt* end of his rifle. Aha! Here is the *piece de resistance!* My *eye!* Here, Benedict, *you* screw it in! Those *Kickapoos* are *not* so very *accurate* when it comes to *eye* gouging...but, after Dr. *Williams* created *this* eye for me...why you can't *imagine* how *grateful* I've been ever since! Looks *absolutely* like the *real* thing, don't you think?

NARRATOR
(REVERB) "I now began very *clearly* to perceive that the *object* before

me was nothing more *nor* less than my *new* acquaintance, Brigadier General John A. B. C. *Smith*. The manipulations of *Benedict,* his servant, had made, I *must* confess, a very *striking* difference in the *appearance* of the personal man. The voice, however, *still* puzzled me a bit...but even *this* apparent mystery was *speedily* cleared up."

BUNDLE
Benedict, you *rascal*...I really *do* believe you would let me go out *without* my *palate!*

NARRATOR
(REVERB) "Hereupon, the servant, *grumbling* out an apology, went up to his master, *opened* his mouth and *adjusted* therein a somewhat *singular*-looking machine...in a very *dexterous* manner, that *I* could not altogether *comprehend.* However, in an *instant*, it altered the *entire* expression of the General's countenance. When he again *spoke,* his *voice* had resumed *all* that rich *melody* and strength which I had noticed upon our *original* introduction."

GENERAL
Ugh! Damn the bastards! *Ugh!* Damn the *vagabonds!* Pardon me, Miss, but...you see, the *savages* not only *knocked* in the *roof* of my mouth, but took the trouble to cut *off* at least *seven*-eighths of my *tongue.* If it wasn't for Signor *Bonaventura*...I don't know *what* I would have *done* without him. I can recommend you to him with *confidence* and *assure* you that I have the *greatest* pleasure in so doing.

NARRATOR
(REVERB) "Well, I *acknowledged* his kindness in my *best* manner, and took *leave* of him at *once*, with a *perfect* understanding of the *true* state of affairs...and with a *full* comprehension of the *mystery* which had *troubled* me for so long. It was a *clear* case. Due to the valuable *privileges* we now enjoy while living in this age of *mechanical* invention, everything *broken* upon and *within* this legendary *celebrity* had been *replaced.* The fact was...there was *nothing* left of the *original* Brigadier General John A. B. C. *Smith.* Evidently, all that *was* the man...was *now* used up."

END

THE PREMATURE BURIAL
By Edgar Allan Poe
Adapted By Dan Bianchi

CAST – 1m/1w
SYNOPSIS – A carnival side show offers a look into the prospect of being buried alive.

(CARNIVAL MIDWAY CROWD, SOUNDS)
CALLIOPE MUSIC BACKGROUND

CLEM
Ladies and gentlemen, *step* right up, step right up...not you kid, you're too young...ladies and gents, *step* into that tent and you'll *witness* before your eyes, *Greta*...the one and only *surviving* human being who was *once* buried prematurely...that's right, she was *buried alive* folks, buried alive. And, she rose from the dead...not unlike *Lazarus* or, for that matter, our *Lord* and Savior. That's right...see the girl raised from the dead for only a quarter. Two bits to hear her tell the story herself.

Now, gather round...gather round, that's it....not you kid, get lost.. Now, you sir...yeah, you...you must agree that to be buried *alive* is, *beyond* question, the most *terrifying* misery to have ever *fallen* upon a human being, am I right? You know I am. And, it's happened a lot *more* frequently than *you* might imagine.

Why, my Daddy always said...the boundaries which divide *Life* from Death, are at *best* shadowy and vague. Who shall say *where* the *one* ends, and *where* the *other* begins?

MUSIC

Now, you take that *disease* when a person *appears* to be dead but really *isn't? Narcolepsy,* that's what it's called. Look it up if you don't believe me. And, and...haven't *you* heard of people being pronounced *dead* and coming *back* to life? Of *course,* you have. Why, I was reading a *book,* just last week...and in it, it *said* that there have been *hundreds* of authenticated *cases* of *premature* death pronouncements. That means, buried *alive,* folks...buried *alive.*

For instance, there was this case in *Baltimore.* Just three years ago. The *wife* of an eminent *Congressman* was *seized* with a *sudden* illness.

Fell right down. Those high falutin doctors didn't know what to make of it. After *much* suffering, she died...*or* was *supposed* to have died. Don't faint, lady...not yet. It gets better later on.

So, as the story goes...*No* one suspected that this woman was *not* actually dead. I mean, she *looked* dead to anybody who saw her. Her face had that *pinched* and *sunken* outline, y'know? The *lips* were white, *rigid.* The *eyes* lost their shine. Her body was *cold* as ice. No pulse. Sounds dead to me. How about you, sir?

EERIE MUSIC

Well, for the next *three* days her body was *unburied* lying in *state* at the family home. I know what you're thinking...was she embalmed? Nope! Then, the *funeral* was held. The lady's body was *deposited* in her family vault and it *remained* there, *undisturbed,* for *three* years.

Three years? Now, I know what you're gonna ask...but, no, she didn't walk out of that tomb three years later. No. But, ya see, the tomb was *reopened* then to allow for *another* deceased family member. But...*imagine* the *shock* for the dead woman's *husband,* who, *personally,* opened that door.

(IRON DOOR CREAKS OPEN)

Listen to that! You hear that? That's that iron door *creaking* open and just then...a *shrouded* object fell *rattling* within his arms! It was the *skeleton* of his wife!

(MAN SCREAMS)

Where you running off to, mister? There's more to my story! It was only the *skeleton* of his wife. Now, how did that happen, you may ask? Well, I'll tell ya. Ya see, the family figured that, three years earlier...she had *revived* within *two* days *after* her entombment....

(SCRATCHING, MOANING, SOBBING ECHOES)

I can hear her now. She must have *struggled* within the coffin and caused it to *fall* from a ledge to the floor...

(COFFIN SMASHED)

...where it had *smashed* open and she e*scaped* from it. On the *steps,* ya see, they found this wooden *plank,* broken *off* from the coffin, which she had used to *strike* the iron door to raise attention. But, I guess nobody heard her. In her *weakened* condition, she probably *fainted* or *died,* possibly through *sheer* terror.

SILENCE

Sheer terror, folks. I know *I'd* die from *sheer* terror if *I* was locked in a tomb! How about you, sir? Or, you, madame? I *know* what you're thinking. When do we get to see Greta...the walking dead girl? Well, for only a *quarter,* you can go *right* in there and *see* her for yourself. Don't take *my* word for it. Listen to her *true* story and you'll *know* what it feels like to be terrified, but you'll *never* know what it feels like to be *buried* alive. At least, let's *hope* not!

MUSIC

Now where was I? Oh, yeah...ya see, that *woman*...whose skeleton fell into the arms of her *husband* when he opened the door to that *tomb?* Her *shroud* had become *entangled* in some of that sculpted, scrolled *iron* work on the door, ya see... and *so* she died there and remained standing *upright,* as she *rotted* away for the next *three* years. Until her *husband* had opened that iron door and...

(WOMAN SCREAMS)
SILENCE

Oooh wee! Now, there goes another one. And, we haven't even entered the tent yet. But, I don't *blame* that woman for running off. Gives *me* goosebumps just *thinking* about it. But, before we go in to see Greta, the walking dead girl...I'd like to tell you another true story, my Aunt Sue *Ellen* told me.

MUSIC

It was about this rich *lawyer* fella down in Atlanta...and how he died *mysteriously.* that's right, I said, mysteriously. Yep. But, his family...they *refused* an *autopsy* and so he was *quickly* laid to rest. An hour or so *after* the *corpse* had been *buried,* one of the *numerous* gangs of body-snatchers back then...they was all over back then in *less* enlightened times than nowadays.

(GRAVEYARD SOUNDS, DIGGING)

Well, they made their way into the *graveyard,* see? And, they *dug* up that there *lawyer*...and *sold* his body to a local *medical* college so as they can cut it up for educational purposes.

Ya see, the *law* only permitted a *certain* amount of *corpses each* year for studying purposes...but, it was *never* enough for all those *students* and doctors. Now, while on the *examination* table, just as the doctor was about to *cut* into the stomach, the body...

(BODY THRASHING ON TABLE, STUDENTS SCREAM)

it started *convulsing,* and *writhing* like a *snake* on a griddle... and then...it just *sat up!* I'm not kidding ya, folks! God's honest truth, it did. And, then, it stepped *off* that table, *gazing* about the room for a few seconds...

(MAN MUMBLES, THUMP)

...and he *mumbled* something and then *fell* like a *rock* down to the floor. For some moments *everyone,* doctors *and* students, *everybody* was *paralyzed* with awe.

SILENCE

What's that you ask...did he *live?* Well, as a matter of fact, he *returned* to his family, who were even *more* shocked. Ya see, *they* had *already* divided the man's *estate* amongst *themselves!*

(GONG)

Well, I guess I can go on all *night* with similar *true* stories. But, now it is time to meet our *star* attraction for all those who pay *full* admission to hear an *astonishing* story from the *only* person in *existence* to have *lived* to tell the tale...right this way, folks...show your ticket, please. That's it, *through* the tent here...hey, *kid,* I thought I told you to get *lost!*

(GONG, CROWD SETTLES)
MUSIC

Ladies *and* gentlemen...I ask you to *think*...how *frightening* it must be to *suspect* that a dearly departed *member* of the family had been *prematurely* buried. But, how much *more* frightening for the *buried* one, no? Even if it *is* possible to escape the grave, how can one live *normally* after that? I mean, just think of the *torture* their mind had to go through ...waking up in their *coffin* six feet *underground?*

And, I'm talking about the *physical* torture, too. The *lungs* giving out ...*suffocating*...breathing in those *stifling* fumes of the damp earth. The *death* garments *clinging* to you. *Waking* to find yourself *stuck* in some narrow coffin? The *absolute* blackness...the *silence?* And, worst yet, realizing *you* are in the *presence* of the *Conqueror* Worm. You try to *think* about the *air* and grass above...*remembering* your dear friends who would *rush* to save you *if* they *only* knew what was happening to you. But, you realize soon enough that *they* will *never* know. And, you know that you are *hopelessly* condemned to be *really* dead. I ask you, good people...how can a mere human *being* carry such a *heavy* burden? There must be *nothing* so *agonizing* upon Earth. We can't even *dream* of something *half* so *hideous* in the realms of *Hell.*

And, so, while all of these stories may seem *horrifying,* even as fiction, they are even *more* terrible because they are *true.* Yet, I must admit, *second* hand truth. How much *more* terrifying such a tale of *premature* burial *might* be if it were told by *someone* who had experienced it *firsthand*? Ladies and Gentlemen...I give you *Greta, the living dead girl!*
FANFARE MUSIC
(APPLAUSE)

Greta...tell us about your ordeal...

MUSIC

GRETA
(As if drugged, rehearsed) For several years I've been *subject* to attacks of catalepsy.

CLEM
Catalepsy! Even when the diagnosis of this disease is correct, its causes are *still a* mystery to even the *greatest* doctors.

GRETA
Sometimes I lie, for a *day* only, or even for a *shorter* period, in a state of *deep* sleep. I am *senseless*, motionless.

CLEM
The heart *still* pulsates yet *barely* perceptible. There are *some* traces of warmth and a *slight* color lingers in the cheeks.

GRETA
I can lie in a *trance* for weeks, even *months.* I *appear* to be dead. Doctors have *failed* to determine if I am *suffering.* Even *I* am *unaware* of my condition.

CLEM
Now, *if* a victim's family *and* friends are *well* aware of this catalepsy when it occurs, *then* the victim is, *hopefully,* saved from *premature* burial. And, the *signals* of the sickness are, *luckily,* gradual.

GRETA
When *I* suffer a fit, I *drop* into a phase of *false* sleep. But, you see, I know...I *know* about my condition.

CLEM
But, just think about all of those who *don't* know…who may suffer their *first* attack in an *extreme* form…they would *most* likely be *buried* alive. *Imagine,* all of the hundreds, the *thousands* who had been *buried* alive! Who, without *any* apparent cause, will *sink,* little by little, into a *semi*-comatose state, *without* pain, *without* ability to move.

GRETA
I *still* know what is going on around me. I *know* those who *surround* my bed…until the *crisis* passes.   Sometimes, I am hit *hard* by the disease. I grow sick, and numb, and *chilly,* and dizzy, and *drop* to the floor.   Then, for *weeks,* all is *void,* and black, and silent.   *Nothing,* itself, becomes my universe. Total annihilation.

CLEM
Recovery from these seizures is slow.

GRETA
My *soul* is slow in returning to me.   My memory…

CLEM
Yet, general health appears to be good.
                                                            EERIE MUSIC

GRETA
But, I have become a *morbid* person.   I talk *tirelessly* of *worms,* of *tombs* and epitaphs.   I am *obsessed* with death, and the *idea* of premature burial *possesses* me.   It *haunts* me day and night.   *Night* time *terrifies* me.
                                    (HORSE CARRIAGE APPROACHES)

I see *visions* of an approaching *hearse* as the *sun* sets each evening. When I *do* fall asleep, I *shudder* to think that I might *awaken* to find myself buried alive in a coffin.   My *dreams* are nightmares *beyond* description!
                                    (HELLISH CHAOS, SCREAMS ECHO)
                                                        MUSIC BUILDS

(Becoming agitated)   I dream *every* night like this.   My *nerves* are unstrung.   I live in *perpetual* horror!   I hesitate to *travel* far from my home. I *fear* of being somewhere *far* off, *falling* into one of my *usual* fits and being *buried* before my *real* condition is discovered.   I wonder if even my *closest* friends can be trusted.   Maybe, *one* of them might even be *glad* to see me go. They *promise* me that *they* can be trusted. They *say* that the *only* way I'll be buried is if they *leave* me lie in bed until *decomposition* sets in. *Then,* they will be *sure* I am *truly* dead! *Hahaha!*

(Becoming manic) In the meantime, I've worked out a *whole* list of *elaborate* precautions. *Just* in case. For instance, I had the family vault *remodeled* so it can be *easily* opened from the *inside.* The slightest *pressure* upon a long *lever* that extends *far* into the tomb will cause the iron doors to *fly* back.
(GEARS GRIND, IRON DOOR SPRINGS OPEN)

There are *vents* to allow *air* and light into the room. There is *food* and water. The coffin must be *warm* and *softly* padded and, *most* importantly, the *lid* must be able to *open* from within. Besides all of that...there's a large *bell* with a *rope* that extends through a *hole* in the coffin which must be *fastened* to my hand. *Just* in case.
(BELL TINKLES)

You don't *know* what it's like...to *awaken* from the deep sleep. The *dull* pain. No emotions, just *confusion.* No care, no *hope.*
CHAOTIC MUSIC

A *ringing* in the ears. Slowly, the body comes *back* to life, like tiny electric *shocks* tingling my limbs. *Struggling* to think, to *remember* something. Then, the *blood* flows into the head, the *eyes* open, *terror* pervades *every* pore! I have become *cognizant* of my condition. I *know* I am *not* awaking from an *ordinary* night's sleep. And, then...the *fear,* the *terrible* fear of *knowing* that my *catalepsy* may have been *mistaken* for death. Am I in my *bed?* Or in my *coffin?* My *eyes* cannot *focus* in total darkness ...the terrifying effect is *devastating.*

But, I *cannot* scream. My lips and *parched* tongue move, but *no* voice comes forth. My *lungs* feel as if they are *filled* with *mortar.* No *wonder* I can't cry. My *jaws* are locked. *Why?* They are *bound* by *cloth! Oh God!* I've been *prepared* for *burial!* My *hands,* they are *crossed* on my breast, *move* them...*please,* move them. What's *this?* I *can't* move my arms, the *walls* are too close. *Can't move! Jesus Christ! Help me! I am in a coffin! Aaaaaaahh!*
SILENCE
(SCRATCHING, POUNDING WOODEN LID)

No matter *how* hard I try, I *cannot* open the *lid* that is *six* inches from my face. It won't *budge. Hope,* think *good* thoughts...*don't* be ridiculous. I *have* to escape. *Get out. Help!* Don't use up your energy. Your oxygen. Take a *deep* breath. Wait...what's that *smell?* I recognize it...*earth,* dirt, it smells like *dirt.*

MUSIC

Now, I think...I *must* have fallen into a *trance* when I was out walking in the countryside...and *strangers* must have *found* me...and...and... *maybe* they *buried* me in a *pauper's* grave...yes, I'm *not* in a *metal* coffin with *pillows* and upholstery...no, *this* is all wood, *cheap* wood, *hastily* made...and I can *smell* the earth around me. *Buried* like a dog. I am *not* in a vault. I am in a *grave. Oh my God!* There's no *bell* to warn people. The *lid* doesn't spring open. I *can't* get out. All those *precautions* were for nothing. I am in some *nameless* grave only *God* knows where. *Help! Help! Aaaaaahhhh!*

SILENCE

CLEM
There are *moments* when, even to the *sober* eye of Reason, the *world* of our *sad* Humanity may *assume* the semblance of a Hell...

EERIE MUSIC

But, the *imagination* of man knows *no* bounds and *can* be merciless. At the *same* time, the *grim* reality of being *buried* alive *cannot* just be *regarded* so lightly. A mere *phobia* reserved for *hypochondriacs? Ha!* But, we cannot *allow* them to *defeat* us. These terrible *fears* must be made to *sleep,* at times, to give us time to *breathe* and *hope* and *raise* our courage. They *must* sleep. Or, they will *devour* us.

SILENCE
(APPLAUSE, CROWD MURMURS)
CARNIVAL MUSIC

That's it, folks. Show's over. Please stand and file out through the tent doorway, that's it. Show's over. Tell your friends to come to see and hear for themselves. Thanks for coming, folks...hey, *kid,* how did *you* get in here?

END

NEVER BET THE DEVIL YOUR HEAD
By Edgar Allan Poe
Adapted By Dan Bianchi

CAST – 1m
SYNOPSIS – The Narrator tells us all about his worthless friend Toby.

FUNEREAL MUSIC

NARRATOR
What can I *say* about my dear *departed* friend, Toby *Dammit?* He was a *sad* dog, it is true, and, sure enough, he *died* a *dog's* death. Yes, he surely did.

SILENCE

But, let it be known, he *himself* was *not* to blame for his vices. *They* grew out of a personal *defect* in his mother. *She* did her *best* in the way of *flogging* him while an infant. Why, to her, *babies*, like tough *steaks,* are *always* the better for beating. But, *poor* woman! *She* had the *misfortune* to be *left*-handed, and a *child* flogged *left*-handedly had *better* be left *unflogged.* Don't take *my* word for it. The world *revolves* from right to left, does it *not?* Therefore, it will not *do* to *whip* a baby from *left* to right. It's only logical...if each blow in the *proper* direction drives an *evil* tendency *out*...it *follows* that every *thump* in an *opposite* direction knocks its *quota* of wickedness *in.* How do *I* know this? Well, *I* was often present at Toby's *chastisements*...although, some of you *liberals* might call them *beatings.*

MUSIC
(BABY SCREAMS)

Y'know, *even* by the way in which *he* kicked, I could *perceive* that *he* was getting *worse* and worse every day. At last I *saw*, through the *tears* in my eyes, that there was *no* hope for this *villain* at all. It broke my heart. Why...do you know that, *one* time he had been *walloped* until he grew *so* black and blue in the *face*...he *might* have been *mistaken* as one of those *Africans.* I kid you not. But, the *only* thing that came of it was...little Toby *wriggling* himself into a *fit!* I tell you, I could stand it no longer. Why, one day, I *dropped* to my knees, and, *uplifting* my voice, I *foretold* of his ruination.

SILENCE

The *fact* is...Toby's talent for *depravity* and *corruption* was awful. At *five* months of age he used to get into *such* passions that he was *unable* to articulate. At *six* months, I caught him *gnawing* a pack of cards. At *seven* months he was in the *constant* habit of catching and *kissing* the *female* babies. At *eight* months he peremptorily *refused* to put his signature to the *Temperance* pledge.

MUSIC

Thus, he went on *increasing* in *iniquity*, month after month, *until,* at the *close* of the *first* year, he not only *insisted* upon wearing *moustaches,* but, had *contracted* a *propensity* for *cursing* and swearing, and for *backing* his *statements* by bets.

SILENCE

Through this *ungentlemanly* practice, Toby Dammit's *ruination,* which *I* had predicted, *overtook* him at last.

MUSIC

The vice had grown with *his* growth and *strengthened* with *his* strength, so that, when he came to be a *man*, he could scarcely *utter* a sentence *without* making a wager.

SILENCE

Not that he *actually* bet with money. With *him*, wagering money was a mere *figure* of speech…nothing more. His *expressions* had no meaning attached to them whatever. They were simple if not *altogether* innocent *expletives…imaginative* phrases used to round off a sentence.

For instance, when he said "I'll *bet* you so and so," nobody ever *thought* of taking him up on it…but, still *I* could not *help* thinking it *my* duty to *condemn* him for it. Let's face it, the habit was an *immoral* one, and *so* I told him.

I told him, "Toby, your *gambling* is a *vulgar* habit. I *beg* you to believe me when I say that *all* of society *disapproves* of it."

Now, as *you* folks know, *I* only speak the truth. So, I was not about to lie to Toby. Whether or not the *majority* of society wanted to or not, *gambling* was, indeed, *forbidden* by act of Congress.

MUSIC

Well, I *complained* about his nasty vice, but to no avail. I *protested*…in vain. I *begged*…he *smiled*. I *implored*…he *laughed*. I *preached*…he *sneered.* I *threatened*…he *swore*. I *kicked* him…he *called* for the police.

I *pulled* his nose…he *blew* it, and *offered* to *bet* the Devil his *head* that I would *not* venture to *try* that act of violence *again!*

SILENCE

Poverty was *another* vice which the *peculiar* physical *deficiency* of Dammit's *mother* had *entailed* upon her son. He was *detestably* poor, and *this* was the reason, no *doubt,* that his *expletive* expressions about *betting,* seldom had *financial* backing. No, I will *not* be *bound* to say that I *ever* heard him make *use* of such a *figure* of speech as "I'll *bet* you a *dollar.*" It was usually "I'll *bet* you what you please," or "I'll *bet* you what you dare," or "I'll *bet* you a trifle," or else, more *significantly* still, "I'll bet the *Devil* my head."

"I'll bet the Devil my head." Yep, that saying seemed to please him best …perhaps, because it involved the *least* risk. Ya see, Toby had become *excessively* stingy. *Miserly,* if you know what I mean? So, had any one taken him *up* on his bet…well, his *head* was small, and *thus* his *loss* would have been small, as well. Of course, these are my *own* reflections and I am by *no* means *sure* that *I* am right in *attributing* them to *him.*

MUSIC

In *any* case, the *phrase* in question became his *favorite* saying. *And,* I can tell you, it was terribly *obscene* to listen to a man *bet* his brains like dollar bills. But, Toby Dammit was an *obstinate* person. Try as I might, he could not *understand* the *meaning* of my warnings. In the end, he *abandoned* all other forms of wagering…and gave himself up to "I'll bet the *Devil* my head." In fact, he used it *so* often, he was *wholly* committed to it.

MUSIC

I am always *displeased* by circumstances for which *I* cannot account. Mysteries *force* a man to think, and so *injure* his health. The truth is, there was *something* in the *air* that cause Dammit to utter that *offensive* expression…something in his manner of *enunciation*…which made *me* very uneasy…something which was *odd*…even *mystical,* perhaps? I began not to like it at all. You see, *I* believed Mr. Dammit's *soul* was in a *perilous* state. I resolved *myself* to saving him. Again, I *collected* my energies for a *final* attempt at *dissuading* him from using that *damnable* phrase.

SILENCE

When I had *ended* my lecture, Mr. Dammit *indulged* himself in some *very* confusing behavior. For some moments he remained silent, merely

looking me *inquisitively* in the face.
MUSIC BUILDS

But, presently he *threw* his head to one side, and *elevated* his eyebrows to a great extent. *Then,* he *spread* out the palms of his hands and *shrugged* up his shoulders. Then, he *winked* with the *right* eye. After which, he *winked* with the *left* eye. Then, he shut them *both* up very tight. Then, he *opened* them both *so* very wide that I became *seriously* alarmed for the consequences. Then, applying his *thumb* to his nose, he actually made an *indescribable* gesture with the *rest* of his fingers!
SILENCE

Can you *imagine?*
MUSIC BUILDS

He said, he would be *obliged* if *I* would hold my *tongue!* He wished *none* of my advice. He *despised* all my *insinuations.* He said that *he* was *old* enough to take *care* of himself. Did I *still* think of him as *baby* Dammit? Did I *mean* to say anything *against* his character? Did I *intend* to *insult* him? Was *I* a *fool?* Was my *mother* aware of my *absence* from home? What a *nerve!* Asking if my *mother* knew? How *dare* he! And, then...and *then*...he said that he would be *willing* to bet the *Devil* his *head* that my *mother* did *not* know of my *absence!*

Oh, I can tell you, I was *fuming* mad! But, Mr. Dammit did *not* wait for my reply. Turning upon his heel, he hurried off. It was *well* for him that he did so. *My* feelings had been wounded. Even *my* anger had been aroused. For once, I would have *taken* him up upon his *insulting* wager!
SILENCE

And, I would have *won*...for the fact is, my *mamma* was *very* well *aware* of my merely *temporary* absence from home.

However.../ bore the *insult* like a man. It *now* seemed to me that I had done *all* that could be *required* of me. I *resolved* to *no* longer trouble that *miserable* individual with *my* counsel. I'd just *leave* him to his conscience *and* himself.
MUSIC

Still, because of my own *charitable* character...I could not bring *myself* to give up on *him,* altogether. I even went so far as to find *humor* in some of his *less* reprehensible tendencies. Believe me, there were *times* when I found myself *lauding* his *wicked jokes* with *tears* in my eyes. Yet, *so profoundly* did it *grieve* me to *hear* his *evil* talk.

One day, Dammit and I were out walking and talking for a good hour before we found ourselves in a *seedy* area of the city.
                                                    (THUNDER, RAIN)

And, to make matters worse the *weather* had taken a turn for the worse. So, we found *shelter* in a *dark* hallway of some *condemned* building. By that time, we had been *arguing* about his character, once again...and he, *jokingly,* offered to bet the *Devil* his *head* that he could race to the top of the dilapidated staircase, *three* flights up, in *less* than fifteen seconds. *Really,* now? I could not make up my mind whether to *kick* or to pity him. I yelled, "Go on, you fool, *bet* the *Devil* your *stupid* head!"
                                                    SILENCE

And, then...just as he was getting ready to make the *ascent*...we *heard*...from the shadows...
                                                    (MAN AHEMS!)

I was startled, I must say. I *peered* into the darkness and *there* on a bench, sat a little, lame, *old* gentleman dressed in a black suit, *white* shirt and *red* cravat...his hair *parted* in the middle, rather old-fashioned, I'd say. He was in possession of a rather *large* black leather case, too, the kind *doctors* use. Before I could say a word...
                                                    (MAN AHEMS!)

I turned to Toby who looked just as *surprised* as I was. Do you know what he did *then?* He "*ahem-*ed" right back at the old man!
                                                    (TOBY AHEMS!)

At this, the little old gentleman seemed pleased...God only knows *why.* The old man stood and replied... "I am *quite* sure you will win it, Dammit, but we *are* obliged to have a *trial,* you know, for the sake of mere form.
                                                    (FOOTSTEPS ASCEND STAIRS)

"I will take *my* place up there on the second landing. And, you will go when I say 'one, two, three, and away.' Mind you, start at the word *'away.'* Ready now? One...two...three...*away!*"
                                                    MUSIC
                                                    (FOOTSTEPS RUN UP STAIRS)

My poor friend set off in a strong *stride* up the first flight of steps. All I was thinking was...what if he does *not* make the race upward in *less* than *fifteen* seconds? Yes, what if he does *not?* It's maddening. What *right* had the old gentleman to make *any* other gentleman *run* such a *demanding* race? *If* he had asked *me* to run it, *I* wouldn't do it, *that's* a fact, and I don't care *who* the devil he is!

MUSIC BUILDS

Then, for an instant, I realized what I had said to myself...those words...but, it only occupied my thoughts but for an instant. I was *more* concerned staring up into the stairwell *watching* Toby *nimbly* leap in *bounds* up those *dilapidated* steps. Just as he made a turn on the *second* floor landing heading for the *third* and final flight of stairs...he *disappeared* from my sight, but, I could *still* hear his footsteps and grunting and...was he *really* going to make it in *less* than fifteen seconds time?

(DISTANT SCREAM, THUMPS)
SILENCE

Alas, no...for, *apparently*, Toby had *missed* a stride and slipped, or, perhaps, a decayed wooden step had *splintered* beneath him...in any case, *down he came!* I still could not see him...so, I called out, *"Toby! Are you alright up there?"*

MUSIC

Now...at the same instant, the old gentleman came *limping* quickly *down* the stairs while carrying that big, black *satchel* of his...and he brushed *right* past me, almost *knocking* me off my feet. Then, he was gone out the front door.

I had no time to think, for Dammit *still* lay particularly *still* up there on the dark stairs. Perhaps, his *feelings* had been hurt. More likely, he needed my assistance.

(FOOTSTEPS ASCEND STAIRS)

I hurried upstairs to him where he had *fallen* back down the *third* flight of steps to the *second* floor landing where he lay *very* still. Upon *further* inspection, I found that he had received a *serious* injury...to put it mildly. The *truth* is, he had been *deprived* of his head, which after a *close* search I could not find anywhere. I *did*, however, find that there was a thin, *sharp* wire strung across the stairway just *six* feet from the third floor landing. About *neck* high. It appeared evident that the *neck* of my unfortunate *friend* had come *precisely* into contact with this *fiendish* device.

FUNEREAL MUSIC

So, here lies a *lesson* to all who wish to follow the same path as my friend, Toby Dammit. It is true, *regardless* of the *meaningless* life he led and *despite* my *constant* criticism which had gone unheeded, I could not *restrain* my emotions during his burial and I *bedewed* his grave with my tears. Also, I took it upon myself to design and display a *fake* coat of arms for the name of *Dammit,* to offer his *worthless* family, at least, an *air* of legitimacy. You *might* think that they would be *thankful* for this kind *and* generous gesture, but, think again. Not *only* did they *fail* to show up, *but,* when I sent to them my *very* moderate bill for the *general* expenses of his funeral...the scoundrels *refused* to pay it!

SILENCE

So, I had Mr. Dammit *dug* up at once, and *sold* him for dog's meat.

END

METZENGERSTEIN
By Edgar Allan Poe
Adapted By Dan Bianchi

CAST – 1m
SYNOPSIS – The Narrator tells the tale of two royal families feuding for centuries and how a mysterious horse enacts supernatural revenge.

MUSIC

NARRATOR
As you may know, the families of *Berlifitzing* and *Metzengerstein* had been at *odds* for centuries. Two *illustrious* houses *mutually* embittered by *deadly* hostility. How did this *endless* feud even begin? From an ancient prophecy...

(REVERB) "A lofty *name* shall have a fearful *fall* when, just as the rider *triumphs* over his horse, the *mortality* of *Metzengerstein* shall *triumph* over the *immortality* of Berlifitzing."

SILENCE

(NO REVERB)   So, what does *that* mean? Not much. But, wars between *nations* have begun over more *trivial* causes than this. In any case, since the Middle Ages, these two *European* families *somehow* managed to live side by side, yet, *hating* each other...and, though *each* generation took up *quarreling* over property and government, in truth, *underneath* each argument lay *hereditary* jealousy. You see, the *Berlifitzings* were *less* ancient and *less* wealthy than the *Metzengersteins*. The old *prophecy* seemed to *imply* that the *final* triumph will be awarded to the *more* powerful house, so, bitter *animosity* grew on the part of the *weaker* and *less* influential family.

MUSIC

At the time of *this* story, old *Count* Berlifitzing *hated* the rival family with a passion...yet, he *did* have two *greater* passions...his love of horses and of hunting.

(HUNTING HORN, DOGS BARKING)

Neither bodily *infirmity*, great age, nor mental *incapacity,* prevented his *daily* participation in the *dangers* of the chase.

SAD MUSIC

On the *other* hand, *Baron* Metzengerstein, was only *fifteen* and not yet of age. His father, the *Minister* Of War, died young. His *mother*, the Lady Mary, followed him quickly after. The young Baron *inherited* the royal family name, fortune and *all* the estates, among them, the largest and *most* splendid *Château* Metzengerstein.

(RAUCOUS PARTY, SCREAMS)

Well, rather than *accept* his *lofty* position in a *gentlemanly* manner, the *teenaged* Baron's *demonic* behavior suddenly became the talk of Europe. His *own* people *nicknamed* him *Little Caligula* as he carried out *shameful* debaucheries, *flagrant* treacheries and *unspeakable* atrocities against them, against servants *and* against his royal *enemies!*

(FIRE CRACKLING, MEN SHOUTING, HORSES WHINNYING)

One night…the stables of the castle *Berlifitzing* were discovered to be on fire. *Unanimous* opinion held that the *burning* of his rival's *beloved* horses was just one *more* crime added to the *already* hideous list of *Little Caligula's* offenses.

SILENCE

But, *during* the conflagration in which thirty-*seven* horses perished… the young nobleman sat, *meditating*, in a vast and *desolate* library in the family palace of *Metzengerstein*.

EERIE MUSIC

Around him, hung faded *tapestries* representing the *shadowy* and majestic forms of a *thousand* illustrious ancestors. Rich-*ermined* priests…*pontifical* dignitaries…autocrats… *sovereigns*…

(DISTANT BATTLE SOUNDS, HORSES)

…and those dark, *tall* figures of the Princes *Metzengerstein*…their muscular *war*-horses *plunging* over the *carcasses* of fallen foes! Nearby, *voluptuous* females of days gone by, floated *away* in an unreal dance to the *strains* of *dreamlike* melodies.

SILENCE

But, as the Baron sat there, *imagining* the *horrific* scene which had been taking place at that *very* moment in the stables of the old Count…

EERIE MUSIC

…his *gaze* became *riveted* to *one* tapestry where the figure of an *enormous*, and *unnaturally* colored *war*-horse…represented as belonging to an ancient *ancestor* of his rivals...stood *motionless* like a statue...while its distressed rider was *killed,* run through by the *sword* of a *Metzengerstein!*

The Baron smiled *fiendishly*. And, yet, he became a bit *unnerved*...as he could not *remove* his eyes from that horse. The *longer* he gazed, the more *absorbing* became the spell...and the more his *fascination* grew with that tapestry.

SILENCE

But...at *that* moment...his *stare* was broken by the violent *glare* of a reddish glow *illuminating* the black night on the horizon. He turned to the windows and could see...*off* in the distance...the *blazing* stables of the old Count *Berliftzing!*

EERIE MUSIC

Again, he *smiled* and returned his stare to the *tapestry* on the wall.

CHAOTIC MUSIC INTERRUPTS

But, now...*wait*...what was *this?* The *head* of the gigantic steed...it had *altered* its position! The *neck* of the animal, before arched, as if in *compassion*, over the *prostrate* body of its dying lord...was now *extended,* at full length, in the *direction* of the *Baron!* The beast's *eyes,* before *invisible*...they *now* wore an energetic and *human* expression ...*gleaming* with a *fiery* and unusual red... and the *distended* lips of the *enraged* horse revealed his *gigantic* and *revolting* teeth!

Stupefied with *terror,* the young nobleman *tottered* to the door. As he threw it open, a *flash* of red light, *streaming* far into the chamber, flung *his* shadow with a *clear* outline against the *quivering* tapestry. He *shuddered* to look at that shadow...his *own* shadow...it made him *stagger* in utter *horror* as he recognized its *outline!* Yes, he had just seen that figure in the tapestry! That *shadow* belonged to...the *relentless* and triumphant *murderer* of the fallen *Berlifitzing!*

SILENCE

The young Baron *rushed* away, *out* into the open air. He needed to gather his wits, to *clear* his mind.

(DISTANT MEN YELLING,
HORSE WHINNYING, SNORTING, BUCKING)

But, as he stood on the marble steps, he *noticed* that there was much *commotion* going on at the front gate...*three* of his men were trying to *restrain* a *gigantic* and *fiery*-colored *horse!* Yes, he became *instantly* aware that the mysterious *steed* in the tapestry was the very *counterpart* of this *furious* animal now before his eyes!

MUSIC

He was *told* that the horse was caught, *smoking* and *foaming* with rage. *Apparently*, it had fled from the burning *stables* of the Castle Berlifitzing. But, when the Baron's men *returned* the horse to the castle...the *grooms* there *disclaimed* any title to the creature. *That* was strange, since the horse bore evident *marks* of having made a narrow *escape* from the flames. His *skin* scorched, his mane and tail still *singed* and smoking. *And,* the letters *W. V. B.* were also branded very *distinctly* on his forehead. Surely, it could only refer to *Wilhelm Von* Berlifitzing, a rival back in the *12th* Century, *no?* But, the grooms at his rival's castle were *positive* they had never *seen* such a horse before.

SILENCE

Well, that didn't stop the young Baron from claiming *ownership* of this remarkable, *wild* beast. It was *his* foolish intention to *tame* it for himself.

EERIE MUSIC

Now, it wasn't but *thirty* minutes later when the Baron had returned to his library when he noticed...the sudden *disappearance* of a *small* portion of the tapestry...yes, the area in which the dying *rider* on horseback had been pictured. It was simply no longer there. Once again, the Baron became *unnerved* by this *new* revelation. He became *agitated*...pacing, *muttering,* cursing. He shouted *orders* that the library be *locked* and the solitary *key* given to him.

(DOOR LOCKED)
SILENCE

The *revelations* were not yet *over* for that evening. One of the servants *informed* the Baron of the sudden, *unhappy* death of the old *Count* Berlifitzing. It seemed he, *too,* had *perished* in the flames while trying to *save* his *cherished* horses.

MUSIC

As soon as he had learned of this...the young Baron smiled *wickedly*...
(MEN SHOUT, HORSE WHINNYING, BUCKING)

But, just then, a *further* commotion erupted outside and he *ran* to a terrace overlooking the courtyard, where, below, the huge steed *whinnied* and bucked and *plunged* and kicked, with *intensified* fury! The

Baron's stable hands could not get *near,* much less, *control* the ferocious horse.

SILENCE

From *that* night on...a great *change* came over the *personality* of the young *Baron* Von Metzengerstein.

MUSIC

His life of *debauchery* ended abruptly. No longer could the *gossip* mongers rely on *him* for new scandals. In fact, *he* was rarely to be seen *beyond* the limits of his own domain...and, if he *should* travel into the rest of the world...he was *utterly* companionless...

(HORSE GALLOPING)

Except for that unnatural, *impetuous*, and *fiery*-colored horse...which he *continually* rode.

Numerous *invitations* to balls and festivals, as well as, requests to join *royal* hunts for wild *boar* were sent to him...but, *all* were turned down. Other *noble* families regarded these *refusals* as insults. In time, the requests became *less* frequent and *then* ceased altogether. It was no secret...all of *Europe* knew that the *Baron* preferred the *companionship* of a *horse* to his *fellow* human beings.

(HORSE WHINNIES, SNORTS, GALLOPS)

Indeed, the *Baron* was certainly *attached* to his new charger. Why, some would *swear* that every time the demon horse *burst* into a frenzy, its youthful *owner* seemed to attain *new* strength. Not only that, the Baron's *stable* hands claimed they had seen the creature *leap,* incredibly, *three* times the distance *any* horse could jump. Soon, there was talk that the horse possessed *supernatural* capabilities.

EERIE MUSIC

Truly, it was a *bizarre* and *unnatural* relationship, to say the least. In the *glare* of noon...at the *dead* hour of night...in *sickness* or in health...in *calm* or in tempest...the young *Metzengerstein* seemed *fastened* to the saddle of that *colossal* horse...whose *stubbornness* and *audacious* nature so well suited his *own* spirit. And, *yet,* the Baron had *no* particular *name* for the animal. The horse had its *own* stable which was kept at a distance from the rest. *No* one but the *Baron* could enter the creature's stall. No one but *he* groomed and *fed* the *mysterious* stallion.

SILENCE

There was also one *more* perplexing *fact* added to the *mystery* of this creature. We *know* that *three* grooms had *caught* the steed on the *first* night...thinking it had *fled* from the *fire* at the *Berliftzing* stables. They used a *chain*-bridle and *noose* to capture it. And, yet, not *one* of the three could with any *certainty* affirm that he had, *during* that dangerous struggle, or at *any* period, thereafter, actually placed his *hand* upon the *body* of the beast. No one but its owner had actually *touched* the horse. The strange horse whose *origin* was *still* unknown to all.

MUSIC

Now, as we know, there are noble and *high*-spirited thoroughbreds with a *peculiar* intelligence that draw *special* attention from men *well*-acquainted with horse breeding. They gather around such a horse and *shower* it with *marvelous* praise, pointing at it, as if it were a *four*-footed god.

SILENCE

But, *this* horse, the young *Baron's* horse, was *beyond* such praise. The admiring crowds *it* drew stood, *silently*, with mouths *gaping* in awe.

EERIE MUSIC

At such times, the animal might cause its *admirers* to *recoil* in horror from the deep and *impressive* meaning of its *terrible* gaze...yes, those eyes...staring *back* at them. *Terrifying* eyes. Why, there were even times when the young Baron *Metzengerstein* turned *pale* and *shrunk* away from the those *human*-looking eyes.

SILENCE

However, *no* one could doubt the *extraordinary* affection which existed on the part of the young nobleman for the *fiery* qualities of his horse... although...stable hands *did* notice that their master *never* vaulted into the saddle without an *unaccountable* and *almost* imperceptible *shudder*. And, upon his *return* from every long ride, he bore an *expression* of triumphant *hatred*...that's what *they* called it...and it *distorted* every muscle in his face.

(THUNDER, RUNNING FOOTSTEPS, GALLOPING HORSE)

One *tempestuous* night, Metzengerstein, *awaking* from a heavy slumber, descended like a *maniac* from his chamber...ran to the stable, mounted his horse and galloped away into the forest! Hours went by and his staff became worried as the weather worsened...

(LOUD THUNDER CLAP, FIRE
CRACKLING, FRIGHTENED VOICES)

MUSIC

When, suddenly, a great *explosion* from the night sky *rocked* the Chateau *Metzengerstein,* to its very *foundation*...and *ignited* a terrible, *uncontrollable* fire! All efforts to *save* any portion of the building were *evidently* futile...as the astonished *watchers* stood *idly* about in *silent* and pathetic wonder. At least, human life had been spared.

But, now, a *new* and fearful object soon *riveted* their attention...for up the *long* avenue of aged *oak* trees which led from the *forest* to the main entrance of the *Château* Metzengerstein...
                    (GALLOPING HORSE APPROACHING)
                                        MUSIC BUILDS

...a *steed,* bearing a rider dressed only in *bed* clothes...was seen *leaping* with *such* recklessness ...which *exceeded* the very *Demon of the Tempest!*
                    (DISTANT MAN SCREAMING,
        THUNDER, WINDS, HORSE GALLOPING, WHINNYING)

It was *obvious* to all that the rider had *no* control of the horse. The man's face *contorted* in *agonizing* screams...while convulsively *struggling* to hold on for dear life! The great hooves *clattered* and *resounded* above the *roaring* of the flames and the *shrieking* of the winds! Look, there... with a *single* surge, see how it *cleared* the gate-way...and, again, the *moat*...until, the steed *bounds* far up the *tottering* staircases of the palace...with its now *limp* rider...*disappearing* amidst the *whirlwind* of chaotic *fire!*
                                        SILENCE

The *fury* of the flaming tempest *immediately* died away... and a dead *calm* followed.
                                        EERIE MUSIC

A white flame *still* enveloped the building like a *shroud,* ...and, streaming far *away* into the quiet atmosphere, *shot* forth a *glare* of *otherworldly* light...while a cloud of smoke *settled* heavily over the charred *remains* of the Chateau *Metzengerstein*...a cloud of smoke...in the distinct *colossal* figure of...a *horse.*
                                        END

THE BUSINESS MAN
By Edgar Allan Poe
Adapted By Dan Bianchi

CAST – 1m
SYNOPSIS – Our ridiculous Narrator acting as a sort of motivational speaker addresses his audience.

(DARKNESS)

NARRATOR
There is an old saying… "*Method* is the *soul* of business."
MUSIC
(LIGHTS UP)

Good evening, ladies and gentlemen…my name is Peter *Profit!*
(APPLAUSE)

That's right, Peter *Profit.* I know that *some* of you may be asking…just who in the *Hell* is this Peter *Profit?*
(LAUGHTER)

Well, I'll tell you. He's an *authentic,* original, *dyed*-in-the-wool *business* man. And, to say the least, he is a *methodical* man.
(APPLAUSE, CHEERS)
SILENCE

"*Method* is the *soul* of business." Yessir, words of wisdom. The *method* is the thing, after all. I'm sure you all agree. But, y'know, there are *some* people who think *differently?*
(CROWD MUTTERS)

I *hate* to even *admit* they exist, but, they do. You know the kind…the *eccentric* fool who prattles *on* about *method*, but, he doesn't understand one *iota* of it?
(CROWD MUTTERS)

Am I *right*, sir? *You* know…the kind who follows rules *strictly* to the letter, *by* the book, *follows* the rules…and, *meanwhile*, he *violates* its very *spirit?*
(CROWD ERUPTS)
SILENCE

This fellow is *always* doing the most *preposterous* things in what *he* calls an *orderly* manner. Now, personally, *I* see *that* as a *contradiction,* no? *True* method pertains to the *ordinary* and the *obvious*…the *boring* and mundane. Let's keep it that way. It *cannot* be applied to the *shocking,* the *strange* and unusual.

(CROWD AGREES)

Did *you, sir,* ever hear of a *methodical* jackass?   Or, did *you, madame,* ever hear of a systematical *idiot?*

(LAUGHTER)

No, of course not. I didn't think so. Now, you may ask, "Mr. Profit, how is it *you* have turned out the way you are?" Well, to put it simply, *I* might *not* have turned out the way I am, *but* for a fortunate *accident* which happened to me when I was a *very* little boy.

SAD IRISH TUNE

A good-hearted old *Irish* nurse…whom I shall *not* forget in my will…held me *upside* down one day by my *ankles* when I was making *more* noise than was necessary…and then she *swung* me around *twice* and *knocked* my little head against the bedpost. *Thus*, my *fate* was decided and *I* made my fortune.

SILENCE

"How was *that?"* you inquire. You see, if you know your *phrenology* …right *here* on the *sinciput*…on my *forehead* here…is where a *bump* arose… and, *if* you know your *phrenology*…*that* area there *determines* system *and* regularity in one's life. *I* didn't make that up…I *read* about it in a book, so, you *know* it must be correct. Anyway, it is that *positive* appetite for *system* and *regularity* which has made *me* the *distinguished* man of business who stands here before you today.

(APPLAUSE)

Thank you, thank you. Now…let us move on. If I may, I would just like to *add* that…if there is *anything* on *Earth* I hate, it is a *genius.* Am I right?

(APPLAUSE)

You're damned *right*, I'm right! It warms my *heart* to see *this* many people agree with me. Thank you. Well, as you know, *geniuses* are all *arrogant* asses…and there is *more* than enough *scientific* data which proves *undeniably* that the *greater* the genius, the *greater* the ass…and to this rule there is *no* exception whatsoever. I see you nodding, sir.

You *know* what I am talking about! And, as we *both* know, there is *no* exception...especially, when you try to make a man of *business* out of a *genius*...it can't be done...any more than making *money* out of a Jew...or *nutmeg* out of a pine cone. *Geniuses! Ha!* The creatures are *always* digressing...*deviating* into some *fantastic* vocation, or *ridiculous* speculation, *entirely* at *variance* with the *fitness* of things, or, shall I say...the way things are *supposed* to work? These *asses* have *no* business to even be *considered* as a *business* at all. I *hope* there isn't anyone here *tonight* who *may* be one these asses. How about...let's see...how about *you?* No? *You* aren't one of those asses? *No,* I didn't think so.

Alright, you may ask, "*Well,* Mr. Profit...how do we *know* who may be an *ass?"* Very simply, *you* may tell these characters *immediately* by the *nature* of their occupations. If you ever perceive a man setting up as a *merchant* or a *manufacturer,* or, going into the *cotton* or tobacco trade, or *any* of those *eccentric* pursuits...or, becoming a *dry* goods dealer, or *soap*-boiler, or something of *that* kind... or, *pretending* to be a lawyer, or a *blacksmith,* or even a *physician*...anything *out* of the *usual* way... you may *peg* him at *once* as a *genius,* and then you *must* agree, *according* to the *scientific* data...*ipso* facto, *he* is an *ass.*

(APPLAUSE)

Now, *I* am proud to say that *I* am *not* in *any* respect a genius...but I *am* a regular business man. Here, you *see?* I have a day-book *and* a ledger which should *prove* what I claim to be. They are *well* kept, though *I* fill it in myself...and, as for my *general* habits of *accuracy* and *punctuality,* let's just say...I am not *always* a *slave* to a time-clock. Moreover, *my* occupations have *always* been made to go with the *flow* of the *ordinary* habits of my *fellow* ordinary men...*and* women...such as yourselves.

I want you to know, that, regarding my *current* viewpoints, I don't feel the *least indebted* to my *exceedingly* weak-minded parents...who, beyond any *doubt,* would have made an arrogant *genius* of me...

SAD IRISH MUSIC

...*if* my guardian *angel* had not come, in *good* time, to the rescue. You know of whom I mean...that's right, that *good*-hearted old Irish *nurse* of mine. I owe *everything* to that *smack* in the head she had administered to me.

In biography, the *truth* is everything, and in *autobiography* it is especially so... yet, I *scarcely* hope to be *believed* when I state, *however* solemnly, that my poor *father* put me...this was when I was about *fifteen* years of age...it's *hard* for me to reveal this, but...*he* put me into the *accounting* office of what *he* called...a *respectable* and *successful* hardware business.

(CROWD MUTTERS IN SHOCK)

Yes! Can you *imagine*? *Successful?* *Ha!* Don't make me *laugh!* However, the *consequence* of this *folly* was, that, *two* days later, I had to be sent *home* to my family of *numb-skulls* because I was running a *high* fever. And, on *top* of that, I had a most *violent* and *dangerous* pain in the *sinciput*...remember your *phrenology*? That's right here...the upper portion of my cranium...it regulates system *and* order? Oh, I was nearly a *goner*...touch-and-go for *six* weeks! Why, the *physicians* even gave up on me. It was *highly* traumatic for a boy my age. But, although I *suffered* much, I was a *thankful* boy for the most part. You see, I was *saved* from working in a *respectable* and *successful* hardware business.

(APPLAUSE)
SAD IRISH MUSIC

Oh yes, I felt grateful to the *lump* on my skull which had been the *means* of my salvation...as well as to the *kindhearted* female who had *originally* put these means within my reach.

SILENCE

Now, most boys run away from home at ten or twelve years of age, but *I* waited till I was *sixteen*. I might *not* have left even *then*, if I had *not* happened to hear my *mother* talk about *setting* me up in my *own* grocery store. A *grocery* store? Can you *imagine*?

{LAUGHTER)

Well, *that* did it. I *had* to leave. *I* had to *establish* myself in a *decent* occupation. I couldn't stick around *there* with *eccentric* old people who wanted the *best* for me. The *best?* And, *then* what? The *next* thing *I* knew I'd be running the risk of becoming a *genius* in the end.

(LAUGHTER)

"So, *Mr.* Profit, what did you do?" Well, I'm glad you asked. I *must* say, I succeeded *perfectly* well my *first* time out...and by the time I was fairly *eighteen*, I found myself doing an *extensive* and *profitable* business in the Suit Maker's *Walking*-Advertisement line.

"How did *that* work out, Mr. Profit?" I am *happy* to say, quite well. In fact, I *surprised* myself...in that I was able to *handle* the *difficult* duties of this profession. And, I did that *only* by sticking to *that* system which led me to follow a *scrupulous* method...which characterized my *actions* as well as my *accounts*. But, to be fair, in *my* case it was *method...not* money...which *made* the man... at least, *that* part of him that was *not* made by the *suit-maker* who was my boss.

At nine, *every* morning, I received my *clothes* for the day. Ten o'clock found me in some *fashionable* promenade or other place of public amusement. The precise *regularity* with which I turned my *handsome* person about...so as to *bring* into view *every* portion of the suit upon my back... was the *admiration* of *all* the *professionals* in the trade. Noon never passed without *me* bringing home a *customer* to the house of my employers, Mister *Cutt* and Mr. *Comeagain.* I say this *proudly*, but with *tears* in my eyes...for the firm proved themselves to be the *lowest* of the low. While it *is* true they cheated *and* overcharged customers, I cannot *truly* fault them because that *is* the nature of their business. In fact, as an employee, *I,* too, was *cheated* out of *weeks* of wages...to the point that *I* owed *them* for *my* work hours.

Naturally, we *quarreled* about that little disagreement...but, as we all know, *business* is business, and *should* be done in a businesslike manner. There was no *system* whatsoever in their swindling *me* out of a few pennies. If one is to enact a *clear* fraud, there *must* be a method to it, no? But, *I* learned my lesson. I left at once their employment and formed the *Eye-Sore* Company all by myself...one of the most *lucrative,* respectable *and* independent of the *ordinary* occupations.

My strict *integrity*, economy *and* rigorous business habits, here again came into play. Well, the company took off like a *bat* out of...you know *where!* I found myself driving a *flourishing* trade! In no time, I'd become a *believer* in *Change.* I had *found* my calling...a calling in which I might *still* be doing to this day if *not* for a little *accident* which happened to me during one of the *usual* business operations of this profession.

"What *happened,* Mr. Profit?" Well...as *every* intelligent person knows, whenever a rich, old man or young *heir,* or *bankrupt* corporation gets a *notion* of putting up a *skyscraper* with their name on it...there is *no* way to stop them. And, *that* notion is the *basis* of the *Eye-Sore* trade.

"How did the Eye-Sore Company *work,* Mr. Profit?" I am glad you asked. You see, as *soon* as one of these *building* projects is underway...*my* company would secure a *prime* little lot just adjoining *their* property. This done, we wait until their *monument* to themselves is *half*-way erected...and *then* we pay some *third*-rate architect to design for us an *over*-ornamented *mud* hovel right against it...in other words, *a pig-sty.* Of course, if asked to *remove* such a structure...this *eye-sore* which might *damage* the integrity and lessen the *value* of the monumental skyscraper...well, *that* can't be done without a *bonus* of *five* hundred per cent upon the *prime* cost of *our* lot and building materials.

I ask you, can it be *done?* I put this to the *business* men here tonight. Would it be *rational* to *suppose* that we can *remove* our eye-sore just because someone *asked* us to *do* such a *thing?* For *no* financial *recompense?* Solely, for the sake of social *integrity?* For the sake of...*art* and *architecture?*

(AUDIENCE MUTTERS)

And, *yet,* can you *imagine* ...there *was* one corporation which actually *asked* me to do this very thing...this *very* thing! I did not *reply* to their *absurd* proposition, of course...and they *did* threaten to take me to court. But, I could *not* forsake the general *principle* of the matter and, so, I felt it my *duty* that on the very night I received an injunction...I took black *paint* and covered the *front* of their building with it and...well, as you *may* have read in the papers...these *unreasonable* villains *clapped* me into jail. By the time I was released...The *Eye-Sore* Company was no more.

(AUDIENCE SYMPATHIZES)

But, as a *businessman* through and through...I *learned* from my mistakes. Next, I was *forced* to adventure into a *new* livelihood...The *Assault-and-Battery* business! I admit, it was somewhat *ill*-adapted to the *delicate* nature of my constitution...but, I went to work on it with a good heart...and a spirit full of *gusto!*

SAD IRISH MUSIC

And, I found my *vocation* once *again* alive *and* well in those *stern* habits of methodical *accuracy* which had been *thumped* into me by that *delightful* old Irish nurse of mine...I would indeed be the *basest* of men *not* to remember her well in my will.

SILENCE

By observing, as I say, the *strictest* system in *all* my dealings, and keeping a *well*-regulated set of books, I was enabled to get over *many* *serious* difficulties, and, in the end, to *establish* myself very *decently* in this new profession. The truth is, that...*few* individuals, in *any* line, did a better little business than I.

"And, how did *this* business operate, Mr. Profit" you ask. Well, allow me to just read to you a *page* or so out of my Day-Book...and this will save me the *necessity* of blowing my *own* trumpet...a *contemptible* practice of which no *high*-minded man would consider doing. However, the *Day-Book* is a thing that doesn't lie.

(Reads) "January *1st*...New Year's Day. Met a drunken *stockbroker* named Jones in the street. He will do. Met *another* drunk, Gruff, a wealthy merchant. He will do, too. Entered *both* gentlemen in my Ledger, and opened a *running* account with each.

"Jan. 2nd...Saw Jones at the *Stock* Exchange, and went up and *stepped* on his foot. He *doubled* his fist and *knocked* me down. *Good!* I got up again. I *contacted* my attorney to *sue* for a thousand...but, *he* says a simple knock down *can't* collect more than *five* hundred. Reminder...get *rid* of attorney...*he* has no method or system at all.

"January 3rd...Went to the theatre, to look for Gruff. Saw him *sitting* in a side box, in the second tier, next to a *fat* lady. I observed them closely through an opera-glass, till I saw the fat lady *blush* and whisper to Gruff. Went round, then, *into* the box, and sat *right* next to him and *winked* at the fat lady. I had the *high* satisfaction of finding him *lift* me up by the nape of the neck, and *fling* me over into the pit. *Neck* dislocated, and right leg *capitally* splintered. Went home in *high* glee, drank a bottle of champagne. My *new* attorney says we shall sue for *five* thousand.

"February 15th...*Compromised* in the case of Mr. Jones. Amount entered in journal...fifty *cents.*

"Feb. 16th ... That ruffian, Mr. *Gruff* made me a present of *five* dollars. Cost of new suit, four dollars and twenty-five cents. Net profit... seventy-five cents."

Now, as you businessmen here tonight will admire...*here* is a *clear* gain, in a very *brief* period, of *no* less than *one* dollar and twenty-five cents! And, I solemnly *assure* you, these were just *two* examples which were taken at random from my Day-Book.

(APPLAUSE)

It's an old saying, and a *true* one, however, that *money* is *nothing* in *comparison* with health. Am I right? I found the *physical* work of my profession somewhat *too* much for *my* delicate state of body...if you *know* what I mean? As you *might* imagine, I was knocked *all* out of shape. So, what was I to *make* of that? Banged up and bruised so much that when my *friends* met me in the street, they couldn't tell that I was *Peter Profit* at all!

(LAUGHTER)

True! So, it occurred to me that it would be *best* if I could, in *some* way, *alter* my line of business. I turned my attention, therefore, to *Mud-Dabbling,* and continued it for some years.

"What in the *world* is Mud-Dabbling, Mr. Profit?" Well, as I was to find out…the *worst* of this occupation is, that *too* many people take a fancy to it, and the *competition* is stiff. Every *ignoramus*, every *idiot,* every *jackass* who hasn't *brains* enough to make his way as a walking advertiser…or an *eye-sore* proprietor…or a *salt-and-batter* man, that's the street lingo for *assault and battery*, folks… thinks, of course, that *he'll* do very *well* as a dabbler of mud. But, believe me when I tell you…I *never* lie…that he can *never* be *more* wrong if *he* thinks he needs *no* brains to mud-dabble. I see you nodding, sir…evidently *you* know where I am *going* with this, am I right?

Believe me, there was *nothing* to be made in this new business *without* method. I did only a *retail* business myself, but my old habits of *system* carried me *swimmingly* along.

"How does this *mud-dabbling* work, Mr. Profit?" Well…first, I *select* my location, you see? That, alone, takes *great* deliberation. Preferably, where two main streets intersect. Then, I take care to have a *nice* little puddle at hand, which I could get at in a second. By these means I got to be *well* known as a man to be trusted… and *this* is one-*half* the battle, let me tell you, in *this* line of work. Now, if someone *needs* to get *over* that puddle…without *ruining* their new pantaloons or trousers…well, it will cost them a *nickel*, maybe *more* if he is wearing a new, *clean* pair of boots. I never met *anyone* who refused. If I *had* met with refusal, *I* wouldn't have put up with it. Never imposing upon *any* one myself, I didn't *need* to hire anyone for such work…*I* did it all myself. Now, the *best* places to do such work were often out *front* of banks. But, the banks, you see, well…they look *down* upon *entrepreneurial* enterprises such as *mud*-dabbling. They must have worked *overtime* to convince the police to shut me down.

"Could you not *retaliate*, Mr. Profit?" Believe me, I *would* if I could. If it were a *person* involved, I'd have given him a good *knocking* about. But, *banks,* as you know, are *not* individuals, but corporations…and *corporations,* it is very well known, have neither *bodies* to be kicked nor *souls* to be damned.

Never one to *quit* my vocation as a businessman...I was therefore *induced* to adapt that line of work into *Dog*-Spattering...a somewhat *similar* profession as *Mud*-dabbling, if *not* as respectable. My location, to be sure, was an *excellent* one, being mid-town... and I had a *good* stock of *black* soot. My little dog, *too,* was quite *fat* which is *certainly* beneficial. *Pompey* was his name. He had been in the trade a *long* time, and, I may say, *well* understood it.

Our general routine was this...Pompey, having *rolled* himself well in the gray mud, would *sit* in a doorway...until he would observe a *dandy* approaching in *bright* boots. He would then *proceed* to greet him... and give the boots a *rub* or two with his *filthy* body. Then the dandy would *swear* very much, and look about for a *shoeshine* man. There I would be, *full* in his view, with *black* polish and brushes. It was only a minute's work, and then came a *nickel* or two. This did *moderately* well for a time...in fact, *I* was not greedy, but my *dog* was. I allowed him a *third* of the profit, but *he* was *advised* to *insist* upon half. This I couldn't stand...so we *quarreled* and parted.

(CROWD SYMPATHIZES)

Tut-tut! You see before you a *businessman* who does *not* quit when *faced* with such *dire* circumstances. I next tried my hand at the *Organ-Grinding* profession for a while, and may say that I made out *pretty* well. It is a plain*, straightforward* business, and requires *no* particular abilities. You can get a street organ for a mere song. This done, you have only to *stroll* along, with the organ on your back, until you see a group of sightseers...*tourists.* Then you stop and grind. They will gladly offer coins so that they may *think* they are participating in some quaint *ritual* which they can tell their friends all about back home.

"But, what if there are no *tourists* that day, Mr. Profit?" Good question. One can *never* depend on *foreigners*, am I right? So...to *assure* yourself of a profit...one should take a *hammer* to the inside workings of the organ. And, *then,* when one *grinds* away at it...in the *proper* neighborhood...a window opens, and somebody *pitches* you a coin or two to "Hush up and go away," or words and phrases of a *similar* meaning. I am *aware* that *some* grinders have actually continued to *play* on as the offerings *continued* from neighbors *forced* to listen to the *cacophony* produced by the broken organ. *Some* of those grinders left with broken noses, as well. *I,* for one, was *not* such a grinder. A dollar was quite *enough* to make me leave.

I made a *killing* at this occupation, but, *alas,* somehow, I was not *quite* satisfied, and so finally abandoned it. The truth is, I labored under the *disadvantage* of having no monkey.

(LAUGHTER)

Well, good people, I was now out of employment for some months...

(CROWD SYMPATHIZES)

Have no fear, after some time I *succeeded* in procuring a situation in the *Sham*-Postal Service. Ah, sir, am I to believe *you* are well *acquainted* with this profession? Very good. Well, then you *must* know that the duties, here, are simple, and not altogether *unprofitable.* For example...very early in the morning I had to make up my packet of *fake* letters. Upon the *inside* of each of these I had to scrawl a few lines on *any* subject which occurred to me as *sufficiently* mysterious...*signing* all the letters with *elaborate* but fake signatures...my *penmanship* being impeccable. Having folded and *sealed* all, and *stamped* them with bogus postmarks...New Orleans, *Bengal,* Botany Bay, or any other place a *great* way off...I set out, forthwith, upon my daily route, as if in a very great hurry. I *always* called at the big houses to deliver the letters, and receive the postage due.

"Do people actually *pay* this fee, Mr. *Profit?"* All I can say to that is...*indeed* they *do!* People are such *fools* when they receive something *unexpectedly,* am I right? *Nobody* hesitates at *paying* for a letter...and especially for a *package* that may contain *unknown* wonders from Mr. *Dobson* or Mr. *Tompkins.* Yes, those were the two *false* names I invented as the *mysterious* senders.

Now, while it was *no* trouble for the *bearer* of such *unexpectedness* ...*me*... to run round a corner *before* the *receiver* had time to open their worthless parcel, there *was* a *downside* to this profession. You see, I had to *walk* so much and *so* fast and so *frequently,* I could hardly breathe by the end of the day. I was *forced* to do so in order to *vary* my route. It stands to reason, that, in *this* profession, one *cannot* use the *same* route every day.

Besides, *I* had *serious* scruples of conscience. Yes, hard to believe, but, it's true. I couldn't *bear* to hear *innocent* individuals abused. Unbeknownst to *me,* at the time, it turned out that there really *was* a *Mr.* Dobson and a *Mr.* Tompkins and the way the whole town took to *cursing* them was really *awful* to hear. In any case, *I* washed my hands of the matter in *disgust.*

Before I leave the podium, I would like to tell you about my last speculative, yet, *highly* lucrative business...*Cat-Growing.* It is well known...the city, *nay,* the whole *country,* has become *infested* with cats...so much so of late, that a *petition* for *relief* was brought before the Legislature. The Assembly was *unusually* well-informed, and, having passed many other *wise* and wholesome laws, it has now signed, *unanimously,* the *Cat-Act.* In its *original* form, this law offered a *premium* for cat-*heads*...ten cents a head.   But, the *Senate* succeeded in *amending* the main clause...so as to substitute the word *"tails"* for *"heads."* This amendment was so *obviously* proper, that, for the first time in a long time, the *House* concurred with the Senate and *passed* the new amendment. *Tails it is!*

As soon as the *governor* had signed the bill, *I* invested my *whole* estate in the purchase of Tom cats, Tabby cats *and* all *kinds* of alley cats. At first I could only afford to *feed* them mice...which *are* cheap enough... but, the cats *multiplied* at such a *marvelous* rate...that, once *again,* my sympathetic *nature* won the day and I *indulge* them in oysters and turtle. Their *tails,* at a legislative price, now bring me in a good income... for I have discovered a way to *run* my business *year* round. It *delights* me to find, too, that the animals *soon* get accustomed to the thing, and would rather have their appendages cut off than otherwise. I consider *myself,* therefore, a self-made man, and I am *now* bargaining for a seat in the State Assembly *or* Senate... *either* will suffice for a man who is well equipped for politics. I hope that *all* of you here tonight feel much the same way and I pray that you vote for me in November! Thank you and good night!

ELECTION MUSIC
(CHEERS, APPLAUSE)
END

A DESCENT INTO THE MAELSTRÖM.
By Edgar Allan Poe
Adapted By Dan Bianchi

CAST – 3m
SYNOPSIS – A sailor tells how he and his sea-faring brothers faced a terrible whirlpool in the ocean.

MUSIC

NARRATOR
Three years ago it was…I'll never forget it. Had it *ever* happened to mortal man? None, cepting me, the *only* one I know who *ever* survived to tell of it. *Six* hours it was, I endured *six* hours of deadly terror. It's broken me up body *and* soul, I tell ya. I know, *to you,* I am an old man. But, I profess to you…I am *not.* You see these white *hairs?* It took less than a *single* day to change *these* hairs from *jet* black to white…a day to *weaken* my limbs and to *unstring* my nerves…so that I tremble *now* with every move I make. What's *worse,* every *shadow* frightens me.
(SEA BIRDS, WAVES ON SHORE)

Look out *there*…what do you see as *far* as the eye can roam? The *sea,* yes. *Blue* as ink. Looks calm, no? But, look *below* now…to the waters *crashing* on the rocks down there *below* the cliff. To the *surf* reared high up *beating* itself into foam on the black boulders…over and over, *howling* and *shrieking* forever. Now, look out there…you see that little *dot* sitting there about *six* miles out? That there is an island. Nothing much to it…*hideously* craggy and barren…just *full* of dark rocks. It's called *Moskoe* Island. I don't even know *why* anyone bothered to *name* it, but, *that's* what it is called…*Moskoe* Island.
(ROARING WAVES)

Listen now…sounds like the *moaning* of a vast herd of *buffalo* upon the prairie, don't it? It's those *waves* down there, *chopping* away at the cliff. Convulsing and heaving, *boiling* and hissing…*swirling* and *plunging* into a *murderous* brew. Look *Northeast* there…a *whirlpool*…and *there,* another! Must be a *dozen* of em. But, there is only *one* called the great whirlpool of *Maelstrom*…which lies out *there* near *Moskoe* Island.

I'd guess the depth of the water there is between thirty-six and *forty* fathoms…*impossible* for a vessel to pass near it without the risk of *splitting* on the rocks, which happens even in the *calmest* weather. The ship hasn't a *chance* once it finds itself within the *vortex...swallowed* up and carried *down* to the bottom, and there *beaten* to pieces against the ocean floor! A little while later, its *fragments* are *thrown* up again.

Fishing boats, *pleasure* yachts and *cargo* ships have *disappeared* into that whirlpool...they get *too* close and it's *too* late to escape its reach. Why I've even seen *sperm whales* pulled down by it...hard to describe their *howlings* and *bellowings* in their fruitless struggles to *disengage* themselves.

Once, the largest ship in existence, the *Regalia...it* came too close, too close. It *tried* to pull away, but it wasn't strong enough...like a feather in a hurricane, round and *round* it went...and within *minutes* disappeared into the brine.

SILENCE
(SEA BIRDS, WAVES ON SHORE)

My two brothers and me, we once owned a 70 ton schooner, fully rigged...used to sail it out *that* way because *there* was good fishing. Out of *all* the fisherman on this coast, we *three* made a regular business of going out to *fish* near *Moskoe* Island.   The fish out there can be got at *all* hours, *if* you know where to look.   The choice spots, ya see, are over among the rocks. *That's* where you'll get the finest variety and *plenty* of em.   Why, we often got in a *single* day, what others could not scrape together in a week. Made good money, too.

But, *we* knew the tides, ya see...giving us about *fifteen* minutes time to push *across* the main channel...far *above* the whirlpool and then drop *anchor* on the *far* side of Moskoe Island. The *eddies* are not so violent over there. After filling our nets we'd do the *same* coming back, *timing* ourselves by the tide. We *seldom* made a miscalculation.

Twice, during *six* years, we couldn't get back to port because of that *damned* Maelstrom. We were *forced* to stay all night at *anchor* on account of a *dead* calm, which is a rare thing. *Once* we had to *remain* out there nearly a *week, starving* to death. A gale blew in and made the channel *too* boisterous for us to even *think* of crossing it.

MUSIC

But, the *unforgettable* day I am now telling you about was the *tenth* day of July, *1888.* All that morning into *late* afternoon, there was a gentle and *steady* breeze from the south-west. The *sun* was shining brightly. I'm telling ya, Why, the oldest *seaman* among us could not have *foreseen* what was about to happen.

The *three* of us...my two brothers, *Tom* and Ansel, *and* myself...had crossed *over* to the islands about *two* o'clock P M., and had soon nearly loaded our catch with fine fish...

                                    SILENCE
                        (WAVES AGAINST SAILING VESSEL)

TOM
I'm thinking we've got enough *fish* out here to fill *three* more ships!

ANSEL
It's the biggest catch *we've* ever made, I'm sure of it.

TOM
Well, it's just about seven...we'd better weigh and start for home.

NARRATOR
(REVERB)   "We set out with a *fresh* wind on our starboard quarter...never *dreaming* of danger. There wasn't the *slightest* reason for apprehension. All at once..."

TOM
Do you *feel* that breeze? Look at the sails...

ANSEL
It's coming *down* from the North. That's never happened before.

TOM
I don't like the looks of this. Making me feel ...

ANSEL
Why don't we return to where we were *anchored* all day and wait it out?

TOM
Oh, Jesus! Will ya look at *that!* Look *astern!* Out *there* on the horizon...
                                    MUSIC

NARRATOR
(REVERB) "And, there we saw the *whole* horizon *covered* with a singular *copper*-colored cloud that *rose* with the most *amazing* velocity."

ANSEL
The breeze has headed off...the sea is dead calm...we're drifting in
every direction.

(THUNDER)

TOM
No matter with that...*here it comes!*

NARRATOR
(REVERB) "We did not have *long* enough to think about *anything*. In
less than a *minute* the storm was upon us!
(RAIN, WIND, WAVES, THUNDER)
CHAOTIC MUSIC BUILDS

"The sky became suddenly *so* dark that we could not see each other on
deck! Such a hurricane, well, it's *folly* for me to describe it. I'd *wager*
that the *oldest* seaman alive *never* experienced anything like it."
(THUNDER, WOOD CRACKING, CRASHING)

TOM
Watch out, Ansel! The main mast is giving way!

ANSEL
Aaaaahhhhhhhh!

NARRATOR
(REVERB) "After that, the *other* mast went as well...*both* of em looked
as if they'd been *sawed* off! It *took* my youngest brother with it! He had
lashed himself to it for safety.
(STORM, WINDS, THUNDER CONTINUES)

"The ship was *completely* underwater at one time. Rolled over, *upside*
down, tossed back and forth as if it was *light* as a feather. How my *elder*
brother escaped destruction I *cannot* say...for I never had an
opportunity of asking him. I *threw* myself flat on deck, with my feet
against the narrow gunwale of the bow... and with my hands grasping
a *ring*-bolt near the *foot* of the fore-mast. It was mere instinct that
prompted me to do this...which was undoubtedly the very best thing I
could have done. I know I had no time to think about it.

"As I've said, at one point, we were c*ompletely* deluged and I held my
breath, and *clung* to the bolt. When I can stand it no longer I *raise* myself
upon my knees, still keeping *hold* with my hands, and thus get my head

clear. Presently our little boat *gives* herself a shake, just as a dog does in coming out of the water. That's what it's like. Like *ridding* itself from the ocean.

"Just as I am now *trying* to clear my head…and *collect* my senses…I feel somebody *grasping* my arm. It's my elder brother, and my heart *leaps* for joy, for I thought for sure he had gone *overboard!* But, the *next* moment all this joy is turned into *horror*…for he puts his mouth close to my ear, and screams out the words …"

TOM
Moskoe maelström!

NARRATOR
(REVERB) "Well, no one will ever know what I'm feeling. *Shaking* from head to foot. I know what he *means* well enough! I *understand!* We are now bound for that *murderous* whirlpool and *nothing* can save us!

TOM
We're doomed!

NARRATOR
(REVERB) "The sky is still black as *pitch* in every direction."

TOM
Look! There!

SOFT MUSIC

NARRATOR
(REVERB) "Overhead there *bursts* out, all at once, a circular *rift* of clear sky…as *clear* as I've ever seen…and of a deep *bright* blue…and through it…there blazes forth the *full* moon with a glow that I've *never* seen before. It lights up *everything* about us…but, *oh God*, what a *scene* it lights!

CHAOTIC MUSIC SWELLS
(THUNDER CRASH)

TOM
(Distant, Yelling) *Can you…!*

NARRATOR
(REVERB) "The *din* has so increased, I can't hear my brother although we both scream at the top of our lungs. Then, looking pale as *death,* he

holds up one of his fingers, as if to say 'listen!'

"At first, I cannot make out what he means...but, soon a monstrous thought flashes upon me. I look at my pocket watch...then, fear fills every pore in my body...and I fling the watch into the sea! The time...we have run past seven o'clock! The Maelstrom should be in full fury now!
MUSIC BUILDS
(WAVES CRASHING LOUDER)

"So far, our boat has ridden the swells and stayed upright...but, now ...the gigantic sea bears us with it as it rises up...up...as if into the sky! I can't believe that any wave can rise so high. And, then down we come with a sweep, a slide, and a plunge, that makes me sick and dizzy, as if I am falling from some lofty mountain-top in a dream.

"But, while we are up I throw a quick glance around...and in that one glance... I see our exact position in an instant. The Moskoe Maelstrom...the whirlpool, it's about a quarter of a mile dead ahead! I shut my eyes in horror!

"Soon, we are enveloped in foam...I can feel the boat making a sharp half turn to larboard... and then, we shoot off in its new direction like a thunderbolt! The roaring noise of the water is deafening...whistling like a shrill shriek...like a thousand steam vessels letting off steam all at once! We are now in the belt of surf that always surrounds the whirlpool ... another moment and we'll plunge into the abyss! The boat isn't even sinking into the water...it's sort of skimming along on the surface...and on one side is the fathomless Maelstrom...and on the other side is the ocean...a huge writhing wall between us and the horizon.

"Now, this is strange, ya see...because now, as we are in the very jaws of perdition...I feel more composed than when we were only approaching it. Having made up my mind to hope no more... I got rid of a great deal of that terror which unnerved me at first. I suppose it is despair that is holding me together.

"It may look like boasting, but what I tell you is truth. I began to reflect how magnificent a thing it was to die in such a manner...and how foolish it was of me to think of so paltry a consideration as my own individual life...in view of so wonderful a manifestation of God's power. The maelstrom? A thing of beauty? I do believe that I blushed with shame when this idea crossed my mind. But, after a little while I became possessed with the keenest curiosity about the whirlpool itself. I wanted to *explore* its depths, even at the *sacrifice* I was going to make...I actually felt *sad* that I should *never* be able to tell my old *companions* on shore about the *mysteries* I should see. Of course, *thinking* about such things at a *time* like that...*might* be thought of as a *bit* fanciful. Perhaps, the *revolutions* of the boat *racing* around the whirlpool might have *rendered* me a little light-headed.

"So, there we are...my brother and me and the ship...going *round* and round...and I notice we are being *drawn* down further into the vortex ...the *walls* of the black ocean *rising* up around us. The wind and spray *blinding* us...the *roar* deafening...the *air* being *sucked* up like a vacuum ...*strangling* us...*robbing* us of our *vitality*, our thoughts. But, we're still *alive*.

"How *often* we've been *round* the circuit of the belt it is *impossible* to say. We *career* round and round for perhaps an hour, *flying* rather than floating, gradually drawing *nearer* and nearer to the *middle* of the surge...closer to its *horrible* inner edge.

"All this time I have *never* let go of the ring-bolt. My brother is at the stern, *holding* on to a small empty *water*-cask which had been securely lashed...it is the *only* thing on deck that had *not* been swept overboard. As the brink of the pit approaches...he *lets* go his hold upon this cask, and *makes* for the ring *I am holding to...and...!*"

TOM
Let go! Let me on to it!

NARRATOR
(REVERB) "In the *agony* of his terror, Tom tries to force *my* hands off the ring...as it is not *large* enough for *both* of us to grasp! I...feel a deep *grief* when I see him attempt to do this. I mean, I *know* he is at *this* moment, a *madman*...a *raving* maniac through *sheer* fright. I don't care, however, to *fight* over it. Ya see, I *know* it can make no difference whether *either* of us hold on at all. So, I let *him* have the bolt, and I go *astern* to the cask.

"Scarcely have I *secured* myself in my *new* position, when we give a *wild* lurch to starboard, and *rush* headlong into the abyss. I mutter a hurried *prayer* to God...*all is over.*

"As I feel the *sickening* sweep of the descent, I *instinctively* tighten my *hold* upon the barrel, and *close* my eyes. For some seconds I *dare* not

open them while expecting *instant* destruction. And, I am wondering
...*why* am I *not* already drowning?   More time passes. *Good Lord!* I'm
still alive?   The sense of *falling* has ceased.   The vessel seems to be
traveling *much* the same, although *somewhat* sideways. So, I gather
what's *left* of my courage and open my eyes to *see* what is what.

"*Never* shall I *forget* the *sensations* of awe, of *horror,* and of *admiration*
with which I *gaze* about me. The boat appears to be *hanging*, as if by
magic, midway down, upon the *interior* surface of a *funnel* vast in
circumference...*extraordinary* in depth, and whose perfectly *smooth*
sides might have been mistaken for *ebony!*

"I *still* see it...*rapidly* spinning, *bewildering* it is...*gleaming* with a sort of
ghastly radiance...like *light* beams shooting forth...as the rays of the full
moon...*stream* in a flood of golden *glory* along the black walls...and *far*
away down into the *innermost* recesses of the abyss.

"*Confusing?* Oh yes. A *terrific* grandeur, it is, *bewildering*. But, I turn
my gaze away *instinctively* to peer *downward* to see...an *unobstructed*
view. The ship is now *lying* on its side...*we* on deck are *practically*
standing upright, yet *clinging* to its surface. Centrifugal *force,* is what it
is called. Yes.

"Down below us, way down...the *mist* rises so I *cannot* see *any* bottom
to this funnel. We are spinning *so* fast now, my *brain* is dizzy. But, as I
look about the *walls* of the Maelstrom...I perceive that *our* boat is *not*
the *only* object *whirling* about...above *and* below us are visible
fragments of vessels...*large* masses of building timber...*trunks* of
trees...*pieces* of house furniture, *broken* boxes, *barrels!* It is as if we
are in the *center* of a *tornado* of water!

"But, *now*...a *new* thought enters my mind...a new *hope.* I remember
such *fragments* found on the *shore* of Moskoe Island...and perhaps...
they had once entered the *whirlpool* at a *late* stage of the tide...and, for
some reason, they did *not* descend to the *bottom* of the vortex...and as
the tide turned *slowly*...*they* might have been *released* by the whirlpool
back into the ocean! Can it be *possible?*

"But, to stay on board the ship...it's *too* heavy. No, the maelstrom will
never release it! I *must* try to escape as a small fragment. So, with little
hesitation, I *lash* myself *securely* to the water cask I am holding onto
...and *cut* it loose...I must *throw* myself *and* cask into the water. But,
first, I *signal* to my brother to *follow* my direction...to *grab* a barrel that

is floating by...to make him *understand!*

"But, he just *shakes* his head despairingly...and *refuses* to move from his position at the ring-bolt. It's *impossible* to reach him...there is no time. And, so...I *resign* him to his fate and fasten *myself* to the cask and, without another moment's hesitation...I *fling* myself into the swirling *sea!*

SILENCE

"The result was *precisely* what I had *hoped* it might be. As is evident, I am here *now* to tell you this tale...obviously, you can see that I *did* escape...and since I've *told* you the method I used to *achieve* my escape... I will bring my story *quickly* to conclusion.

MUSIC

"After I had jumped, it took about an *hour* for the *entire* ship, *including* my brother, to plunge *headlong*, at once and forever*, into* the chaos of foam below. I still *clung* to the cask...and, luckily, it wasn't *long* before a great *change* took place in the whirlpool. The *slope* of the sides of the *vast* funnel became less and *less* steep. The *gyrations* of the whirlpool grew less and *less* violent. The *bottom* of the abyss seemed *slowly* to *rise* up, to even out. The sky was clear, the *winds* had gone down, and the full *moon* was setting in the West...when I found myself on the *surface* of the ocean, in *full* view of the shoreline from where we had sailed. I could *also* see where the *Maelstrom* had been. Still, the sea *heaved* in mountainous waves from the after-effects of the hurricane.

"I was carried *violently* into the current that *hugged* the coastline...and in a few minutes I entered the *fishing* grounds where, hours later, a *boat* picked me up. I was exhausted from *fatigue* and speechless. Those who *drew* me on board were my old *mates* and daily companions...but *they* knew me no more than they would have known a *traveler* from the *spirit*-land. My *hair* which had been *raven*-black the day before, was as *white* as you see it now. They say *too* that my *face, my expression*, my *personality*...it's changed. I've told them my story...I could tell they didn't *believe* it. I've now told it to you. What do *you* think of it?"

END

AUTHOR

DAN BIANCHI has spent over 40 yrs in theater, film and fine arts. Awards include: 2014 NY Innovative Theatre Award Lifetime Artistic Achievement; 3 times Best Director Off Broadway with his Threepenny Theatre Co. (shared with Sir Peter Brook; Charles Ludlam; Julie Taymor); Billy Rose Musical Theater Award; ASCAP Musical Theater Award; National Endowment Grant; MacDowell Fellowship, The Beckett Prize (twice), The National Writers Guild Screenwriting Award. He's founded two international theater companies, written/directed over 30 plays/musicals, worked as screenwriter in Hollywood, directed 7 motion pictures with members of the Royal Shakespeare Co.. In 2002/3 he founded and ran VIDEOTHEATRE, NYC's only DV dedicated venue screening independent features and shorts. Dan is also a Fine Artist who has exhibited his works at MOMA NYC; MOMA Australia; Brazil; Germany; Museum of Non-Conformist Art, Russia, etc. A born NYer, he lives in Greenwich Village with his wife and daughter.

He founded RADIOTHEATRE in 2004 and has since produced 80 live shows, over 600 performances at NYC and U.S. venues. Since 2004, Dan has been nominated for a 2010 Drama Desk Award, won 2 NY Innovative Theater Awards for Best Sound and Best Music. Radiotheatre has been nominated for 13 NYIT Awards including Best Performance Group five yrs in a row. He is the most produced living stage writer in NYC.

He has also published 12 books of his adaptations of classic horror and sci-fi literature for the stage. His most recent book is a history and collection of stories from the legendary NYC story telling group, The Lights Out Club, which he hopes to bring to the stage soon. "MANHATTAN MACABRE: 200 Years of Strange Tales From The Lights Out Club" 390 pg. www.thelightsoutclub.com

FOR A COMPLETE LISTING OF RADIOTHEATRE PRODUCED SHOWS IN NYC, ARTICLES and REVIEWS, PLEASE SEE web site: www.radiotheatrenyc.com

Have you heard of The Lights Out Club? No? Well, for the first 140 years of its existence, society wasn't supposed to know about it. It all began back in 1796, when Alexander Hamilton, one of America's founding fathers, had just given the new nation its first sex scandal which had left him temporarily unemployed. He retreated to Manhattan, his home town, to lick his wounds. During that time, he was able to convince six prominent New Yorkers to entertain themselves each week by sharing tales of terror by the light of a solitary candle. For an extra jolt, they would meet in dark, out-of-the-way, often, dangerous places. Their spooky tales were based upon personal experiences, or, true events which had taken place in NYC. As the group grew, the secret membership was by reference only and restricted to New Yorkers. By the 1800s, they were known as The Lights Out Club. To this day, this legendary, influential group has continued on, attracting members from all walks of life, from school teachers to politicians, cops, athletes, vaudevillians, gangsters, authors and Hollywood superstars ...everyone, it seems, has a terrifying story to tell...and loves hearing them, as well. Past members include MARK TWAIN, EDGAR ALLAN POE, ORSON WELLES, LEGS DIAMOND, RODNEY DANGERFIELD, ENRICO CARUSO, NORMAN MAILER, SOPHIE TUCKER, ROD SERLING and dozens more. Now, for the first time ever, THE LIGHTS OUT CLUB has authorized long-time member, DAN BIANCHI, to collect, catalog, record and transcribe its tales to the written page, and, to edit and conserve hundreds of weird stories of New York's ghosts, creatures, haunted houses and strange incidents, all of which have taken place in real NYC locations...and, often concern historical figures and events. Here are eerie tales of old Manhattan which have not seen the light of day since the first night they were told by the light of a solitary candle!

ALSO BY DAN BIANCHI AT HOUSE OF FEAR

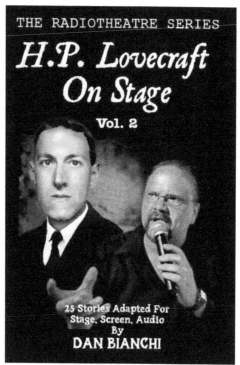

THE RADIOTHEATRE SERIES
H.P. LOVECRAFT ON STAGE VOL. 2
$19.95 NOW ON SALE at AMAZON

Based on live shows previously produced by the critically acclaimed, award winning performance group Radiotheatre, THE RADIOTHEATRE SERIES presents classic tales of Horror, Science Fiction and Adventure adapted into simplified scripts available for stage, screen and audio productions.

H.P. LOVECRAFT ON STAGE VOL.2 includes - THE TRANSITION OF JUAN ROMERO; THE RATS IN THE WALL; THE EVIL CLERGYMAN; THE CURSE OF YIG; THE STRANGE HIGH HOUSE IN THE MIST; HERBERT WEST, REANIMATOR; MAN OF STONE; OUT OF THE AEONS; HE; THE HORROR AT MARTIN'S BEACH; BEYOND THE WALL OF SLEEP; THE UNNAMABLE; THE WHISPERER IN DARKNESS; THE TERRIBLE OLD MAN; THE HORROR IN THE MUSEUM; THE DIARY OF ALONSO TYPER; THE BEAST IN THE CAVE; THE CALL OF CTHULHU; THE HAUNTER OF THE DARK; WHAT THE MOON BRINGS; DISINTERMENT; THE HORROR IN THE BURYING GROUND; THE TREE ON THE HILL; HYPNOS; MEDUSA'S COIL

THE RADIOTHEATRE SERIES
H.P. LOVECRAFT ON STAGE VOL. 1
$19.95 NOW ON SALE at AMAZON
Based on live shows previously produced by the critically
acclaimed, award winning performance group Radiotheatre,
THE RADIOTHEATRE SERIES presents classic tales of Horror,
Science Fiction and Adventure adapted into simplified scripts
available for stage, screen and audio productions.

H.P.LOVECRAFT ON STAGE Vol. 1 includes:
COOL AIR; THE MOON BOG; THE THING ON THE DOORSTEP;
THE BOOK; THE DUNWICH HORROR; THE THING IN THE
MOONLIGHT; FROM BEYOND; THE MUSIC OF ERICH ZANN;
THE FESTIVAL; PICKMAN'S MODEL; THE COLOR OUT OF
SPACE; THE OUTSIDER; ARTHUR JERMYN; TWO BLACK
BOTTLES; THE SHUNNED HOUSE; THE SHADOW OVER
INNSMOUTH; THE HOUND; THE PICTURE IN THE HOUSE;
THE CATS OF ULTHAR; THE LURKING FEAR; THE TOMB;
DAGON; THE STATEMENT OF RANDOLPH CARTER; THE
HORROR AT RED HOOK; THE WHITE SHIP

Made in the USA
Middletown, DE
15 April 2020